"In a world where everyone is a theologian, urban legend[s] tongue as conventional wisdom, spoken with the confiden[ce] self-evident. Combining the head of a theologian and the heart of a pastor, [Wi]t- mer tackles these urban legends head-on by thoughtfully engaging Scripture and drawing on church history. Using his characteristic humor, Wittmer firmly but graciously leads the reader from myth to biblical truth in a way that is accessible to a wide range of readers."

Matthew S. Harmon, *professor of New Testament studies, Grace College and Theological Seminary*

"Too many people think theology is boring or scary, an arcane ritual for senile scholars shuffling down corridors of dusty old tomes. Dr. Wittmer upends such misperceptions in this infectious book, crackling with humor and bursting with pastoral wisdom. I left encouraged that the great things of the gospel are always relevant to our lives because they are so good, true, and beautiful."

Hans Madueme, *associate professor of theological studies, Covenant College*

"Mike Wittmer is a clear and engaging writer. His short, pithy explorations of popular cultural ideas about the Christian faith would make excellent starting points for discussion in Bible study groups or adult Sunday school classes. By no means will everyone agree with his theological position on every issue, but I guarantee that the ensuing discussion will generate intelligent conversation about important matters of our faith."

J. Richard Middleton, *professor of biblical worldview and exegesis, Northeastern Seminary at Roberts Wesleyan College*

"Michael Wittmer's *Urban Legends of Theology* is a sound guide through the maze of confusions and half-truths that plague modern-day Christians as they read popular religious literature, search for answers among unrefereed blogs on the Internet, and listen to the emotive words of popular religious music. This work is written in a comprehensible and often winsome way to keep the reader engaged while at the same time adroitly unraveling forty of the more misleading claims made about God, creation, and salvation, replacing them with carefully tuned answers."

Richard A. Muller, *senior fellow, Junius Institute for Digital Reformation Research, and P. J. Zondervan Professor of Historical Theology (emeritus), Calvin Theological Seminary*

"Among Christians, partial truths and total falsehoods about God, theology, and Christian living travel via casual conversations, worship songs, books, and even Bible studies and sermons! Michael Wittmer tackles several of the most popular urban legends that appeal to our craving for brevity, simplicity, and speed, yet leave us spiritually malnourished. With earnestness, candor, humor, and above all, a careful handling of the Scriptures, Wittmer invites us to scrutinize the slogans, clichés, and bits of 'common knowledge' that too often go unexamined. Herein is the fruit of biblical and theological scholarship serving a pastoral end: helping readers more fully worship and rest in Jesus Christ."

Keith W. Plummer, *dean of the School of Theology, Cairn University*

"There is no end to the making of theological myths. Thankfully, Michael Wittmer has written an accessible and clear book to help Christians think biblically about the most important—and often misunderstood—theological questions. This an excellent addition to B&H Academic's wonderful Urban Legends series."

Brandon D. Smith, *assistant professor of theology and New Testament, Cedarville University, and cofounder of the Center for Baptist Renewal*

"The Urban Legends series is excellent, and with the publication of Michael Wittmer's recent contribution to the series, *Urban Legends of Theology*, it has become even better! In this book, he teaches the truth of theology by addressing the legends, forty of those theological doctrines popularly believed though not true. This book is an excellent and ideal companion to teaching the truth of theology by responding to the legends of theology. We are in Wittmer's debt for teaching theological truth through legend, and this book should be used widely in the church and the classroom."

Gregory C. Strand, *executive director of theology and credentialing, EFCA, and adjunct professor of pastoral theology, Trinity Evangelical Divinity School*

"Mike Wittmer always makes theology accessible and enjoyable, and this book is no exception. Here, he takes on a variety of problematic statements, myths, errors, and sometimes heresies while pointing us to a better and more biblical way. You may not agree with his take on every theological point here, but you will be challenged to think about, to wrestle with, and to better understand the beauty and complexity of the Christian faith. Prepare your minds for action!"

Trevin Wax, *vice president for research and resource development at the North American Mission Board; visiting professor at Wheaton College; and author of* The Thrill of Orthodoxy, Rethink Your Self, *and* This Is Your Time

"In Mike Wittmer's class, I learned that God is 'the greatest possible being.' That means that our mistakes about him are not simply wrong—they are worse than who God really is. *Urban Legends of Theology* doesn't just correct our theological mistakes. It improves our vision of God, helping us truly know, fully love, and completely live for his glory. Take and read!"

Matthew Westerholm, *associate professor of church music and worship, The Southern Baptist Theological Seminary*

URBAN LeGeNDS OF

THEOLOGY

URBAN LEGENDS

OF

THEOLOGY

40 Common Misconceptions

MICHAEL WITTMER

ACADEMIC
BRENTWOOD, TENNESSEE

Urban Legends of Theology
Copyright © 2023 by Michael Wittmer

Published by B&H Academic
Brentwood, Tennessee

ISBN: 978-1-0877-5607-3

Dewey Decimal Classification: 230
Subject Heading: CHRISTIANITY / JESUS CHRIST / CHURCH

Cover design by Darren Welch and Emily Keafer Lambright.

Cover illustration by Gustave Doré, from *The Divine Comedy* by Dante Alighieri, Canto 23, sourced from Realy Easy Star / Alamy.

Printed in the United States of America
2 3 4 5 6 7 8 9 10   BTH   27 26 25 24 23

For the fun and generous family of Cedar Springs Baptist Church:
I love you and I like you.

Contents

x

Contents

Part III

Introduction

I thank David Croteau for inviting me into this Urban Legends series. David's excellent idea was winsomely achieved in *Urban Legends of the Old Testament, Urban Legends of the New Testament,* and *Urban Legends of Church History.* I enjoyed and learned from each, and hope my contribution will keep the momentum going, at least until *Urban Legends of Middle School Ministry.* Spoiler alert: those are not legends. I was there. Every bit of it is true!

I will not repeat what earlier *Urban Legends* said in their introductions, except to say that an urban legend is something popularly believed—in the church or culture or both—that is not true. Some legends are more wrong than others, and some are more damaging than others. Some legends will rob you of peace and joy while others will damn you to hell. We must discern one from the other so we know how to handle each. Briars and wolves are both detrimental to sheep, but not in the same way. Wise shepherds gently guide sheep away from dense thickets, whereas they shoot wolves dead. Likewise, some of these legends will merely scratch your faith, while others will have you for lunch. Still others are setups, meant to slow your walk so you are easier to catch.

I arranged these forty myths in theological order, assigning roughly equal numbers to the categories of God and Theological Method, Humanity and Sin, Jesus and Salvation, and Church and Last Things. (The church was short-changed but not because I am an evangelical. I simply ran out of room.) I followed the *Urban Legends* tradition of scattering ten lesser "mini myths" throughout, and I added my own wrinkle, six "suburban legends" that are updated versions of the urban legend. Think of them as urban legends that moved out to the burbs, trying to make a go of it in the twenty-first century. Some should be evicted from the neighborhood while others should be shot on sight, gently.

That makes fifty-six myths and legends in all. As much fun as it is disman-tling some of these, it is more important to replace each with truth. Please do not skip past the application that concludes each chapter. These application sections are not cutesy wrap-ups. They are the point. Deconstruction is only the first, and by far easiest, part of following Jesus. Anyone can deconstruct, even those who do not believe in him. As we tear down these legends, we must give ourselves wholly to the truth that supplants them, lest we become wise as demons (Jas 2:19).

This is not a book to wave in someone's face for misstating doctrinal points. This book aims to comfort your faith, pull back the covers, fluff the pillow, and invite you to rest in Jesus. If theology does not lead you to trust Jesus more, if it does not make you want to curl up in the cradle of his grace, you are doing it wrong. You are not following the truth but, quite possibly, an urban legend. Maybe one of these.

PART I

———

God and Theological Method

———

CHAPTER 1

It Is Important to Believe in Something, and It Does Not Matter What

The Legendary Belief

In the Netflix drama *The Crown*, the elderly mother of Prince Philip left her convent in Athens to live in Buckingham Palace. Her religious ascetism clashed with the worldly life of her son, who rarely attended church and was unsure that God existed. The mother's heart yearned for her floundering son, and she asked, "How is your faith?"

"Dormant," Philip replied.

She sighed. "That's not good. Let this be a mother's gift to her child, and one piece of advice. Find yourself a faith. It helps. No. Not just helps. It's everything."[1]

Unraveling the Legend

This poignant moment seems profound, until you listen carefully to what was said. "Find yourself *a* faith"? What if it is not the true faith? Does any faith serve equally well? How can faith be "everything" if we are believing in the wrong thing?

The mother's counsel echoes a common contemporary theme: "It's important to believe in something, and it doesn't matter what." But such advice is bound to disappoint. Have you seen a child holding a "We believe" sign at a Detroit Lions game? He passionately believes in something, but by the time he is ten, he will learn conviction is no substitute for competence. What he believes in matters far more than how strongly he believes it, and soon enough he will become just another cynical fan in Michigan.

---

[1] *The Crown*, season 3, episode 4, "Bubbikins," directed by Benjamin Caron, Netflix, 2019.

The mother's advice is also dangerous. Faith means to trust, rely, commit. We believe in something when we lean in and give ourselves to it. If this is so, wise believers only commit to what they know, not to what they do not. You would not jump out of a plane if you weren't sure whether your backpack held a parachute or a picnic. You would not pull out into a blind intersection with a shout, "Shut your eyes, kids! We're going for it!" You would not agree to an operation if the surgeon said she had never seen what you have, but she felt lucky, so why not?

In every area of life, we know that what we believe in matters a lot.

Every area except one.

As far as I can tell, God is the only topic where modern folks assume that what we believe matters less than how much we believe it. Popular songs encourage us that anything is possible if we'll only believe. A rising number of people describe themselves as "spiritual but not religious."[2] They are spiritual enough to believe in a higher power, yet they refuse to limit themselves to any religious system. They may have had a mystical experience, perhaps involving drugs, sex, or an exquisitely wet burrito. They have discovered "their truth," and they want the same for you. So, they knowingly put a nonjudgmental hand on yours and say, "It's important to believe in something, and it doesn't matter what."

What You Kant Know

To understand how modern society got here, it is important to know a little about Immanuel Kant. And to understand Kant, you need to know something about David Hume.

The modern world began in the sixteenth century and hit its stride with the rise of Enlightenment philosophy in the eighteenth century. Modern thought demanded proof for its beliefs. This rigorous method enabled science to unlock nature's laws, leading to vaccines, airplanes, and Amazon Prime, but it proved lethal for belief in God. In his *Dialogues Concerning Natural Religion,* David Hume (1711–1776) noted the difficulty in proving that our world had a Creator. If the earth's beauty points to an intelligent designer, then the evils of our world indicate such a being does not exist. The evidence seems mixed. Hume thought enlightened, modern people should put their money where their mouth is. They professed to believe only what they could prove; since they could not prove God exists, in Hume's opinion they should be honest enough to give up that belief.

---

[2]   Michael Lipka and Claire Gecewicz, "More Americans Now Say They're Spiritual but Not Religious," *Pew Research Center*, September 6, 2017, https://www.pewresearch.org/fact-tank/2017/09/06/more-americans-now-say-theyre-spiritual-but-not-religious/.

Hume's skepticism alarmed the ethicist Immanuel Kant (1724–1804), who said Hume woke him from "his dogmatic slumbers." Kant had been teaching ethics on autopilot, giving the same lectures year after year. Then he read Hume and realized Hume was right. It was impossible to prove there is a God. And if there is no God who rewards righteousness and punishes sin, how could Kant continue to teach morality? Why should people be good if there was no judgment day? Wouldn't everyone do whatever they could get away with?

Kant had to rescue belief in God from Hume's skepticism. Ethics demanded it. But he couldn't deny Hume was right. He could not prove, and so he could not know, that God existed. Kant's solution to his dilemma remains with us today and is a primary source behind our urban legend, "It's important to believe in something, and it doesn't matter what."

Kant's solution was to separate faith from knowledge. He thought he might continue to have faith in God even though he could not know God. Kant divided our world into two realms: the lower world of knowledge, which he called the phenomenal realm; and the higher world of faith, which he called the noumenal realm. The phenomena are the superficial aspects of our world that science can prove and thereby know, while the noumena are the deeper truths that we cannot know yet must believe. For example, our eyes can observe sunlight glittering on the leaves of an apple tree and study the chemical process of photosynthesis. We can break down the elements of an apple into carbohydrates, water, and sugars. These are facts we can know. But the essence of the apple tree lies deeper, beyond the reach of our senses. We believe there must be some underlying point that unites the tree's bark, flowers, and fruit. We can't see, touch, or prove it, so we can't know it. But we can still believe it is there.

Kant's noumenal realm included the essences of apple trees and the essences of all other things, including the self. Most important for our purposes, the noumenal realm also included God. Kant agreed with Hume that we could not prove God, but he said that simply highlighted the limits of our knowledge. As our eyes are unable to penetrate the bark and wood to find the essence of an apple tree, so we are unable to penetrate the heavens and know the first thing about God. This is not God's fault. He is simply too high for any mere creature to know. But that's okay. We may not be able to say anything about him, but like the essence of an apple tree, we are still permitted to believe in him. And we must: otherwise, everything would be permissible. Ethics would be impossible.

Kant meant well. He tried to rescue God from Hume's skepticism, but there was not much left of God after the rescue. If God cannot be known, then he becomes a fill-in-the-blank deity in which we are all free to believe whatever we prefer. If we have been hurt by men, we can say God is Mother and Daughter rather than Father and Son. If we enjoy gluttony, greed, or sexual immorality, we can set aside the biblical commands and say our God condones such acts. If we don't think a loving God would send people to hell, we can revise how we want the afterlife to go. Heaven and hell can become whatever we want them to be. No one can say we're wrong because no one really knows. Any religious belief is possible because divine revelation is impossible.

That is the problem. Kant pushed God high enough to be safe from Hume's skeptical attacks, which meant Hume was also safe from God. The unknowable God cannot penetrate Hume's world to say who he is and how he wants Hume to live, because if he could reveal himself then he would be knowable and no longer a noumenal belief. The upshot is that modern people are permitted to believe in God, as we're permitted to believe in the essence of apple trees (or any noumenal idea), but we cannot say we know anything about him, or her, or it. It is still important to believe in some deity—because how else could we ground morality or the meaning of life?—but it doesn't matter what.

Kant's separation of faith from knowledge opened the door to religious pluralism. Why is everyone permitted to believe in whichever deity floats their boat? Because no one knows any of them. None are known to be right, so none can be known to be wrong. We are free to be "spiritual but not religious," which, if you think about it, isn't a significant improvement from modern secularism. It's a short step from "There is no God" to "Any god will do." Why do people think they're free to believe in all the gods? Because they don't really believe in any. Secularism and pluralism are two sides of the same coin.

Transcendence and Immanence

The answer to Immanuel Kant's separation of faith from knowledge is something that a man named Immanuel, or "God with us," should have understood. Christian theology begins with the ontological gap between the Creator and his creation. God transcends us in every way. He is infinite; we are finite. He is eternal; we are temporal. He is immutable; we are unstable. God isn't a larger, better version of us. He exists in a wholly other dimension that explodes all our categories. No human concept or construction can ever convey the magnitude of his glory. As King Solomon prayed at the dedication of his gleaming temple, "Even heaven, the highest heaven, cannot contain you, much less this temple I have built" (2 Chr 6:18).

And yet, Christian theology combines this transcendence with an equal emphasis on God's immanence. God is the incomprehensible I AM, yet he is also Immanuel, God with us. We must not cheat God's transcendence to make room for his immanence, nor cheat his immanence to highlight his transcendence. God is not half transcendent and half immanent, nor 75 percent transcendent and 25 percent immanent. He is 100 percent transcendent and 100 percent immanent, both high above us and here with us (Isa 57:15). If God is not fully transcendent, he is not God. If God is not fully immanent, he cannot be known.

When people say, "It's important to believe in something, and it doesn't matter what," we might compliment them on their high view of God's transcendence while also asking if they think this supremely powerful God is able to reveal himself. If he cannot, perhaps they should reconsider whether their God is high enough! We might stress that faith in God is too important to be blind and confess how lost we'd be without his revelation. Here's the bottom line: Is the Bible God's revelation or not? The transcendent God is far more than he can express in Scripture, but he is not less or different than what he reveals there (this is the topic of our next chapter).

Application

Consider the predicament of modern people who believe there is a God but that he cannot be known. How can they know who they are, how they got here, where they are going, or what they should do in the meantime? There's a reason Jesus calls them "the lost" (Luke 19:10).

Our hearts should brim with compassion for these friends, and gratitude to God for giving us his Word. Ancient people trekked to the oracle at Delphi to receive a word from their god. Others butchered animals to inspect their entrails. How much easier for us! We have multiple copies of God's true Word, in superb translations, scattered around our homes. Have you read it today? Now would be a good time, before starting chapter 2. Take a moment to hear from God. Because you believe in something, and you know exactly what.

——

Theology Puts God in a Box

The Legendary Belief

Time magazine interviewed Katharine Jefferts Schori when she was elected bishop of the Episcopal Church in the United States of America. The interviewer asked her, among other things, whether belief in Jesus is the only way to heaven. Jefferts Schori replied, "We who practice the Christian tradition understand him as our vehicle to the divine. But for us to assume that God could not act in other ways is, I think, to put God in an awfully small box."[1]

Unraveling the Legend

Putting God in a box is usually associated with conservative Christians. We think we know what God is like, and we may too confidently proclaim what he will or will not do. There is a reason Presbyterians laugh knowingly when their preacher channels Saint Peter shushing other Christians in heaven, "Please be quiet around the Presbyterians. They think they're the only ones here." The joke works equally well in Baptist, Methodist, and Pentecostal churches. Wisconsin Synod Lutherans might not get it, which makes it even funnier (just kidding, Lutheran friends).

But progressive believers risk taming God too. They say, "My God would never _____," and then fill in the blank with "tell his people to slay Canaanites," "condemn homosexual acts," or "send anyone to hell." Who's got the "awfully small box" now? Jefferts Schori seems to embrace Western culture's leveling of the world's religions, in which more than one can get the job done. Rather than accept what Jesus said about himself, "No one comes to

---

[1]   Jeff Chu, "10 Questions for Katharine Jefferts Schori," *Time*, July 10, 2006, http://content.time.com /time/subscriber/article/0,33009,1211587-2,00.html.

the Father except through me" (John 14:6), she attempts to stuff God into her pluralistic box.

So, this chapter's urban legend isn't entirely mythical. It has been spotted in the wild. Limiting God is a live danger, on both the right and the left, for those who claim to know him. But it's not a necessary bug of the theological task. The legend lives on, but only in poor theology, not theology per se. Theology done right does not cram God into its own box.

God Seizes the Initiative

Conservative preachers and theologians are said to limit God when we declare that he will punish forever sinners who do not repent and believe in Jesus. But rather than limiting God, this statement is an example of God limiting us and what we may say about him. It's nearly a direct quote from Scripture. Paul says Jesus will return from heaven and take "vengeance with flaming fire on those who don't know God and on those who don't obey the gospel of our Lord Jesus. They will pay the penalty of eternal destruction from the Lord's presence and from his glorious strength" (2 Thess 1:7–9).

Theology cannot plausibly be accused of stuffing God into a box when it binds itself to divine revelation. Putting God in a box requires taking the initiative, but sound theology doesn't initiate anything. It responds to God's initiative in his revelation. All revelation comes from God. He is the source, the agent, the speaker of his divine word. Theologians get into trouble when we surmise that we are the knowing subjects and God is the object of our knowledge. This is exactly backwards. God is the subject of theology. He is the actor; we are the objects who receive his word. His revelation apprehends, constrains, and acts upon us (Heb 4:12–13). He is in the driver's seat; we are along for the ride.

False theology storms heaven to capture God and imprison him in a system that seems safe and manageable. It crams its idol into a box it can live with. True theology confesses that God seizes the initiative. All that we know originates with him. If he did not speak, we would know nothing about him.

God Is More Than He Reveals

Orthodox theology starts with revelation, then stays with it the whole way through. Those who accuse theology of putting God in a box often remind us that God transcends what he has revealed. Yes. Of course. But this transcendence itself is only grasped by revelation.

Human reason suggests God transcends us in quantitative ways. He is more of whatever good we possess. We have knowledge; God must have all knowledge. We have power; God must have all power. We are somewhere; God must be everywhere. God is omniscient, omnipotent, and omnipresent. This is true, yet these perfections are the narrowest tip of an infinitely deep iceberg. God's inner knowledge, power, and presence are vastly more unfathomable. Consider that the omniperfections are relative. They require an external world that God has knowledge and power over. But God has an eternal knowledge, power, and presence that exist independently from any created thing. He is infinite knowledge, power, and presence within himself.

Reason tells us God's mystery is quantitative; revelation proclaims God's mystery is total and dimensional—that he exists in an unapproachably glorious, wholly other plane of reality. The "I AM WHO I AM" (Exod 3:14) cannot directly express himself to his beloved creatures without annihilating them. He must conceal himself in a burning bush, thick cloud, or pillar of fire, for our protection. If God were to open himself to us, revealing his glory and beauty without a buffer, we would incinerate on the spot. We wouldn't even leave a stain.

Reason led Moses to ask God to show him his glory. *Our relationship is becoming intimate, let me see you!* God revealed that Moses would not survive a face-to-face encounter, so he covered Moses in a crevice with his hand and permitted only a glimpse of his glory that trailed behind (Exod 33:18–23). Reason demands that God defend his justice to Job or to Esau and Pharaoh. Revelation says God's thoughts are higher than our thoughts, "how unsearchable his judgments and untraceable his ways!" and who are we to question him? (Isa 55:8–9; Rom 11:33; Job 38:1–2).

God Is Not Less Than He Reveals

Revelation assures us that God is qualitatively, dimensionally more than he can reveal to us finite creatures, but also that he is not less or different than what he reveals. God is wholly concealed in his revelation, so we depend entirely on him for what he wants us to know. Yet at the same time God is wholly revealed to us. What he tells us about himself is true; he does not hold back.[2]

This paradox is most apparent in Jesus. The Son of God "is the radiance of God's glory and the exact expression of his nature" (Heb 1:3). The Son cannot reveal himself directly without destroying the person who sees him. When the Son gave his closest earthly friend a heightened view of his glory, John said, "I fell at his feet like a dead man" (Rev 1:17). The Son of God can only safely reveal himself through the cover of the human nature of Jesus. And yet the Son

---

[2] Karl Barth, *Church Dogmatics* II/1, trans. T. H. L. Parker, ed. G. W. Bromiley and T. F. Torrance (Edinburgh: T&T Clark, 1957), 179–254. While I disagree with Barth's overly subjective view of revelation, this section powerfully describes the importance of grounding all knowledge of God, including knowledge of his mystery and hiddenness, in his revelation.

shines through. John proclaims, "The Word became flesh and dwelt among us. We observed his glory, the glory as the one and only Son from the Father" (John 1:14). Jesus's human body and soul fully reveal God while simultaneously buffering us from being consumed by his glory.

Our transcendent God stoops to our level to communicate in creaturely forms, using flesh and words that we can understand. John Calvin said God accommodates himself to our "slight capacity," as a nurse might lisp to an infant.[3] How do you communicate with a newborn? You make surprised, happy faces and say "goochie goo." There's a depth (hopefully) to your person that you cannot begin to convey, yet something true about you does get through. The baby blinks and gurgles and smiles back at you. Message received.

The gap between God and us is immeasurably wider than the gap between us and a baby. To communicate with us, God must stoop further than we can imagine. He makes a surprised, happy face and hands us the Bible. We study its pages to learn who God is and what he is like. We learn much, but we never take even a halting, baby step toward closing the infinite gap. We read "God is love" (1 John 4:8) and know it is the truth. But it's also baby talk. God is infinitely more loving than we will ever comprehend.

This is analogous to the difference between a square and a cube. If a three-dimensional cube entered a two-dimensional world, the people in that world would see only a square. There is a height to the square that the flat-landers would never comprehend. And yet what they understand is still true. A cube is a square. It's just more than a square. It's squares all the way up into its higher, impenetrable dimension.

Figure 2.1: The Square and the Cube

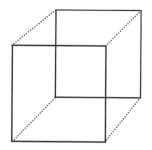

In a similar way, Jesus fully reveals God. He told Philip, "The one who has seen me has seen the Father" (John 14:9). God is the cube, which means he is also the square (Jesus). Within the person of Jesus, the divine Son is the cube,

---

[3] John Calvin, *Institutes of the Christian Religion*, I.13.1, trans. Ford Lewis Battles, ed. John T. McNeill (Philadelphia: Westminster, 1960), 121.

and the human nature of Jesus is the square. Jesus completely reveals God, in the sense that God is not other than or different from what we see in Jesus. We know God truly through Jesus now, and we will know him even better when we see Jesus face-to-face. Imagine having forever to climb the heights of Jesus's beauty, love, and grace! We will never reach the peak, so we will never get bored. There will always be some new facet of Jesus to discover, and each discovery will line up perfectly with what Jesus has already revealed. We will never be ambushed by what we learn, wondering how this trait or that state-ment matches what we already know. We will never know Jesus exhaustively, though we do know him truly. Even now.

Application

We cannot comprehend how God is both transcendent and immanent, hidden and revealed. If we could explain this tension in a way that left no loose ends, we would not be creatures. We would have escaped the bounds of finitude and entered God's realm. There would no longer be a Trinity but a Quaternity—four of us divine persons—and that would be bad for everyone else! So, we gladly claim our creaturely place and confess the mystery of God.

We cannot comprehend the tension, but we need both to be true. And Scripture teaches both. Isaiah 55 explains that God's Word is both fully tran-scendent and fully immanent.

Verses 8–9 express the heavenly mystery of God:

"For my thoughts are not your thoughts,
and your ways are not my ways."
This is the Lord's declaration.
"For as heaven is higher than earth,
so my ways are higher than your ways,
and my thoughts than your thoughts."

Verses 10–11 express the earthly effectiveness of his revelation:

"For just as rain and snow fall from heaven
and do not return there
without saturating the earth
and making it germinate and sprout,
and providing seed to sow
and food to eat,
so my word that comes from my mouth
will not return to me empty,
but it will accomplish what I please
and will prosper in what I send it to do."

We avoid putting God in a box if we begin with revelation and hold firmly to it all the way through. Revelation teaches that God is wholly concealed, far above what he can convey to creatures like us. And revelation teaches that God is wholly revealed in what he conveys. He is more than he can express, but he is not different, and he is not less. God does not fit into anyone's box. But if he's a cube then he's also the square. Let his revelation shape you.

CHAPTER 3

Faith Begins When Knowledge Ends

The Legendary Belief

My friend came from a non-Christian background to become a leader in the evangelical world, so I was interested in his journey to Jesus. He said he came to faith by extensively researching the Bible. He evaluated its manuscript tradition, checked it for internal consistency and coherence with outside sources, and ultimately determined it was historically reliable. He knew he could trust it. But this knowledge only took him so far. From this secure foundation he faced a choice: Would he stop at the edge of his knowledge, or would he step out beyond what he could verify and believe that Jesus rose from the dead? He gathered himself and took the leap of faith. He chose to believe what he could not prove and so could not know. He bet his life on the resurrection of Jesus Christ.

Unraveling the Legend

My friend is a fine Christian, so this process of conversion worked for him. Praise God! But I think his journey made two mistakes: supposing that (1) knowledge requires proof and that (2) faith begins when knowledge ends. This chapter addresses both errors, particularly the latter, which has become a widespread urban legend.

My friend took his leap of faith reluctantly. He wished he could prove that Jesus's tomb was empty, but there was no way to know for sure. He resigned himself to jump because what else could he do? The risk for not believing was everlasting damnation. By contrast, many Christians seem to celebrate the separation of faith from knowledge. They think they only have faith when they pass beyond what they know and take risks for God. They encourage Faith Promise offerings, when Christians pledge more money than they can humanly give; Faith Budgets, in which churches spend money they do not have; and Faith Ministries, which depend on Faith Promise and Faith Budgets.

During spring semester of my first year in seminary, my school devoted a week of chapels to imploring God to supply the funds we needed to pay our bills and remain open. I was moved by the experience, until I learned the school did this every spring. They were a faith venture that did not think they were relying on God if they had money in the bank. A subsequent president decided this was no way to run a school, and he raised money for endowments so professors and students could focus on their studies.

Believe What You Know

What is faith, and what is its relation to knowledge? Chapter 1 argued that faith means to commit and that wise believers only commit to what they know, not to what they don't. It's true that knowledge by itself is not enough. Demons know many truths about God—truths that make them tremble—yet they don't have faith (Jas 2:19). We only have faith when we commit to what we know. Knowledge is not sufficient for faith. But it is necessary. We cannot believe what we do not know.

The apostle Paul wrote that everyone who puts their faith in Jesus will be saved, then adds, "And how can they believe without hearing about him? . . . So faith comes from what is heard, and what is heard comes through the message about Christ" (Rom 10:13–17). John Calvin noted that faith is "a firm and certain knowledge of God's benevolence toward us, founded upon the truth of the freely given promise of Christ, both revealed to our minds and sealed upon our hearts through the Holy Spirit."[1] Faith throws all its weight on what it knows to be true—that God is every bit the gracious Savior revealed in the face of Christ.

Faith does not begin when knowledge ends. Faith clings to knowledge the whole way through. This is true for saving faith that comes to Jesus and for sanctifying faith that subsequently follows him. God never tells anyone to commit to anything that may or may not be true. He always tells people to rely on what they know. Read Hebrews 11, the Bible's Faith Hall of Fame. Every one of these champions demonstrated their faith either by claiming a divine promise or obeying a divine command. Sometimes both. Abraham "did not know where he was going," but he knew that God told him to go and promised him the land (vv. 8–9). He did not know why God had told him to sacrifice Isaac or exactly how this episode would end, but he knew God had commanded him, and he believed that if worse came to worst, God would keep his promise and raise Isaac from the dead (vv. 17–19).

---

[1]   Calvin, *Institutes* III.2.7, 551 (see chap. 2, n. 3).

Faith doesn't know how all the details will work out, and in that sense it does take a risk. But it is the risk of commitment, not the risk of ignorance. You may have heard preachers helpfully compare faith to sitting in a chair. There is always a risk to sitting in a chair, especially in a room of junior high boys. We must transfer our weight to the chair, and if the chair isn't sturdy or if it's pulled out at the last second, we will hit the floor. Yet unless the chair was hastily assembled from Ikea or we've eaten too many waffle cones stuffed with mint chocolate chip ice cream, we assume the chair will support our weight. We commit to the chair in a commonsense union of faith and knowledge.

The same union holds for our Christian life. Some popular books mistakenly urge believers to leap far beyond what our knowledge can support. *The Prayer of Jabez* said we should "step out in faith" and "challenge God's power," taking big risks that force him to come through for us and perform miracles in our lives. "It's a frightening and utterly exhilarating truth, isn't it? As God's chosen, blessed sons and daughters, we are expected to attempt something large enough that failure is guaranteed . . . unless God steps in."[2]

Read that sentence again. Isn't it shockingly similar to how Satan tempted Jesus? The devil took him to the top of the temple and said, "If you are the Son of God," attempt something so big that on your own you will certainly fail. "Throw yourself down from here." Take the leap of faith and trust God to step in and save you. Jesus did not fall for it. He said jumping off the temple would not be a sign of great faith. It would be sin because he would be testing God (Luke 4:9–12).

What is the difference between trusting God and testing God? If we have a promise from God that we are claiming or a command from God that we are obeying, then it is an act of faith to claim that promise and obey that command. If we don't have a word from God—if we're merely trying to prove God's power or love—then stepping out is not an act of faith but a foolish act of sin. It is not our job to test God. He already knows he is good. God tests us. Will we believe his promises and obey his commands? Faith is not about jumping off temples. It is the daily act of depending fully on what God has revealed in his Word.

It is More Than You Think

Since we are relying on what God has revealed, we may safely claim we are relying on what we know. Philosophers define knowledge as justified, true belief. To know something, we must (1) believe it, (2) our belief must be true, and (3) we must be justified, or within our epistemic rights in believing it.

---

[2] Bruce Wilkinson, *The Prayer of Jabez* (Sisters, OR: Multnomah, 2000), 15–16, 34, 47, 53.

Modern philosophers, such as René Descartes and John Locke, said justification requires sufficient evidence. We cannot claim to know what we cannot prove.

Recent philosophers, led by Alvin Plantinga, think this is naïve. Many facts we know, such as what we ate for breakfast and that other people have minds, cannot be proved. Yet we would go crazy if we doubted every memory, and we would not stay married long if we doubted our spouses have a mind. The modern demand for proof is foolishly restrictive. Rather than treat our beliefs as guilty unless proven innocent, why not adopt a credulity disposition—a temperament that assumes our beliefs are true unless we have good reason to doubt them?

Plantinga argues that we are warranted in thinking our beliefs are true as long as we are justified in believing our faculties are functioning properly in their correct environment according to a design plan that is successfully aimed at truth. I realize that is a mouthful, and I encourage you to read his *Knowledge and Christian Belief* to learn more. Plantinga's point is that belief in God supplies warrant for each of these elements. We who believe in God may rightly assume our minds and senses are functioning properly, they are well matched for this world, and they are intelligently designed to discover truth. Consequently, we are well within our epistemic rights to give our beliefs the benefit of the doubt. We may assume that whatever we are inclined to believe is true, unless we have good reasons for doubting it.[3]

What about belief in God? Well, do you believe God exists? Is it true that God exists? Then congratulations, you may say you *know* God exists. The Bible agrees. Only a fool says, "There is no God" (Ps 14:1; 53:1), since God has revealed to everyone "his invisible attributes, that is, his eternal power and divine nature." These "have been clearly seen since the creation of the world, being understood through what he has made. As a result, people are without excuse" (Rom 1:19–20).

What about the Bible? Well, do you believe Scripture is God's Word? Is it true that Scripture is God's Word? If you say yes, then congratulations. You may say you *know* the Bible is God's Word. Plantinga incorporates insights from John Calvin to explain that the Bible is self-authenticating. Simply put, when we read the Bible, we hear the voice of God. Calvin said this happens because the same Spirit who wrote the Bible bears witness to it, opening our ears to recognize that the Bible is what it claims to be. He explained, "For as God alone is a fit witness of himself in his Word, so also the Word will not find

---

[3]   Alvin Plantinga, *Knowledge and Christian Belief* (Grand Rapids: Eerdmans, 2015). This is a simplified version of his acclaimed *Warranted Christian Belief* (New York: Oxford University Press, 2000). There he argues that only theists have the right to claim knowledge, for those who do not believe in God lack warrant for their beliefs (p. 240).

acceptance in men's hearts before it is sealed by the inward testimony of the Spirit."[4]

If we know the Bible is God's Word, then we also know it is true. God does not lie, and he doesn't get facts wrong, so the biblical account of Jesus's resurrection must be true. We were not present when Jesus's body jolted awake. We did not see him sit up, stretch, and fold the strips of linen that bound his head. We did not see him step over and around the unconscious guards as he left the tomb. Yet we may say, on the authority of God's Word, that we *know* Jesus rose from the dead. When we put our faith in Jesus, we are not taking one step beyond what our knowledge can support. We are entrusting our lives to what we know is true.

Application

Faith does not begin when knowledge ends. Neither does faith begin before knowledge starts. You may have heard the expression, "Faith seeking understanding," popularized by Anselm in the eleventh century. This phrase might sound like faith is a shot in the dark. Take a flyer. Believe in something, even if you do not know whether it is true. This is not Anselm's intent. He merely meant to oppose the idea that faith requires proof and argument. He thought reason is better on the back end, as a servant that probes and explains our beliefs, rather than on the front end, as a master that must give permission for us to believe. Faith may not begin with full understanding, but it does begin with knowledge. The faith that seeks understanding rests on what it knows to that point.

If we believe what we know, then knowledge is the fuel of faith. Our faith cannot travel further than our knowledge takes us. Knowledge by itself is not enough. We can have a tankful of gas and not go anywhere. But we won't get far down the road without it. If we run out of knowledge, our faith runs out of gas.

Faith does not begin when knowledge ends. It clings to knowledge throughout its entire journey. Do you want a robust faith? Believe what you know; it's more than you think.

---

[4]   Calvin, *Institutes* I.7.4, 79 (see chap. 2, n. 3).

CHAPTER 4

Theology Is Western and White

The Legendary Belief

I teach theology in an evangelical seminary. While striving to be diverse and relevant to contemporary issues, I cover the traditional loci through their historical development in the church. I believe it is important to teach the Great Tradition as it has come to us, and since key cities on that journey include Rome, Paris, Wittenberg, Geneva, Heidelberg, London, and Nashville (one of these is not like the others), this approach is increasingly criticized as a white European male-centric model. Critics say the Great Tradition is not sensitive enough to the needs of minority students, who may be unfamiliar with the classical vocabulary and would profit more from practical issues such as suffering and justice. They allege that traditional theology is too male, too Western, and too white.

Unraveling the Legend

Like most academic disciplines, vocational theology has historically been dominated by men. I omitted "male" from the title of this urban legend because that part is true. Thankfully this is beginning to change, as more women are finding their voice and support for a theological vocation. May this trend continue!

Theology may for a while longer be the domain of men, but it has never been exactly Western or white. The first seven councils of the Great Tradition met in what today is modern Turkey, in the *Eastern* church. Our understanding of the Trinity and the two natures of Jesus comes from the Eastern councils of Nicea, Constantinople, Ephesus, and Chalcedon. The theologians who contributed most to the orthodox view were from the Asian lands of Cappadocia (located in today's east-central Turkey): Basil the Great, his younger brother

Gregory of Nyssa, and their friend Gregory of Nazianzus.[1] Any responsible discussion of the Trinity or the divine Son must rise in the East.

But isn't theology hopelessly white? Well, consider this surprising fact. The most important theologian of the Western church is Augustine. The most important theologian of the Eastern church is Origen. Both were Africans.

Out of Africa

The church began in the eastern end of the Roman empire and spread west. Paul started from Jerusalem, a Middle Eastern city, and traveled northwest, through Antioch (Syria) and Asia (Turkey) to Greece, Rome, and perhaps Spain. Other missionaries went southwest into Africa. Philip met an Ethiopian eunuch who brought the gospel to what is today southern Egypt and northern Sudan (Acts 8:26–40). Various traditions say John Mark was martyred in Alexandria, but not before establishing a church in the Jewish community there. These efforts paid off, as northern Africa became the center of Christian theology from the second through fifth centuries.

Africa's leading city was Alexandria, a storied intellectual powerhouse that became the dominant theological force in the Eastern church. Its theologians included Clement, Origen, Athanasius, Didymus the Blind, and Cyril. Africa's second city was Carthage, which became the theological center of the Western church. It produced such giants as Tertullian, Cyprian, and Augustine, who moved farther west and made Hippo a fifth-century center of Western Christianity.

The African Tertullian supplied the terms *trinity, substance,* and *persons* that the ecumenical councils used to express trinitarian doctrine. The councils themselves were patterned on earlier African councils, and the spark that ignited the whole conciliar sequence came from Africa, in a dustup between the Alexandrian bishop Alexander and his presbyter Arius. Nicene orthodoxy was championed in the middle of the fourth century by the African Athanasius, who opposed the Arians and wrote *On the Incarnation of the Word.* Athanasian orthodoxy was confirmed by the African Augustine's *On the Trinity,* still the foundational trinitarian text in the West. The doctrines of the Trinity and Christology were built on the language of Africans, defended by Africans, and promoted by Africans.

In *How Africa Shaped the Christian Mind,* historian Tom Oden noted the editors working on his Ancient Christian Commentary on Scripture series were "astonished" to learn how much early church exegetes such as Chrysostom and Ambrose relied on earlier African writers like Didymus, Cyril of Alexandria,

---

[1]   Ninety-seven percent of Turkey lies in Asia and only three percent in Europe. In the first century, the territory of what today is western Turkey was known as the province of Asia (2 Cor 1:8).

and especially Origen. Africans didn't merely influence theological development; they drove biblical interpretation too.[2]

Some might object that these African theologians lived in North Africa rather than south of the Sahara. Augustine was an ethnic Berber who likely had olive skin, similar to a modern-day Libyan. On the other hand, Athanasius was nicknamed the "Black Dwarf" because he was short and had a dark complexion. But why should this matter? Oden noted it is unwise to focus on skin color. "How black were the Christians of North Africa? Black enough if blackness is understood in terms of intergenerational suffering and oppression. If black is defined by color, a trip to Numidia or Nubia or Ethiopia settles the chromatological argument." Oden added that we shouldn't privilege sub-Saharan Africa as "the real Africa." The continent is one. "North Africa is no less African than sub-Saharan Africa."[3]

If North Africa was the cradle of Christian thought, then Christianity did not enter Africa by missionaries sent from America. Africa is where Christian theology grew up. Only later did it migrate to Europe, and from there to America. When nineteenth- and twentieth-century missionaries brought the gospel to Africa, they were not introducing something foreign. They were bringing the good news of Jesus home, back to where it began.

Pushed into Europe

Why did the center of theology shift from Africa to Europe? It shifted in part because Europeans learned from Africa, modeling their universities on the third-century learning community gathered around Alexandria's famous library and their monasteries on the rigorous piety honed in the communes and hermitages of African deserts. In part, it shifted because Europeans appreciated Augustine, Cyprian, and Tertullian, reading their works in Rome and other major cities immediately after publication. But as often happens in history, the decisive cause was war.

As Augustine lay dying in 430, the Vandals besieged his hometown, Hippo. Many Christians fled to Europe to escape the invasion. Two years later, Vandals took the city and held North Africa until the seventh century, when Muslims swept from Arabia through North Africa and up into Spain. Their advance into Europe was stopped by Charles Martel at the battle of Tours in 732, but they have retained control of North Africa ever since. With Hippo, Carthage, and Alexandria in Muslim hands, the center of Christian thought naturally

---

[2] Thomas C. Oden, *How Africa Shaped the Christian Mind* (Downers Grove, IL: IVP Books, 2007), 29, 45–46. See also Justo González, *The Story of Christianity*, vol. 1, *The Early Church to the Dawn of the Reformation*, 2nd ed. (New York: HarperOne, 2010), 199.

[3] Oden, *How Africa Shaped*, 69, 79–84.

moved to the safety of Europe. There it remained for the next millennium, until English Protestants brought their religious fervor to America. The theologians of the Middle Ages, Reformation, and Modern Era were largely Europeans or Americans of European descent, but this owes more to the Muslim invasion than to white supremacy. If North Africa had remained in Christian hands with its churches, monasteries, and libraries intact, how differently would theology have developed in the West?

Perhaps a lot. The vigorous devotion of the African church may have avoided the medieval corruptions that ignited the Reformation and the rationalism that secularized theology in modern European universities. Of course, the Africans may have encountered other problems, as their fervent passions flared into the errors of Donatism, Montanism, Manicheism, and Gnosticism. Yet much of Christian theology may have remained the same. The classical theism of the Middle Ages relied on Scripture, Greek philosophy, and the church fathers of Africa and the East. These were in place long before Anselm and Thomas Aquinas came on the scene. In many ways these medieval theologians were imitating the ideas—and in Anselm's case even the style—they found in Augustine.[4] Likewise, the European Reformers believed they were channeling the soteriology of Augustine and the ecclesiology of Cyprian. French theologian John Calvin cites these two Africans more than anyone else in his *Institutes of the Christian Religion.*

Theology's Great Tradition does not need to be deconstructed to become relevant to minorities. It is already less Western and less white than you might think. Are you interested in the issue of justice? You could start with Basil's *Address to the Rich,* Gregory of Nazianzus's *Oration 14: On the Love of the Poor,* or Gregory of Nyssa's attack on slavery in *Homily 4 on Ecclesiastes.* Wondering how to bear unjust suffering? Read Tertullian's *Apology* or *To the Martyrs.* Asking where is God when your world collapses? That was Augustine's project in *The City of God,* as he attempted to make theological sense of Rome's fall. We do need minority, non-Western voices to write theology for the twenty-first century, but they don't need to start from scratch. Our theological tradition began with them, and it welcomes them home.

Application

Diversity is a high value and a significant good. Who has not benefited from hearing another person's perspective? Even if we ultimately disagree, we learn much from seeing the world through others' eyes. At the same time, the more

---

[4] Thomas Aquinas is justly criticized for relying too heavily on Aristotle. However, the writings of this seminal philosopher were discovered and brought to Aquinas and the West by Muslim Arabs, who were neither Western nor white.

we share our differences, the more we realize we are very much the same. This is true of all humanity, which finds its unity in Adam (Acts 17:26), and it is truer of Christians, who are united in the Last Adam. Jesus "is our peace" who reconciles Jew and Gentile, East and West, black and white into "one body through the cross" (Eph 2:14–16). If I am in Jesus and you are in Jesus, then what we have in common far outweighs what distinguishes us.

We must not overemphasize our differences. The Christian faith is a historical faith, which means it is inherently particular. The Church of the Annunciation in Nazareth is built around an early church grotto whose altar reads, "The Word was made flesh here." The events of the gospel happened there, not in the West. But they happened there for everywhere. The historical truth that Jesus is a Middle Eastern man does not prevent him from saving Americans like me. The historical truth that Christian theology was nurtured in Africa and central Asia does not lessen its significance for Europeans and Americans, any more than the historical truth that Europeans further developed the Great Tradition in the medieval and Modern eras makes it irrelevant for Brazilians and Filipinos. The Africans, Asians, Europeans, and Americans who labored on their portion of the tradition were not perfect, and we may disagree with some of their theological moves. But we ignore them at our peril.

There is no need to remake the theological wheel. Beginners in theology may not be familiar with the traditional terms, but that is true with any subject. Anything worth learning—including how to order a light iced venti vanilla latte with three pumps, soy milk, caramel drizzle, one shot of espresso, no whip, and extra foam—requires comprehending a new vocabulary and grammar. Newcomers might be intimidated by theological terms such as *perspicuity, justification, compatibilism, passibility*, and so forth, but give them enough time and they will inevitably grapple with the same concepts. They may not come to them through the same historical controversies that shook late medieval and modern Europe, but they will eventually ask and answer similar questions.

There is no need to reject the theological wheel. We might give it a different spin, taking it out for a ride in a fresh and promising direction. But each new road must bring us back to the old way, a way that is white and Western, and richly black, brown, African, and Middle Eastern. Theology's Great Tradition is still chugging down ethnically diverse avenues. Chinese, Australian, and Nigerian theologians are developing and applying theology to their indigenous populations. As they remain faithful to theology's Main Street, their contextualized contributions will drive our understanding of God and his ways further down the road until we reach our final destination, when "a vast multitude from every nation, tribe, people, and language" will praise our glorious God together (Rev 7:9).

CHAPTER 5

Doctrine Divides. Love Unites

The Legendary Belief

Theological liberalism arose in the nineteenth century as modern Christians attempted to make peace with the rising naturalism of their world. By the first decade of the twentieth century, theological conservatives had seen enough. They banded together and published a series of books called *The Fundamentals* that defended the foundations of the Christian faith: the inerrancy and infallibility of Scripture; the virgin birth and deity of Jesus; his substitutionary atonement; and his literal, physical resurrection and literal, physical return.

These truths should not have been controversial to anyone who knew what the church had always believed. Yet theological conservatives lost every denomination that the liberals contested. The liberals won by steering the conversation away from theology and onto acts of service. A favorite slogan was "Doctrine Divides. Service Unites." Or often, "Doctrine Divides. Love Unites." As Harry Emerson Fosdick put it in his defiant sermon, "Shall the Fundamentalists Win?," intolerant conservatives were foolishly "driving in their stakes to mark out the deadline of doctrine around the church, across which no one is to pass except on terms of agreement." How dare conservatives "deny the Christian name to those who differ" with their traditional opinions! Fosdick concluded, "Opinions may be mistaken; love never is."[1]

Unraveling the Legend

Fosdick and his liberal supporters were partially right. Doctrine does divide. Doctrine separates Christians from Muslims, Hindus, and Buddhists. Within

---

[1]   Harry Emerson Fosdick, "Shall the Fundamentalists Win?," *Christian Work* 102 (June 10, 1922): 716–22.

Christianity, doctrine separates conservatives from liberals, orthodox trinitarians from unitarians, and biblical sexual ethics from the LGBTQ+ lobby. While these divisions are necessary, Fosdick did finger a worrisome danger in conservative churches. Christians who valiantly defend the faith against liberalism might turn their weapons on each other. To a man with a sword anything might seem a tempting target to slay, and churches have tragically split over Bible translations, degrees of separation from the world, and the granular, disputable elements of eschatology.

But doctrine not only divides. It also unites. Have you attended an international church in a foreign city? Expats from across the world gather to worship Jesus. They might disagree about politics and economics and international disputes, but they believe the same truths about Jesus, and these doctrines bind their hearts together. Their gatherings are a preview of heaven's throne room, where "a vast multitude from every nation, tribe, people, and language" shout their doctrinal praise, "Salvation belongs to our God, who is seated on the throne, and to the Lamb!" (Rev 7:9–10).

As with doctrine, so love may both unite and divide. Love unites when we set aside our differences to serve each other or, even better, serve others together. When churches jointly staff a tutoring program or build a food pantry for their community, their cooperation fulfills Jesus's prayer for unity, "that the world may know you have sent me and have loved them as you have loved me" (John 17:23).

But love also divides. Western culture proudly proclaims, "Love is love is love is love." But this slogan is not as inclusive as it sounds. First, its proponents don't really mean it. They do not really think all "love" is equal. Most people still frown on adults having sex with children, and anyone having sex with animals—regardless of whether they say they love them. Not all "loves" are allowed. Most would not simply shrug and say, "Well, love is love" were their spouses to engage in extramarital affairs. Any love worth having must say no to lesser, illicit loves that cheapen or threaten it. Second, the tolerance implicit in "Love is love is love is love" is most intolerant toward anyone who might disagree. As I write this, it is an open question whether Christian parachurch organizations will be allowed to operate according to the loving commands of God's Word. We may soon be forced to choose between violating our consciences and going out of business. From a conservative Christian perspective, nothing has been more divisive than Western culture's postliberal notion of love. Fosdick might be chagrined to learn where his liberal leanings on love have led.[2]

---

[2]   Fosdick foresaw the dangers of "cancel culture," presciently warning that liberals might become equally intolerant. "Speaking, as I do, from the viewpoint of liberal opinions, let me say that if some young, fresh mind here this morning is holding new ideas, has fought his way through, it may be by

Grace and Truth

The divisiveness of love signals that kindness always comes with specific beliefs. No one loves from nowhere, generically, untethered from doctrine. Love must be defined. *What is love? Which acts count as loving? Who decides?*

Start with the self, allowing each person to define love from the ground up, and you'll get the toxic sludge that is dissolving Western civilization. Love means whatever the majority or loudest voices say it means, and since people are fickle, the standard is continually changing. Today's revolutionaries become tomorrow's old guard, to be canceled and replaced by a new round of radicals. Letters are periodically added to LGBTQ+ (that's what the plus sign is for), and those who stop at the *L* or the *G* will be run over by the *T* and the *Q*, which themselves will be rolled over by whatever letters come next.

But why start with the self? Why not let God define love for us? John explains, "Love consists in this: not that we loved God, but that he loved us and sent his Son to be the atoning sacrifice for our sins" (1 John 4:10). God's love rescues us from sin, providing forgiveness for sin's penalty and freedom from sin's power. But what is sin? Everyone has a doctrine of sin. Everyone believes certain acts are evil and deserve punishment. But each of us see only a slice of the world, and only from one perspective. Our take on right and wrong is bound to be incomplete, if not outright mistaken. So, wise people take their cues from God. He created and redeemed us, and he alone has the right and the insight to declare what is good and bad for us.

What is sin? Whatever the Bible says. What is love? Whatever rescues us from this sin. Our rescue requires grace; God must want to forgive. Our rescue requires truth; God must know what he is doing. He must not forgive acts that aren't sins or give free passes to sins that need to be owned. It's no coincidence that love's climax is the cross of Christ, who embodies both "grace and truth" (John 1:14). Jesus isn't grace *or* truth but grace *and* truth. Without truth, grace smooshes into sappy sentimentality that is easily pushed around. It lacks backbone, like a mom making excuses for her "amazing" run-of-the-mill son who is "too busy" to remember her birthday. Without grace, truth turns into a stern taskmaster that is perpetually disappointed. It lacks heart, like a drill sergeant relentlessly pushing recruits past their breaking point. Grace and truth are not opposites. They are two sides of the same coin. Grace needs truth to effectively save people. Truth needs grace or no one is saved.

---

intellectual and spiritual struggle, to novel positions, and is tempted to be intolerant about old opinions, offensively to condescend to those who hold them and to be harsh in judgment on them, he may well remember that people who held those old opinions have given the world some of the noblest character and the most rememberable service that it ever has been blessed with, and that we of the younger generation will prove our case best, not by controversial intolerance, but by producing, with our new opinions, something of the depth and strength, nobility and beauty of character that in other times were associated with other thoughts." See Fosdick, "Shall the Fundamentalists Win?"

Switch out grace and truth for love and doctrine, and you'll see that just as grace without truth isn't grace and truth without grace isn't the truth, so doctrine without love isn't Christian doctrine and love without doctrine isn't Christian love. Doctrine and love must never be pitted against each other. They are left and right wings that keep our faith aloft.

Suburban Legend

"Western theology builds fences while Eastern thought digs wells."

An updated version of the doctrine versus love myth asserts, "Western theology builds fences while Eastern thought digs wells."[3] Advocates allege conservative Christians fixate on doctrine because they are products of a Western culture that is preoccupied with fences and boundaries. One author explains:

> Most Americans want dandelion-free lawns and roads with clear lanes prescribing where to drive and where not to drive. . . .We listen to classical music based on a scale with seven notes and five half steps. Each note "has a fixed pitch, defined in terms of the lengths of the sound waves it produces." A good performance occurs when the musicians hit the notes precisely.
>
> In contrast, many Eastern cultures have little concern in everyday life for sharp boundaries and uniform categories.[4]

Is this true? I lived in Beijing and attended many concerts there. Do you know what the Chinese call an orchestra that is not hitting their notes precisely? Warming up. The moment the concert begins, Eastern musicians count their rests and play in tune like any Western symphony orchestra. Easterners understand—and live by—boundaries. The most fiercely guarded boundary in the world lies between North and South Korea. The redemptive event of the Old Testament is a group of Middle Easterners crossing a boundary into the Promised Land. The Bible itself is an Eastern document, and it clearly defines the beliefs and practices that distinguish the family of God from those outside. Easterners as well as Westerners know every meaningful set has a boundary. Every husband and wife know who is and who is not in their marriage. Every soccer match separates one team from the other and the athletes from the fans in the stands. That boundaries are a Western idea is just not true.

And it is doubly untrue that conservative Christians focus on doctrine because we want to police the boundary, evicting intruders who don't belong.

---

[3] Proponents of this slogan say Western culture privileges bounded sets while Eastern culture prefers centered sets. Unlike American farmers, who build fences to keep their cattle in, ranchers in the outback of Australia dig wells that attract their animals to stay nearby. No fences are required. This difference in style seems to be entirely an accident of geography. Does anyone doubt that Australian farmers in congested areas would build fences and American ranchers in the vast open stretches of Australia would dig wells?

[4] David Livermore, *Cultural Intelligence* (Grand Rapids: Baker Academic, 2009), 171.

Some "policing" is necessary for every meaningful set. Even liberal groups have conditions for membership, or they would not be much of a group. Conservatives focus on doctrine because we focus on Jesus; doctrine is simply what we believe about him. If someone said they love Jesus, then went on to describe him as a Vietnamese woman known for her lemongrass soup, we would immediately correct him. We would say that Jesus is the divine Son of God who added a full human nature, becoming the Middle Eastern Man who died for our sins, rose from the dead, ascended to heaven, and is returning in glory any day now. Everything in that sentence is doctrine. Everything in that sentence exudes love. Doctrine is not the opposite of love. It's not even in tension with love. Doctrine is necessary to give shape to our love, directing our hearts to the object of our love.

Every meaningful set has both a center and a boundary. Jesus is the center of our faith, and doctrine tells us about him. Nothing is more important than Jesus. But the boundary matters too. When the Philippian jailer begged Paul and Silas, "Sirs, what must I do to be saved?" they didn't ask why a Mediterranean man was so obsessed with boundaries. They led him to the center: "Believe in the Lord Jesus, and you will be saved." The man and his family believed Paul's doctrine, and they crossed the boundary into the family of God (Acts 16:30–34).

Application

I have a theory about the doctrine-love canard. See if it fits your experience. While we need both, it seems people are tempted to privilege one or the other depending on the hand they are dealt. If they believe they have a winning hand, they are quick to enforce doctrine. Notice today how many liberals insist that everyone think like them when it comes to homosexual and transgender issues. But when we suspect our hand is weak, either because our interpretation is out of step with Scripture (liberals) or because the culture is against us (conservatives), we tend to lead with love. Liberals say, "Let's love instead of fretting about doctrine," and conservatives say, "It's unloving to force your doctrine on me."

Not long ago, when most churches opposed homosexual practice, homosexual activists asked for conversation. *Can we have a seat at the table? Can this issue be discussed?* Christians who agreed to dialogue were criticized for compromising with evil. Why legitimize an abomination? Now that the tables have turned and LGBTQ+ supporters have the upper hand, conservative Christians are asking for dialogue, and their liberal interlocutors worry about legitimizing an offensive viewpoint. *Why give intolerant bigots the time of day?*

No one is truly against doctrine. Those who say they are may well be biding their time until they gain power. Then they may become the fundamentalists that Fosdick warned about, in the other team's jersey.

CHAPTER 6

The Bible Is Our Only Authority

The Legendary Belief

Brian McLaren suspected that his theologically liberal book *A New Kind of Christianity* would be controversial, but he said some of the criticism took him by surprise. He noted that "the review by Scot McKnight ends with the statement that we should read the Bible through the lens of church tradition and the creeds, when I thought that part of the evangelical ethos was that the Bible trumps all human formulations."[1] *Isn't the Bible our only authority?*

Unraveling the Legend

McLaren's comment commits the logical fallacy of the false dualism. He presents two options as if they are the only possibilities and suggests we must choose between them. Either the Bible is most important, or we should use the church's creeds to interpret it. Since everyone would say the Bible is most important, they must agree that we should not use church tradition to understand it. But why assume this is a case of either/or? Isn't it a both/and? Protestant theologians believe we must say both things: "The Bible trumps all human formulations" *and* "We should read the Bible through the lens of church tradition and the creeds." To appreciate why we need both, we must understand the Roman Catholic and nonconfessional ditches on either side of our theological road.

---

[1] Lynn Garrett, "McLaren Book Kicks Up Controversy," *Publishers Weekly*, March 30, 2010.

Two Opposite Errors

The Roman Catholic Church teaches that Scripture and tradition are two equal streams of authority. The Second Vatican Council declared, "Both sacred tradition and Sacred Scripture are to be accepted and venerated with the same sense of loyalty and reverence. Sacred tradition and Sacred Scripture form one sacred deposit of the word of God, committed to the Church." The "teaching office of the Church" stands under this united word of God, where it has the solemn task of authoritatively interpreting both Scripture and tradition, with its official declarations becoming part of the Church's ongoing, developing tradition. Vatican II concluded that "sacred tradition, Sacred Scripture and the teaching authority of the Church . . . are so linked and joined together that one cannot stand without the others, and that all together and each in its own way under the action of the one Holy Spirit contribute effectively to the salvation of souls."[2]

Figure 6.1: Roman Catholic Authority

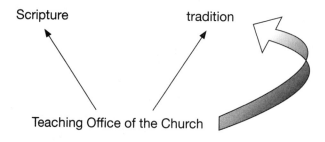

Scripture   tradition

Teaching Office of the Church

While Roman Catholics show deference to Scripture by placing "tradition" in lower case, Protestants believe they still elevate tradition too highly. Scripture and tradition are not equal streams of authority, but, as McLaren said, "the Bible trumps all human formulations." Yet in veering away from the Roman Catholic error, McLaren overcorrects and runs his car into the opposite ditch. Here, given his sharp disagreements with theological conservatives, McLaren might be surprised to learn that his careening faith has crashed alongside some of his most ardent fundamentalist critics.

These Christians mistake the Reformation cry *sola scriptura* for *solo scriptura* or *nuda scriptura* ("only Scripture" or "naked Scripture"). They agree with McLaren that we should not "read the Bible through the lens of church tradition and the creeds" because the Bible is our only authority. We must read the Bible straight, unfiltered by centuries of human accretions. If

---

[2] *Dogmatic Constitution on Divine Revelation: Dei Verbum*, November 18, 1965, II.9–10, https://www.vatican.va/archive/hist_councils/ii_vatican_council/documents/vat-ii_const_19651118_dei-verbum_en.html.

only that were possible! No one reads the Bible from nowhere. We all are products of a past that began centuries before we were born, and those who are least aware of this past are most at its mercy. As we will learn in later chapters, those who don't know how Platonic philosophy or Freudian psychology or American self-reliance or postmodern liberalism or expressive individualism have influenced their minds will not realize when they are reading these into the biblical text.

So they end up in strange, heretical places. Brian McLaren dismissed church tradition, then wrote two chapters on Jesus in *A New Kind of Christianity* and never once mentioned that Jesus is God. Shouldn't that be the first thing any Christian would say? On the opposite end of the theological spectrum, fundamentalist churches that won't observe Pentecost Sunday because it's too "Catholic" don't flinch at celebrating the Fourth of July. They might even recite the Pledge of Allegiance in church, with their right hand over their heart. They force Jesus to share his worship space with a human product—in this instance a nation—which is the sort of thing a theological liberal would do. For better or sometimes worse, every church will have a tradition. Why not use the Great Tradition that has been handed down to us?

Sola Scriptura

The Reformers used the phrase *sola scriptura* to say that Scripture is our highest and final authority. They did not mean Scripture is our only authority. As God's Word, Scripture is the *norma normans non normata* ("the norm of norms that is not normed"). The Bible is the standard that judges everything else. It does not stoop to be judged by any other standard. Yet there are lesser authorities that because they are judged and shaped by Scripture are indispensable to helping us read it. These *norma normata* ("norm that is normed") include the Apostles' Creed, ecumenical councils and creeds, denominational confessions and catechisms, and individual church fathers and theologians.

Figure 6.2: Protestant Authority

Scripture: final authority

↑
|
|

tradition: lens to read Scripture

Apostles' Creed
Ecumenical councils & creeds
Denominational confessions & catechisms
Church fathers & theologians

The Apostles' Creed arises from the Roman church's baptismal creed. We have snippets from early baptismal creeds, each resembling the others and what we find in the Apostles' Creed. When we recite the Apostles' Creed, we are going back about as far as we can, to stand shoulder to shoulder with the first Christians. The baptismal creeds were written to weed out heresy and preserve the orthodox faith. Before converts could receive baptism, they had to recite "I believe in God the Father Almighty, Creator of heaven and earth. I believe in Jesus Christ, his only Son, our Lord, who was conceived by the Holy Spirit and born of the virgin Mary."

These standardized baptismal creeds were the early church's rule of faith. Before they collected the canon of the New Testament, the early Christians possessed the church's creed. When around 211 the bishop Serapion of Antioch learned that a church in Rhossus, Syria, was using the gnostic Gospel of Peter, he told them to stop by appealing to their rule of faith. Gnostic gospels were clearly heretical because they violated several lines in the creed: God as Creator; Jesus as conceived and born, suffered, crucified, died, and resurrected; and the future resurrection of our bodies.

The church used this rule of faith to determine which books met the standard of orthodoxy required of the New Testament canon. And the church still uses this rule to rightly interpret these New Testament books. If you interpret a biblical passage in a way that disagrees with the Apostles' Creed, you can be sure you are reading it wrong.

Second only to the Apostles' Creed are the ecumenical councils and the creeds they produced. Such councils are impossible to pull off now, since the Eastern church split from the Western church, the Western church split into Roman Catholics and Protestants, and Protestants split into denominations that split yet again and again. Some split into nondenominational churches, which risk losing the tradition this chapter urges us to keep. The church seems hopelessly fractured, yet all Christians must esteem the first four councils—Nicea (325), Constantinople (381), Ephesus (431), and Chalcedon (451)—that mapped the orthodox landscape of the Trinity and the two natures of Jesus. The Eastern Orthodox subscribe to these four plus three more, Roman Catholics to those seven plus fourteen more in the West, and some aberrant fundamentalists and liberals subscribe to none. It is hypothetically possible to disagree with one of the first four councils, as none are equal to Scripture, but I have never seen it successfully done. Pastors who dare to take on Nicea or Chalcedon based on Scripture end up regretting it.

After ecumenical councils come lesser confessions and catechisms that are important for distinct denominations. Southern Baptists subscribe to the Baptist Faith and Message, Presbyterians to the Westminster Confession and Catechisms, Lutherans to the Book of Concord, Dutch Reformed to the Belgic

Confession and Heidelberg Catechism, and so on. None of these think their creeds govern Christians outside their denominations. They use their statements of faith to preserve the doctrinal distinctives, unity, and integrity of their church.

Last are individual church fathers and theologians. Their authority is far removed from the ecumenical creeds and councils, and we may safely disagree with them on many issues, as I sometimes do. But we must always be cautious and respectful. We should disagree charitably, as if we were speaking to their face. Just because they are dead does not mean we get a free pass to twist or ignore what they said.

The most important theologian in the West is Augustine. In many ways the Reformation was a fight over him. Roman Catholics claimed to follow the letter of Augustine's soteriology while Protestants, led by an Augustinian monk named Martin Luther, argued that they followed his spirit. If Augustine had lived then, Luther argued, he would have taken their Protestant side. After Augustine, in chronological order, come other significant theologians: Irenaeus, Tertullian, Cyprian, Athanasius, Basil, Gregory of Nyssa, Gregory of Nazianzus, Anselm, Thomas Aquinas, Martin Luther, John Calvin, Jonathan Edwards, and C. S. Lewis.

That last name is a humorous nod to American evangelicals, who sometimes make too much of a good thing. They may not be able to locate a biblical chapter and verse for a specific doctrine, but if C. S. Lewis said it, that might be enough. For a joke that cuts a little too close to home, here is the functional order of authority found in a few evangelical churches: (1) red letters, (2) C. S. Lewis, (3) black letters, (4) Chris Tomlin, (5) the Apostles' Creed.

Evangelicals should remember that we and Roman Catholics share much the same heritage. My ordination paper mentioned that wise Christians read Scripture through the lens of tradition, including Augustine, Calvin, and Aquinas. The last name was a tough sell for my Baptist audience, as they knew too many Roman Catholic schools named after him. I said that while we disagree with Aquinas on many things, we cannot responsibly discuss the doctrine of God without engaging his version of classical theism. And since he lived more than 200 years before the Reformation, Aquinas belongs as much to our Protestant heritage as he does to the Roman Catholics.

Application

You do not have to read the Bible alone. You should not read the Bible alone. Read the Bible through the lens of the Apostles' Creed and from what you know about the first four councils and the confessions and catechisms of your denomination. The creeds of the church are not higher than Scripture, but they are higher than you. If you think you have found something in the Bible that you have never seen before, and your pastor and trusted friends have never seen it, you may have a heresy. You are probably going to need to let it go. Or better yet, kill it.

The goal of preaching and teaching is to be creative in delivery and entirely unoriginal in content. As Vincent of Lérins said in the fifth century, we must take care to "hold that which has been believed everywhere, always, and by all people." This goal seems impossibly difficult now that centuries have separated churches from each other. We have fewer items that everyone agrees on. But those centuries have also delivered a longer, more richly developed and tested tradition. We understand God's Word better now as we stand on the shoulders of those who read it before us. And if we read the Bible well, our children will understand even more.

___

CHAPTER 7

A High View of Scripture Turns the Bible into an Idol

The Legendary Belief

Philosopher Carl Raschke thinks it is a grave error to say the Bible has no errors. He wrote, "Inerrancy is an idolatry of the text. It is bibliolatry plain and simple, inasmuch as it cannot see beyond the logical lattice of the text to encounter the Other who is ever calling us into his kingdom and before his throne."[1] In simpler words, if we think the Bible is perfect (at least in its original manuscripts) we will be tempted to worship it rather than the God who gave it. John Caputo agrees. "I am not an idolater. . . . I take the second commandment very seriously and I do not put false gods—like books (biblical inerrantism) or the Vatican (papal infallibility)—before God, who is the 'wholly other.'"[2] Raschke and Caputo fear that a high view of Scripture turns the Bible into an idol. We become worshipers of a book rather than the personal God.

Unraveling the Legend

When I returned to China for a second year of teaching, I brought a study Bible for my friend who was eagerly growing in Christ. I'll always remember his wide smile as he opened his present. He clutched the Bible to his chest and thanked me profusely. As he walked to his bicycle, he gingerly placed his Bible in the basket, as if it were a carton of eggs, and promised it would never touch the ground. His reverence convicted me. I fling Bibles into backpacks and drop them on the floor without thinking twice. Sometimes I set my coffee on one. That is probably okay, though I respect my friend's awe for the Word

---

[1] Carl Raschke, *The Next Reformation* (Grand Rapids: Baker Academic, 2004), 135.
[2] John Caputo, *What Would Jesus Deconstruct?* (Grand Rapids: Baker, 2007), 110.

of God. He has an extremely high view of Scripture, but it is certainly not an idol. His reverence is something to admire.

Word of God

The people I know with a high view of Scripture do not use it as an idol that blocks them from "encountering the One" behind the text. The Bible is how they connect with the One who wrote it. Consider a woman whose husband was sent to the Vietnam War (this illustration works best before email and video chats). She writes a letter every single day, and when the mail arrives, she runs to the mailbox and rifles through the envelopes for one with his handwriting. She has saved all his letters in a shoebox, and she reads and rereads her favorite lines deep into the night. If you caught her savoring a worn and tear-smudged letter, you would not say, "What's wrong with you? If I didn't know better, I'd say you cherish these letters more than you love your husband!" She'd look at you as if you were crazy, or at least never in love. "Are you serious? I don't love these letters instead of my husband! I love these letters because of my husband. They are my only link to him!" In the same way, everyone I know who cherishes the Bible does so because it is their connection to Jesus. The Bible is how Jesus speaks to them. They want to hear their Lover's voice.

Any good thing can be distorted, so it is possible to value the Bible in a way that does not lead us to God. Some say this happens when people use the Bible as an end in itself. Perhaps a child memorizing verses for quiz team, a graduate student preparing for a university career in Hebrew and Near Eastern Studies, or an armchair "Berean" raising his hand during the Bible study to mansplain the difference between expiation and propitiation. But I don't think that's quite it. These people are not using the Bible as an end. If they are misusing Scripture, it's because they are twisting it into the service of a lesser, selfish good. They are using God's Word to feather their own nest, enhance their reputation, build a career, or bring home the trophy to fawning adults who are loudly impressed with the Bible knowledge of the next generation. I was a quiz team champion, so I know the temptation of which I speak. My problem wasn't that my view of Scripture was too high. It was too low. I was using God's Word to make me look good.

Jesus lit into the Pharisees for the same reason. Jesus never criticized his opponents for their high view of Scripture. He railed on them for using God's Word for their own selfish ends. "They do everything to be seen by others: They enlarge their phylacteries and lengthen their tassels. They love the place of honor at banquets, the front seats in the synagogues, greetings in the marketplaces, and to be called 'Rabbi' by people" (Matt 23:5–7). Jesus didn't criticize the Pharisees' high view of Scripture, because his view was even higher. In an argument with them, Jesus cited Scripture, calling it "the word of God" that "cannot be broken" (John 10:35). He meant it. Elsewhere he said that "not the smallest letter or one stroke of a letter will pass away from the law until all things are accomplished" (Matt 5:18). He once based an entire argument on a verb tense. Jesus noted that God said, "I am the God of Abraham and the God of Isaac and the God of Jacob." Not "I *was*" their God but "I *am*" their God. This means these patriarchs will rise again, for God "is not the God of the dead, but of the living" (22:31–32).

It is impossible to have a higher view of Scripture than Jesus has, so if anyone needs to worry about turning the Bible into an idol, it would be him. Think about it. Do you have a higher view of the Bible than Jesus has? No. Do you think Jesus is guilty of bibliolatry? No. Then you are probably safe. You may have many other problems, but a too-high view of Scripture isn't one of them.

It is unhelpful and unserious to play God off against his Word, as if a high view of Scripture may block us from loving and serving him. Sometimes when I leave the house, I give my children instructions to do a job before I return. If I come home to find the task unfinished and my kids playing *Mario Kart*, I will not be impressed if they say, "Dearest Father, we remembered what you said, but then we considered how much we love and respect you, and how we don't want your words to get in the way of our blossoming relationship. We set aside your word because we care about you! Nothing will ever come between us!"

I would probably say I'm not falling for this again, then remind them that my words are me. You do not respect me if you don't respect my words. If you disobey my words, you are disobeying me. Similarly, there is no daylight between the Word of God and Jesus, and between Jesus and his Father. "In the beginning was the Word, and the Word was with God, and the Word was God. He was with God in the beginning" (John 1:1–2). It is simply not possible to think too highly of God and his Word, whether that Word is Jesus or the Bible.

Suburban Legend

"Our authority is the Spirit speaking through the Word."

Another way some register their fear of worshiping a book is to say, "Our authority is the Spirit speaking through the Word."[3] This sounds good. Who could object to the authority of the Holy Spirit? But note how this slogan decouples the Spirit from the Word. Unlike the Reformers, who insisted that our authority was

---

[3]   Our authority is "the Spirit speaking in or through Scripture," and the Bible is authoritative because "it is the vehicle through which the Spirit speaks." Stanley Grenz and John Franke, *Beyond Foundationalism* (Louisville: Westminster John Knox, 2001), 65, 114–15. "The ultimate authority in the church is not a particular source, be it Scripture, tradition, reason, or experience, but only the living God." John Franke, *The Character of Theology* (Grand Rapids: Baker, 2005), 78.

equally the God who speaks and the Word that he says, this view says our ultimate authority is only the Holy Spirit. The Bible is not that authority but is merely a vehicle through which the Spirit speaks. The Bible is not on the same level as the Spirit. As if God's Word could have less authority than God himself!

This separation of the Spirit from his Word leads to a subjective muddle. If our authority is not the Bible but the Spirit speaking through the Bible, who is to say when the Spirit is speaking and what he is saying? Proponents answer this is the role of the church. God's people gather to hear together what the Spirit is saying to them through the Bible. But surely entire churches have misheard before and will mishear again. How do we know we are not being led astray by a lying spirit, a charismatic pastor, mysticism, fatigue, or something else?

And if our authority is the Spirit speaking, why limit ourselves to the Bible? Why can't the Spirit speak authoritatively through other sources? Karl Barth claimed that "God may speak to us through Russian Communism, a flute concerto, a blossoming shrub, or a dead dog."[4] Stanley Grenz and John Franke said, "The Spirit's voice can conceivably resound through many media, including the media of human culture." We must "listen intently for the voice of the Spirit" in "the world, bubbling to the surface through the artifacts and symbols humans construct."[5] Evangelical theologians Brad Harper and Paul Louis Metzger provide an example. They write that "when Don Henley of the Eagles . . . proclaims in his song 'Heart of the Matter' that undeserved forgiveness is the only thing that can save us from self-destruction, we can know that we are hearing the voice of God."[6] *Really?* I am all for forgiveness, but how would I know this song is the voice of God? Shouldn't we save this honor for the divinely inspired Bible?

Here's one way this high view of Scripture matters. The Bible does not proclaim "undeserved forgiveness" in general. It proclaims Jesus. Satan would happily give everyone an experience of forgiveness, so long as they did not experience the forgiveness of Jesus. Forgiveness alone never saved anyone from everlasting destruction. Only Jesus does that. And he uses the Bible's proclamation about him to do it.

Application

If the Bible is the inspired Word of God, then we must use it. The most important part of each day is when we read God's Word and pray. Our noisy world competes for our attention. Our phones ding with urgent texts and harmless diversions. Who can resist another cat video? But soon we've followed one

---

[4] Barth added, "We do well to listen to Him if He really does." Yet he helpfully cautioned that "we cannot say that we are commissioned to pass on what we have heard as independent proclamation." Karl Barth, *Church Dogmatics,* trans. G. W. Bromiley, vol. I.1, *The Doctrine of the Word of God* (Edinburgh: T&T Clark, 1975), 55.

[5] Grenz and Franke, *Beyond Foundationalism,* 162.

[6] Brad Harper and Paul Louis Metzger, *Exploring Ecclesiology* (Grand Rapids: Brazos, 2009), 115.

click to another until we're rapidly thumbing between news, emails, tweets, and recipes for authentic Tuscany bruschetta. The Bible looks much less interesting, lying motionless on the table beside us. Is it really alive?

Yes! God's Word makes things happen. He speaks, and a universe appears from nowhere. He speaks, and the dead are raised to life. He speaks into your life, but only if you move into range of his voice. Put down your phone, close your laptop, and pick up the living Word of God. What is he saying to you?

CHAPTER 8

Jews, Christians, and Muslims Worship the Same God

The Legendary Belief

Our Jewish tour guide had been comically pro-Israel. "See those hills over there, where the shadows fall? That is Palestinian land. Now look to the right, where the mountains are bathed in sunshine. That is Israeli territory." So, I was a bit surprised when, during our walk through the old city of Jerusalem, he stopped and said, "Of course, Jews, Christians, and Muslims worship the same God." I instantly spoke up. "We may agree that God is one, but that doesn't mean we are worshiping the same One." He wanted to respond, but perhaps remembering his Israeli obligation to preserve the goodwill of American evangelicals, shook his head and continued our tour.

Unraveling the Legend

Years later, I stand by my reflexive response. I agree with Karl Barth, who noted that monotheism is nothing more than "the religious glorification of the number 'one.'" Believing that God is one might even become a catalyst to viciously attack him. Barth reminds us that "Jewish monotheism" crucified Jesus.[1]

But the issue is more complicated. To answer the question sufficiently, we must analyze what we mean by "same." Philosophers break down "sameness" into two parts: reference and sense. Reference indicates the object we are pointing to and sense is the content or meaning that we assign to the object. For example, Clark Kent and Superman are the same referent yet possess a

---

[1] Barth, *Church Dogmatics*, ed. G.W. Bromiley and T.F. Torrance, vol. II.1, *The Doctrine of God* (Edinburgh: T&T Clark, 1957), 448, 453. Note that Barth, who was writing during Hitler's reign, was not blaming all Jews for the death of Jesus. He simply observed that the Jewish leaders confessed to killing Jesus because he said he was God (Matt 26:65; John 10:33; 5:18).

different sense. Lois Lane may glowingly describe Superman to Clark Kent without realizing she is talking to the same person. (If she and Superman went on a double date with Clark Kent and another woman, they would only need a table for three.) Conversely, identical twins may share a similar sense yet different reference. A hoodwinked teacher may think she is supervising Jimmy when she is talking with Johnny.

This chapter will examine both aspects—referent and sense—regarding Jews and Christians and then Christians and Muslims. Do these religions refer to the same divine being? If so, does our sense of this being overlap enough to say we are worshiping the same God? Do we merely understand the one God differently, or are we speaking of an entirely different God?[2]

Jews and Christians

Whether Jews and Christians worship the same God is thorny because Christianity arose from within Judaism. We share the same Scriptures and understanding of God until Jesus came and our paths diverged. What should we make of a religion that accepted God's progressive revelation of himself until he reached his most personal and climactic moment?

Perhaps it is like courtship. A wise man does not spill all his secrets on the first date. He tests the water, slowly revealing more of himself as she accepts what she has seen and heard so far. Many relationships have their moment of truth. *There is something you should know about me.* The man takes her hand and bares his deepest soul. (This is a man we are talking about, so what he shares may be mostly about football, spicy wings, or monster trucks. The point is that he *means* it.) What if the man shares something personal and the young lady responds by breaking off the relationship? She ghosts him, deletes his texts, and reposts her picture on Match.com. Would you say that she still accepts him, just not that last part? Or would rejecting that last part mean that she does not accept him at all? What would he say?

No analogy is perfect, but this one clarifies the problem with Judaism. This foundational Abrahamic faith is not merely missing the upper stories of God's progressive revelation. It smashed the cornerstone, Jesus Christ, and so its building has toppled over (Acts 4:10–12; 1 Pet 2:4–8). The religion that brought the climax of God's revelation has itself rejected that revelation. Judaism is not merely guilty of bad timing—waiting for the Messiah they already missed. They crucified the Lord of glory. So, while they misunderstood, they didn't exactly miss him (1 Cor 2:8).

---

2   To explore this question further, from four different angles, see Ronnie P. Campbell Jr. and Christopher Gnanakan, eds., *Do Christians, Muslims, and Jews Worship the Same God?* (Grand Rapids: Zondervan, 2019).

Judaism and Christianity may seem to share the same sense of God. Both agree the true God is one, his name is Jehovah, and that he sent prophets to his people whom he redeemed from Egypt. But Judaism rejects the hermeneutical key that alone makes sense of Israel's story. As a mystery novel explains earlier events in its final chapter, so the Gospel of Luke ends with Jesus teaching his disciples how "the Law of Moses, the Prophets, and the Psalms" were all about him. "Then he opened their minds to understand the Scriptures" (24:44–45). Don't miss the implication: if we do not start with Jesus, we will misunderstand the whole Bible.

I conclude that the Jewish and Christian senses of God are only superficially the same. The heart of who God is—a triune fellowship of Father, Son, and Spirit who sent the Son to become a Man who died on the cross for our sin and rose again—is not shared by both faiths. Consider how Saul of Tarsus massively reconfigured his Jewish faith when he met Jesus on the road to Damascus. If the Son of God must be crucified for Saul's sin, what did that imply about the depths of human depravity, our need for grace, and the inability of religious rules and rituals to save? Paul realized he was far worse than his Jewish faith had taught him. His best features were nothing but garbage compared to "the surpassing value of knowing Christ Jesus my Lord" (Phil 3:8).

The question of reference requires similar nuance. To reuse our geometric example from chapter 2, if Judaism is a two-dimensional square, Christianity is a three-dimensional cube. Christianity's new revelation added to the Jewish faith without contradicting it. So, the first Christians told their Jewish audience they were talking about the same God. The Jewish God had now revealed himself to be the Father who raised his crucified Son from the dead (Acts 13:16–41). As Paul explained to a Jerusalem mob, "The God of our ancestors [had] appointed [him] to know his will, to see the Righteous One, and to hear the words from his mouth" (22:14).

As time wore on and Judaism repeatedly and categorically rejected God's revelation of himself in Jesus, the common reference between Judaism and Christianity became harder to sustain. If Christians declare that God is a Trinity of love revealed in Jesus, and Jews insist that is blasphemy, are we still speaking about the same God? A cube is a square all the way down. If someone rejects the cube, can they still believe in their square? Not as before. Progressive revelation raises the bar of what we must believe about God. There's no going back to simpler times. The Jewish people's continued rejection of God's revealed sense meant they were also losing their grip on his reference. They knew less about God than before Jesus came.[3]

---

[3]   The square to cube analogy in chapter 2 illustrated how God can be more than he reveals while not being less. A cube is at least a square. I am using the analogy here to illustrate what happens when people of the square reject the higher knowledge of the cube. They may protest that the status of their square has

Christians and Muslims

The gap between Christianity and Islam is much wider than between Christianity and Judaism. Unlike Christians, who followed the Jewish Scriptures and said their God was the fulfillment of Israel's hopes, Muhammad highlighted the many doctrines that he believed the Christians got wrong. He taught that the Bible is a corrupted, human book that cannot be trusted. Jesus is not God, God is not a Trinity, and Jesus did not die on the cross for our sins. We are not born in sin, and so we may achieve salvation through the discipline of good works and keeping the five pillars of Islam. The first of these is the Muslim profession of faith: "There is no god but Allah [the Arabic term for God], and Muhammad is his prophet."

Is Allah the same God as the Christian God?

Let's start with sense. If we begin with general revelation, it might seem that Christians and Muslims have much in common. Both agree that God is one and that he is the uncaused, eternal, omniscient, and omnipotent Creator and Sustainer of every created thing that exists. Muslims even call God the "All-Merciful One." There seems to be enough similarity that in 2007 Muslim scholars published "A Common Word," an olive branch to Christians that emphasized how both religions taught their adherents to love God and neighbor. The Yale Center for Faith and Culture responded with "Loving God and Neighbor Together," which agreed this common ground was "not in something marginal" but "in something absolutely central to both," in their "fundamentals of faith." From this shared perspective Christians and Muslims might participate in "deep cooperation" that might "achieve religious peace between these two religious communities" that would lead to "peace in the world."[4]

I am for world peace, but as we saw in the discussion of Judaism, it makes all the difference if we start with God's climactic revelation in Jesus. Islam teaches that God's nature so utterly transcends us that all we can ever know about him is his moral will. He may be merciful towards those who do good, but in his justice he might not. There is no way to know for sure. All we can do is try our best and pray that when Allah weighs our works, he puts his thumb on the side of our good efforts. How vastly different is our Christian God! Jesus reveals that God is both transcendent and immanent, a triune community of persons who love us as they love one another (John 15:9). This Trinity of

---

not changed, but this seems unlikely. How plausible is it that all the squares in the cube are wrong except their square on the bottom? The progressive revelation of the cube means they no longer simply believe in their square. They also disbelieve in all higher squares. In sum, if God is not a cube (Christianity), how likely is it that he is still a square (Judaism)?

4   The website "A Common Word" is devoted to the Muslim letter and its responses. See https://www
.acommonword.com/. The Muslim letter can be read at https://www.acommonword.com/the-acw
-document/ and the Yale response at https://www.acommonword.com/loving-god-and-neighbor
-together-a-christian-response-to-a-common-word-between-us-and-you/.

love supplies a dramatically different understanding of God the Creator (see chapter 9) and his overwhelming power. The Son of God does powerfully subdue his enemies, yet he also humbles himself to become a man and die on the cross for our sin. These highs and lows are not contradictory, for God uses the humiliation of his Son to exalt him as the sovereign Lord of the universe (Phil 2:5–11). In sum, while Muslims and Christians might superficially agree that God is uncaused, eternal, and omniscient, we disagree strongly about what it means for God to be one, loving, merciful, and even the all-powerful Creator. The character of each deity is vastly different. We do not share the same sense of God.

What about reference? If Christianity is a cube and Judaism is a square, then Islam is a circle. It lacks the common foundation that Judaism and Christianity share (its holy book is the Koran), so its sense and reference are even further removed. I readily concede that all three religions intend to speak of God. This is important, because their attempt to refer to God supplies enough common ground to have a conversation. If we were not intending to speak of the same being, how could we reasonably dispute about him? Yet this partial reference is the most I can concede. Because neither Jews nor Muslims intend to speak of the triune God revealed in Jesus, the core of everything they say about God is untrue. The God they refer to does not exist. The errors in their sense of God prevent them from properly referring to him.

Application

In answering the question, Do Jews, Christians, and Muslims worship the same God? this chapter skipped over the first part to focus on the end of the question: What do we mean by *same*? My answer: the three religions have partially similar referents (in that all intend to speak of the one God) and entirely different senses. Perhaps equally important is the question's first part: What do we mean by *worship*? True worship is the successful adoration of God. Successful worship must aim at the right deity, which requires holding the right beliefs. That's what this chapter has been about. But it also requires regular and purposeful adoration. The facts in our heads must move our hearts to bend our knees. Saving faith starts in our ears—"faith comes from what is heard" (Rom 10:17)—and settles into our legs. Theology must lead to worship, or we're doing it wrong. What posture most accompanies your practice of theology? A stamping foot? A jabbing finger? Crossed arms? Let us make it the bowed knee.

CHAPTER 9

God Created the World Because He Was Lonely

The Legendary Belief

One of my favorite songwriters is Michael Card. He went to seminary, and it shows. His songs are biblically rich and spiritually deep, but no one's perfect. As I sang along with "That's What Faith Must Be," I stumbled over a line that basically said God created our world because he longed for fellowship.[1]

Wait. What? God didn't enjoy fellowship before he made the universe? Did God create the world because he was lonely?

Unraveling the Legend

It is easy to get sloppy when talking about the Trinity. Although I know better, I sometimes slip and mention "the person of God." I might say something like "Disobedience to God's commands rejects the person of God." No. This is wrong. God is personal, but he is not a person. He exists as three persons in one essence. As chapter 1 explained that God is both fully transcendent and fully immanent, so here God is both fully one and fully three. He is one and three in different ways, but he is one and three always.

Theologians disagree about how best to describe the relation between God's one essence and three persons, yet all orthodox theologians follow the balanced parameters of the Athanasian Creed: "We worship one God in trinity and the trinity in unity, neither blending their persons nor dividing their essence."[2] Notice how the Creed states the same thing in reverse: unity in trinity

---

[1]   Michael Card, "That's What Faith Must Be," track 4 on *Present Reality*, Sparrow Records SPD 1155, 1988, compact disc.

[2]   This translation of the Athanasian Creed was adopted by the Christian Reformed Church of North America in 1988. See the website of the Christian Reformed Church at: https://www.crcna.org/welcome /beliefs/creeds/athanasian-creed.

and trinity in unity. We must privilege both God's oneness and his threeness; each gets its turn to be the subject that is modified by the other. In this way we preserve God's threeness—"neither blending their persons," and we preserve his oneness—"nor dividing their essence."

God's oneness and threeness are not merely in tension; each supplies a vital aspect for the other. God's oneness unites his threeness, and his threeness differentiates his oneness. If God were not one, we would be polytheists. If God were not three, we would have the problems this chapter addresses. God's oneness is equally as important as his threeness, but since this chapter corrects the urban legend of a lonely God, it will focus on his threeness. Because God is eternally three persons, he has never been lonely or lacking for fellowship. He is blissfully contented within his one divine being.

If God Were One Person

God is eternal (Gen 21:33; Ps 90:2). He has always existed, which means there was an infinitely long time before he created anything. If God is only one person, then he must have been infinitely lonely. How could he not be? There was no one to speak with or even to look at, forever into the distant past.

A lonely God is a needy God. He would not be contented and happy within himself, so he would not be ready to create. This forever solitary Person would have created our world either as a mistake—maybe he prefers being alone to making room for other people who might not see things his way—or to fill a deep need for companionship. Can you imagine his want ad?

Single Deity, Non-Smoker, Loves Pets (No Cats!). Enjoys Long Garden Walks

How could we worship this God in either case? If he doesn't want us around, then fine. We'll do our own thing. If he's weepy and smothering, we'd make any excuse to gain some breathing space. "It's not you. It's me." Any God who created me to fill a void in his life is no God I would want in mine.

Why Did God Create the World?

If God did not create us to ease his lonely heart, why did he make the world? Perhaps we would get a hint if we knew what he was doing all that "time" in eternity past before creation.[3] But how would we know that? Augustine shared

---

[3] "Time" is qualified because eternity exists outside of time. There is no time (defined as sequence of events) in eternity. Who can understand this?

a joke that was making the rounds in his day: What was the eternal God doing before he created the world? Making hell for those who ask such questions.

We cannot definitively answer the why, but here is what we can say: If God is a Trinity, then he is an eternal community of Father, Son, and Spirit—three divine persons who live in a fellowship of self-giving love. To use Augustine's language, the Father is the Lover, the Son is the Beloved, and the Spirit is the Bond of Love that unites them. Only a triune God can truly love. A single-person God would be either too aloof or too needy to unconditionally give himself to us. But a three-person God has eternally—so always—given himself away to the other persons in the Godhead. Consider what we see in the Gospels: The Father glorifies the Son, the Son glorifies the Father (John 17:1); the Spirit serves the Father and Son (15:26), and the Son has the Spirit's back (Matt 12:32). This eternal circle of exalting and serving the other accounts for the marvelous claim that God is love (1 John 4:8). Our God does not merely have love. He is the personification of love. He is love's essence, and love is his.

This triune God of love does not need to create. He is blissfully contented within himself. But given who God is, a forever community of self-giving lovers, creation is not a surprise. It's the most fitting, appropriate act for a self-giving God to do. God did not create our world to plug a hole in his leaky love bucket. He summoned the love that is shared between the Father, Son, and Spirit and poured it into the void. His love overflowed his triune fellowship and created new others to love.

The same holds true for redemption. God did not need to save us. He would remain blissfully contented within his community of love if he had allowed us to endure the penalty that our sins deserve. But given who God is, a forever community of self-giving lovers, salvation is not a surprise. It's the most fitting, appropriate act for a God of love to do. God did not need to save us to add to his personal satisfaction score. But it's an apt sacrifice for our triune God—three persons who have always put the others ahead of themselves—to do whatever it takes to win us back.

We cannot say completely why God created and redeemed us. Certainly, he created and redeemed us for his glory. But he would have remained equally glorious had he not created or redeemed anyone. Creation and redemption are acts of his will, which means he could have chosen otherwise. But neither is a shock for a triune God of love.

Application

I am tempted not to include an application to this chapter because the beauty of our triune God does not require it. We should be content to study and love him for his own sake, just as he is content to know and love himself for his own sake. And yet the Trinity explains so much about us that I think it's worth the risk. There is much that could be said, but here are two foundational facts that come from being made in the image of a personal, triune God.

First, we are people who need people. You might be a full-fledged introvert, delighted for any excuse to stay in and spend a quiet evening by yourself. Yet after months of COVID quarantine, even you were desperate for human touch. So, you went online. This was a mistake. Social media gives the illusion of companionship—how many online friends are friends in real life?—without face-to-face connection. Seeing other people whom we sort of know smiling with their devoted spouses, adorable children, and homemade sourdough loaf makes us feel empty inside. Why can't we have what they have? Our lives will never measure up to their airbrushed, selective presentation, but we can't turn away. Social media is alluring because our triune, relational God wired us for relationship.

Second, we are people who need to serve people. Social media distorts our relationships. We are not meant to strive and compete with the curated lives of others. We thrive when we follow the example of Jesus and "in humility consider others as more important than yourselves" (Phil 2:3). Our happiest days occur when we set aside our own plans and serve the pressing needs of others. We drive a shut-in to the doctor, sit with children so their mom can keep her appointment, or fix the car for a father struggling to get back on his feet. Why are those moments among our fondest memories? Because that is when we were most like the triune persons who give themselves on behalf of the others. When Jesus said that "whoever loses his life because of me will find it," he was not merely telling us how to have a fantastic afterlife (Matt 16:25). He was telling us how to prosper now. He was saying, "Do you want to truly live? Here's the recipe. Do what we do. Lose your life to find it." Nothing is more alive than our triune God. When we follow his example and set aside our own desires for the sake of the Son, we will find life too.

Why are we people who need people? Why are we people who need to serve people? Because we are made in the image of our triune God of love. We cannot explain the Trinity, but the Trinity explains us.

Mini Myth

"This analogy explains the Trinity."

The profound claim of the Trinity is that God is fully one and fully three. Because God infinitely transcends our creaturely realm, we should not expect to find anything in our human experience that comprehensively explains this. Any attempt will inevitably minimize God's threeness or his oneness. Take the common illustration that the Trinity is like three forms of water: liquid, ice, and steam. The substance remains the same even as it appears in different forms. This is a fine illustration for the ancient heresy of modalism, which minimizes God's threeness by teaching that he is one person who takes three successive forms. First, he appears as Father, then as Son, and now he is present as the Holy Spirit. It's all the same person, revealing himself in three different modes. Like liquid, ice, and steam. The same heresy is present when I compare the Trinity to my own roles as father, son, and brother. I play different parts, but I am only one person. This falls far short of the three distinct persons required by Christian orthodoxy.

Other illustrations commit the opposite heresy of tritheism, which minimizes God's oneness. Some compare the trinity to an egg, apple, watermelon, or pick-your-favorite fruit. We can separate the yolk, white, and shell, yet it remains one egg. We can separate the core, flesh, and peel, yet it remains one apple. We can separate the flesh, seeds, and rind, yet it remains one watermelon. But God's three persons are not parts, and they cannot be separated. The divine persons interpenetrate each other—the Father is in the Son and the Son is in the Father (John 17:21)—so that they are more indivisibly one than any singular thing we can imagine.

Scripture hints at two suggestive analogies. We may find echoes of the Trinity in the sexual union of marital love (Gen 1:27) and in the diverse community of our church (John 17:21–23). As husband and wife join bodies in a loving embrace that produces life, as church members unite in their shared love for Jesus, who is life, so our triune God is the epitome of love and life. Yet marriage and the church are mere shadows of a searingly bright reality that we cannot fathom and never will. God is more one and three than anything we can imagine. We will understand God better when we see Jesus face-to-face, but we will never get our arms around the Trinity and say, "Now I thoroughly understand God. No more questions!" It's a good thing too. God would not be God if we fully comprehended him. We do not explain the Trinity; the Trinity explains us.

———

CHAPTER 10

God Is a Gentleman

The Legendary Belief

The preacher concluded his invitation with a final plea. "What else can God do to prove his love for you? He chose to create you, then sent his Son to die on the cross for you. Even now he is knocking on your heart's door. He eagerly wants to save you, but God is a gentleman. He knows love can't be forced, so he patiently waits, leaving the choice up to you. Won't you open your heart and let him come in?"

Unraveling the Legend

The preacher was alluding to Rev 3:20, where Jesus spoke to the lukewarm church of Laodicea. "See! I stand at the door and knock. If anyone hears my voice and opens the door, I will come in to him and eat with him, and he with me." This probably isn't the best passage to explain Jesus's relationship with unsaved people, as Jesus was speaking to professing Christians who had become complacent, not necessarily those who had not yet followed him. Regardless, Jesus does describe himself as knocking and waiting for those inside to open the door. Doesn't this indicate he is a gentleman? Well, are we sure that knocking is all Jesus does? Or is that only the part we see? Might the Spirit of Jesus be actively working on people's hearts beneath the surface, prompting them to open the door? And aren't we all counting on that?

When people say God is a gentleman, what they seem to mean is that he does not use force or manipulation to get his way. He is content to patiently wait, as the preacher said. But few Christians believe this. How do I know? Because we pray.

Calvinism

When we pray for unsaved or wayward friends, what are we asking God to do? It depends in part on whether we are Calvinists or Arminians. I am a Calvinist, so I will explain that view first. An apt summary for Calvinism is *sovereign grace*. John Calvin led with God's love, emphasizing that God is gracious to sinners like us who don't deserve it. God's grace is sovereign in two ways: he freely chooses whom he will save and those he chooses cannot stop him. His love is irresistible.

Consequently, when Calvinists pray for our unsaved or lukewarm family and friends, we ask the Spirit of God to change their hearts. Transform their wills so they delight in the glorious beauty of the gospel. Make them hunger for Jesus, so they want to obey him. Evidence that God works this way is sprinkled throughout Scripture, from its teaching on election, "He predestined us to be adopted as sons through Jesus Christ" (Eph 1:5), to its emphasis on God's call, "No one can come to me unless the Father who sent me draws him" (John 6:44). God invites all people to come to him, but no one will come unless the Holy Spirit changes their hearts so they want to come.[1]

Arminians respond that this efficacious call is much too strong. How does God change someone's will without violating it? Calvinists reply that is a great question, and since we are mere creatures, we cannot explain it. Nor should we expect to. God is God, and he freely does what he wants. But he must have changed our wills and efficaciously drawn us to himself, for sinners like us would never have come on our own.

Whatever you might think about the Calvinist God, he is no gentleman. He certainly invites everyone to open the door of their hearts—all but the most extreme Calvinists believe in the universal offer of salvation. But while God calls all people to come to him, beneath the surface his Spirit is opening some ears and stirring some hearts to hear and respond. The Calvinist God doesn't only knock; he kicks down the door. He does not wait for spiritual corpses to show signs of life; he awakens the dead (Eph 2:1–10).

Arminianism

If Calvinism can be summarized as *sovereign grace,* Arminianism emphasizes *free love.* Arminians correctly desire to protect the heart of love. God wants us to love him, and since robots cannot love, he gave us freedom. However, the same freedom that enables us to choose God also enables us to rebel against him, and Adam and Eve did.

---

[1] Other verses on election and calling include John 5:21; 13:18; Acts 2:39; 13:48; Rom 8:28–30; 9:7–24; 1 Cor 1:9; 1 Thess 1:4–5; 2 Thess 2:13–14; and 1 Pet 2:9.

All their descendants are born totally depraved. Our bent wills are curved in on ourselves so that we are unable to choose God. Arminians insist we need grace, just not the overpowering, efficacious kind that Calvinists tout. John Wesley posited what he called "prevenient grace." This grace does not compel faith—that would be much too strong—but it does enable faith. God gives prevenient grace to all people, overcoming their depravity and restoring their free wills so they can repent and believe in Jesus. Let's say that depravity pushes a person down to a negative ten. Prevenient grace would then be worth ten points. It brings the person up to neutral so they can choose to follow Jesus if they want.

Arminians believe prevenient grace blankets all people at all times, yet we can ask God to give our wayward friends another, more intense dose. Charles Wesley described this heightened form in his hymn "And Can It Be," in which he compared prevenient grace to a "quick'ning ray."

Long my imprisoned spirit lay
Fast bound in sin and nature's night;
Thine eye diffused a quick'ning ray,
I woke, the dungeon flamed with light;
My chains fell off, my heart was free;
I rose, went forth and followed Thee.

The "quick'ning ray" does not create faith; it makes faith possible. Prevenient grace breaks the chains of sin so our free heart may choose to believe and follow Jesus. How exactly does prevenient grace do this? When Arminians pray for their lost or backslidden friends, what are they asking God to do? I asked my Arminian friends. They say they pray for God to arrange circumstances in their friends' lives that will humble them and awaken them to their need for Jesus. They also ask God to impress certain ideas onto their friends' hearts, to remind them of their sin and the glorious beauty of Jesus. My Calvinist prayers ask God for the same things on my way to also asking the Holy Spirit to change them and make them believe.

But these Arminian prayers assume God is not exactly a gentleman. What would we say about a man who wins a woman's heart by manipulating the circumstances so that all other potential dates fall through? He breaks the timing belt on a rival's car, steals another's cell phone, and distracts another's attention with his gorgeous cousin. He learns hypnosis so he can furtively plant thoughts in his flame's head. Eventually, with no one else to ask her out, and with her heart strangely warming to our scheming friend, she falls in love and marries him. This man may deserve credit for effort, but he is no gentleman! He knows he manipulated his way to love, so it isn't true. If Hollywood made a romantic comedy about this, the movie would end with the man confessing his duplicity and promising to try to win her again, this time for real. [2]

This highlights a crucial difference between creature-to-creature and Creator-to-creature relationships. What would be lethal in a man-woman relationship is par for the course in God's relationship with us. In a way that mere creatures cannot understand, God freely works within our hearts and arranges events without violating our freedom. Calvinists cannot explain how our freedom coexists with God's efficacious call, and Arminians cannot explain how our freedom coexists with God impressing ideas on our minds and causing other options to not work out.[3] In both cases, that mystery is what we should expect. In neither case is God a gentleman, content to do nothing but knock and wait for us to welcome him. Every Christian believes the Holy Spirit eagerly does much, much more. This is why we pray.

Application

This chapter argues that our prayers indicate we believe God powerfully moves in hearts to restore people to himself. The argument could be turned around. Our failure to pray would indicate we do not really believe God answers prayers to save the lost. Here is the big question: What do our prayers—both their existence and their content—say about what we believe about God? If someone read a transcript of everything we said to God today, what would they conclude we believe about God's love and power? Prayer is the proof of faith.

---

[2]   See Roger Olson, *Arminian Theology* (Downers Grove, IL: IVP Academic, 2006). Olson argues that prevenient grace does more than make it possible for a sinner to believe. It actually "communicates the gifts of repentance and faith to the person, who must only accept and not resist them" (163). So rather than generate faith, the person must only receive the faith that the Spirit plants within him. Olson continues, "The soul of the sinner is being regenerated but the sinner is able to resist and spurn the prevenient grace of God by denying the gospel. All that is required for full salvation is a relaxation of the resistant will under the influence of God's grace" (165). Olson says that Arminius posited "an intermediate stage between being unregenerate and regenerate," in which the "freed will, . . . though initially bound by sin, has been brought by the prevenient grace of the Spirit of Christ to a point where it can respond freely to the divine call" (164).

In Olson's view, the Spirit performs many powerful acts within people, bestowing regeneration, faith, and repentance, all without their permission. This may be necessary for salvation, but it is hard to make the case that such divine actions are the work of a gentleman.

[3]   Calvinists typically reconcile divine sovereignty with human freedom by claiming humans possess merely uncoerced choice. We will choose whatever God has decreed, but as long as we want that, we are free enough. Arminians insist that humans must also possess contrary choice, or the freedom to choose between alternatives (also called libertarian freedom). Arminians are right about this, at least when it comes to nonmoral choices (Calvinism rightly notes that our depraved wills prevent us from making perfectly righteous choices—i.e., our motives are never entirely pure), but they can't fully explain how this libertarian freedom fits with the ungentlemanly acts of God. Their best effort is Molinism, which relies on the concept of divine middle knowledge. See Kirk R. MacGregor, *Luis de Molina: The Life and Theology of the Founder of Middle Knowledge* (Grand Rapids: Zondervan, 2015).

If you want to know what you really believe—not merely what you think you ought to believe—check your prayers.

Mini Myth

"Arminians have no assurance of salvation."

Arminians believe a free will restored by prevenient grace is never lost, so our salvation might be. We remain free to follow Jesus or not, and people who are born again today may fall away tomorrow and lose their salvation. "Lose" is not quite the right word, as Arminians don't think we can accidentally lose our salvation like we might misplace our car keys. But they do say we can apostatize, willfully choosing to walk away from the faith.

Since this apostasy is a purposeful decision, it doesn't seem fair to say that Arminians have no assurance of salvation. They may not know with certainty that they will persevere in their faith to the end, yet they can know that right now they are following Jesus and relying on him for their forgiveness of sin. Arminians possess a limited form of present assurance. As long as they continue in their faith, "established and firm," they can know they have been reconciled to God (Col 1:22–23).

CHAPTER 11

You Should Pray Like It All Depends on God and Work Like It All Depends on You

The Legendary Belief

Preachers who affirm the insights of both Calvinism and Arminianism tend to chalk up the differences to a division of labor. They might say, "I can't explain how God's sovereignty and human responsibility fit together. I just know that I want to pray like a Calvinist and evangelize like an Arminian." Or "I want to sleep like a Calvinist and work like an Arminian." If they want to avoid theological labels and express the point in a memorable meme, they will say, "I want to pray like it all depends on God and work like it all depends on me."

According to the New Catechism of the Roman Catholic Church, this last phrase originated with Ignatius of Loyola (1491–1556). The catechism concludes with comments on the Lord's Prayer. Going line by line through the prayer, when the catechism comes to "Give us this day our daily bread," it shares this nugget of wisdom from Ignatius, "Pray as if everything depended on God and work as if everything depended on you." The catechism emphasizes the prayer part. Its next sentence reads, "Even when we have done our work, the food we receive is still a gift from our Father; it is good to ask him for it with thanksgiving, as Christian families do when saying grace at meals."[1] This seems exactly right. But what about Ignatius's line about work? Does God really want us to work like it all depends on us?

Unraveling the Legend

The apostle Paul didn't think so. He told the Christians in Philippi to "work out your own salvation with fear and trembling. For it is God who is working

---

[1] *Catechism of the Catholic Church* (Liguori, MO: Liguori, 1994), §2834.

in you both to will and to work according to his good purpose" (Phil 2:12–13). Paul did not separate sanctification into a division of labor, in which God does his thing, we do our thing, God does his thing again, then flips it back to us. Paul commands us to work hard precisely because God is right now working in us. We should pray and work like it all depends on God. Because it does.

Why Try?

This urban legend intends to inspire effort. "Start your day with prayer, as if your day depends entirely on God. Then leave your house with the mindset to work, as if your day depends entirely on you. Your attitude will determine whether you succeed or fail today. Keep your chin up, and keep plugging away."

But this is not true. The legend concedes as much when it says to pray like it all depends on God. How can it all depend on me if it all depends on him? And why would I even want to pretend that all my success depends on me? That much stress will make me a mess.

Have you seen these funny demotivational posters?

Initiative: The courage to stand up, speak out, and be fired first.

Practice: No matter how much you do it you're probably still not that good.

Never Give Up: Never stop trying to exceed your limits. We need the entertainment.

Mistakes: It could be that the purpose of your life is only to serve as a warning to others.

Persistence: It's over man. Let her go.

Motivation: If a pretty poster and a cute saying are all it takes to motivate you, you probably have a very easy job. The kind robots will be doing soon.

This one is not funny, but it is equally demotivating:

Success: Pray like it all depends on God. Work like it all depends on you.

Think about it. We only attempt what we have a reasonable chance of accomplishing. I will not try out for a professional sport or third chair in a symphony, because why waste everyone's time? But I will gladly prepare a lecture or write a book. I am motivated to try them because I know I can. I am doing one right now.

What gives us a chance of success in the Christian life? Not our own efforts. If becoming holy depended on us, we would have no shot. Why bother? We are too selfish, proud, and lustful to defeat temptation for long. But if God is powerfully working within us, we have every incentive to strive for holiness. If our growth depends on us, our best efforts will certainly fail. But if our growth depends on God, even our feeblest efforts have a chance to succeed.

Christian growth begins when we realize we cannot do what God commands. Not on our own. We must be the ones who obey, yet we will sink if left to ourselves. A good father does not throw his child into the deep end of the pool and say, "Swim like it all depends on you!" Initially he will zip his child through the water, as if the child were swimming. Soon that will not be enough. A growing child will say, "I do, Daddy!" So, the father holds the child afloat, allowing him to flutter kick and doggie paddle his way around the pool. The child is swimming, but only because he is upheld by his father's arms. The child will become a youth who no longer needs his father's support, but you and I never outgrow our dependence on our Father's everlasting arms. Our efforts to please him amount to dependent striving. We must exert effort, but only as we rest in Jesus, laboring from deep confidence in the Spirit's power. If we are stressed, we are doing it wrong.

What about normal human life? Perhaps it is foolish to work like our sanctification depends on us, but don't we have to think that way if we want to get ahead in life or our career? One motivational speaker says our urban legend holds the key to financial success. Wealth comes to those who "Pray like it all depends on God but work like it all depends on you."

I appreciate his appeal to hard work. It is hard to build wealth sitting at home, surfing the Internet in your pajamas. But he invoked prayer, which implies that even our earthly success depends ultimately on the actions of God. These actions are not the special work of the Spirit that Paul mentions in Phil 2:12–13. They are God's general work of common grace that sustains us and the order of our world. But as we learn whenever we endure an economic or social meltdown, God's ordinary providence is essential for our everyday success. Businesses that were built over a lifetime can be lost in one night of rioting, one quarter of quarantine, or one year of risky Wall Street bets that tank the financial system.

We must work hard. Absolutely. But if the success of our work "all depends on us," we will ultimately fail. We cannot supply the stability of nature, culture, and society that is necessary for our success. What a relief! If we work as if it all depends on us, we will break from the strain. It's too much. Finite people are not built for such responsibility. But if we work from the security that our success depends on God, we can serve from a place of confident rest. When we succeed, we thank God for his sustaining grace. When we fail, we rest knowing it was never entirely on our shoulders anyway.

Application

Paul's application for "work out your own salvation . . . for it is God who is working in you" may surprise you. He does not implore the Philippians to lean on the Spirit's supernatural power to reach for the stars. He tells them, "Do everything without grumbling and arguing" (Phil 2:14). That's it? This is what we lean on God for? We may not think this requires God's direct involvement, until we consider how readily we complain and bicker. We may not think this is terribly important, until we consider how much we enjoy living with others in harmony. Paul says God is working powerfully within us to improve the peace and unity in our church community. The sublime surfaces in the mundane.

Speaking of everyday life, what do we believe is the key to our success there? Are we ultimately relying on our hard work or the Spirit of God? Our efforts are important for landing a job, getting a promotion, finding a spouse, and any number of normal human goals. But none of our exertions will pay off without the underlying providence of God. We must pray and work as if our success ultimately depends on him.

Our dependence on God is even more true for Christian ministry. Remember the story of the rich young ruler who went away sad because he wasn't willing to sell everything and follow Jesus? The disciples "were utterly astonished and asked, 'Then who can be saved?'" (Matt 19:25). If a man this impressive cannot enter the kingdom of God, then what hope is there for the rest of us? Jesus answered, "With man this is impossible, but with God all things are possible" (v. 26).

What a uniquely liberating word! We cannot do this. We know that going in, so the pressure is off. God will not hold us responsible for the results of our service to him. Only he can change hearts and raise the dead to life. Our only task is to be faithful, to keep showing up, day after day, proclaiming the Word of truth and pointing to Jesus. What God chooses to do with that Word is entirely up to him. We will not become proud when God blesses, because it is his work. We will not become discouraged when times are lean, because it is his work. We will pray and we will work, because it all depends on him.

Mini Myth

"Calvinists have no incentive to evangelize"

Many people, even some Calvinists, assume the doctrine of election eliminates the need to call people to faith in Jesus. Those God has chosen will be saved and those he has not chosen will not be, and there is nothing we can do about it. The pioneer missionary William Carey encountered this fatalism when he begged an eighteenth-century gathering of pastors to send evangelists across the sea. An older pastor interrupted, "Young man, sit down! You are an enthusiast. When God pleases to convert the heathen, he'll do it without consulting you or me."[2]

This is the extreme fatalism that "work like it all depends on me" seeks to correct. Evangelistic preachers sometimes encourage us to force witnessing opportunities, passing out tracts to waiters and tollbooth operators and asking strangers if they are prepared to meet their Maker. "If you were to die tonight, what would you say when God asks why he should let you into heaven?" We nervously initiate these zero to suddenly eternal conversations because the preacher scared us with a misapplication of Ezek 3:18: If "you don't speak out to warn him about his wicked way in order to save his life—that wicked person will die for his iniquity. Yet I will hold you responsible for his blood." Will God hold us responsible for not warning every lost person who dies and goes to hell? Better not take that chance.

Mainstream Calvinists walk the broad path between these two extremes. We prayerfully seek opportunities to point people to Jesus because nothing is more important. Yet we do not think another's salvation "all depends on me" and that God will hold us responsible for not asking the checkout person if she knows Jesus. Nevertheless, we love Jesus and people, so we remain on the lookout for "gospel appointments." We eagerly share the good news with everyone we can.

Calvinists do not think election eliminates our need to evangelize. Election reinforces it. If God had not chosen anyone, there would be no use sharing our faith. No one would ever respond. But God has chosen some people and who knows, it might be that person (2 Tim 2:10). So it's worth taking a chance. Speak to him and see how God might use it. Rather than remove incentives, God's election and effectual call are the reason evangelism works.

---

[2]   "William Carey," *Christian History* 36 (1992), Christianitytoday.com, https://www.christianitytoday.com/history/people/missionaries/william-carey.html.

PART II

———

Humanity and Sin

CHAPTER 12

This World Is Not Our Home

The Legendary Belief

Attend a Christian bluegrass concert and you may hear the clap-happy lyrics, "This world is not my home, I'm just a-passing through. My treasures are laid up somewhere beyond the blue."[1] Or "Some glad morning when this life is o'er, I'll fly away. To a home on God's celestial shore, I'll fly away."[2] You know this idea has gone mainstream when even Carrie Underwood sings that she does not belong in this world because it's only home for a while.[3]

Rick Warren explains the spiritual point. In his best-selling book *The Purpose Driven Life,* he writes that earth "is not your permanent home or final destination. You're just passing through, just visiting earth. . . . Sadly, many Christians have betrayed their King and his kingdom. They have foolishly concluded that because they live on earth, it's their home. It is not."[4]

Unraveling the Legend

This is extreme language. What is worse than treason? And are we traitors just for thinking the earth is our home? God placed us here. Living on earth was his idea. Seems like he might want us to make ourselves at home.

---

[1] Stove Pipe No. 1 (Sam Jones), vocalist, "This World Is Not My Home," by [Traditional], recorded August 19, 1924, arranged by Albert E. Brumley, 1937. Original words (1919) in public domain; A. P. Carter's arr. ©1931, renewed 1958; Brumley's arr. ©1937 Stamps-Baxter, renewed 1965; acquired by Zondervan 1974.

[2] Albert E. Brumley, "I'll Fly Away," © 1932, renewed 1960 Albert E. Brumley & Sons, admin. by Integrated Copyright Group.

[3] Carrie Underwood, vocalist, "Temporary Home," by Luke Robert Laird, Zachary David Maloy, and Carrie Underwood, track 8 on *Play On.*

[4] Rick Warren, *The Purpose Driven Life* (Grand Rapids: Zondervan, 2002), 48–49.

Genesis 2:7 reads, "Then the LORD God formed the man out of the dust from the ground." The Hebrew term for man is *'âdâm,* and the term for ground is *âdâmâ.* The name Adam means "red dirt." So the most biblically accurate name you could give your child is Clay. Or Dusty. Or Rocky. If you have a girl, try Sandy, Pebbles, or Terra. We are earthlings, for heaven's sake!

God created us in his image to steward the earth on his behalf. His first command was to "be fruitful, multiply, fill the earth, and subdue it. Rule the fish of the sea, the birds of the sky, and every creature that crawls on the earth" (Gen 1:26–28). We stand between God and creation, representing his benevolent reign as we responsibly cultivate the earth for his glory and the benefit of other creatures (2:15). The earth is exactly where God wants us. Where else would you rather live?

Ontology versus Ethics

If you understand what I am about to show you, your Bible and your life will make better sense. You will see why your Christian life redeems rather than obliterates your human life, and why following Jesus does not turn us into angels longing for heaven but disciples who pray for Jesus's return, when he will resurrect the bodies of our loved ones and restore all things (Acts 3:21). We don't ask Jesus to rapture us from the earth. We invite him to come and live with us here, on this redeemed earth (Rev 21:3; 22:20).

Christians mistakenly think this world is not their home because they confuse the philosophical categories of ontology and ethics. Ontology is the study of being and ethics examines morality. To oversimplify, but not by much, we can substitute "things" or "nouns" for ontology and "actions" or "verbs" for ethics. Have you noticed the same words can be used to describe things or actions? The word *rock* is often a noun: "God is my rock"; but it can also be a verb: "The allegations rocked the White House." The words *hammer* and *nail* pair well as nouns—the thing that strikes and the thing that is struck, and as verbs—"The president's opponents nailed him this time, so the president got hammered and went to bed."

Here is an important example from Scripture. John 3:16 says, "For God loved the world" while 1 John 2:15 counters with a command, "Do not love the world or the things in the world." What is going on? These are the same authors, God and John, and the same term, "world" or *kosmos* in Greek. God loves the world but tells us not to? How is that fair?

The hermeneutical key that unlocks this puzzler is the distinction between ontology and ethics. John 3:16 uses "world" ontologically: God loves all the things he has made, especially the human beings. But 1 John 2:15 is not speaking about things. The following verse says, "For everything in the world—the lust of the flesh, the lust of the eyes, and the pride in one's possessions—is not from the Father, but is from the world" (1 John 2:16). What are lust and pride? They are bad actions. They are not things; they are sins. When God and John command us to not love the world, they are not telling us to watch out for things such as fast cars, island vacations, or hot fudge sundaes. They are telling us to hate sin. Only by hating the sins of this world can we fully enjoy the things of this world.

This ontological-ethical distinction is crucial for correctly reading 1 Peter 2:11, "Dear friends, I urge you as strangers and exiles to abstain from sinful desires that wage war against the soul." Many Christians think this verse advocates what I call Martian theology. My Sunday school taught me what many call the "Countdown Song."[5] We kids counted down from ten, then jumped in the air and shouted, "Blast off!" The song goes on to say that God has made a special place—"somewhere in outer space"—for everyone who loves him and does what he says. I loved to sing that song, though if you think about it, its message is bizarre. I am an alien on this planet, biding my time until I can go to my true home in outer space? *Really?*

This is not what Peter says. Read that verse again, with the ontological-ethical distinction in mind. What kind of strangers and exiles are we? We are "to abstain from sinful desires." We are moral exiles, not ontological exiles. The sin in our world—not the world itself—should deeply offend us. Our problem is sin, not stuff. Because we are sinners, we often sinfully twist the good stuff God has made. We may become gluttons who eat too much ice cream, greedy idolaters who assume our value depends on having the biggest and best, and proud bores who flaunt our wealth to validate our status. In each case our problem is not the things themselves but our own evil misuse of them. Everything that God created is good. Every created thing may be rightly and properly enjoyed, and every created thing may be perversely abused. The problem is not with the thing but with our own sinful hearts.

We must distinguish ontology from ethics and think rightly about each one. Too many Christians seem comfortable with the values and entertainment of our world (ethics) yet come to church and sing about how they cannot wait to leave this place (ontology). How much better to resist the perversity of our fallen age (ethics) while resting comfortably in the world that God created for us (ontology)! We belong here, on this planet, fighting the sin that ravages the earth and its inhabitants.[6]

---

5 Dorothy Montgomery, "Somewhere in Outer Space," Gospel Choruses and Songs, https://gospelchoruses.wordpress.com/2014/12/01/somewhere-in-outer-space/.

6 Chapter 6 of *The Purpose Driven Life* creates theological confusion because it unknowingly oscillates between ethical and ontological categories. The chapter is exactly right when speaking ethically of aliens and strangers. We must not adopt "the values, priorities, and lifestyles of the world around us." But the chapter also switches to ontological categories, warning readers they are committing treason for thinking the world is their home and saying the reason "we experience difficulty, sorrow, and rejection in this

You may wonder whether the fall has changed the location of our home. Maybe the earth was originally intended to be our home, but can that still be true of this fallen place? Well, if you return from vacation to find someone has vandalized your house, spraying graffiti on your walls, breaking windows and doors, and slashing your mattress and couch cushions, you would not say, "That's it! I no longer live here. This is not my home." Wouldn't you say instead, "My home! How could this happen to my home!" Similarly, our sin has vandalized the shalom of our home. Our home is broken, yet it is still home. It needs a lot of work, which Jesus will supply when he returns.

Spiritual and Geographical Home

Nothing in this chapter should lessen our desire to be with Jesus. Paul wrote, "I long to depart and be with Christ—which is far better" (Phil 1:23). He said he "would prefer to be away from the body and at home with the Lord" (2 Cor 5:8). Praise God that when we die, we go home to be with the Lord. What a comfort! But we will not be fully home, in every way, until Jesus returns with us to this planet.

Have you ever asked a college student if he is going home for Christmas? If his parents have moved during the fall semester, he will say, "Yes, but it's complicated." He is going home because he will see his parents. But he has never been to this house or the city where his parents now live. He is going home to the right people, but in a new location. Something similar happens when we die. Jesus is our spiritual home. He is *who* we are meant to live with forever. Yet the earth is our geographical home. It is *where* we are to live forever with Jesus. Paul so much wants to be with Jesus that he will happily die to make that happen, yet he says that he would rather be with Jesus by Jesus's return than by his death. Consequently, he closes one letter with the prayer, "Our Lord, come!" (1 Cor 16:22).

The Bible does not encourage us to long for heaven. It stokes our desire to be with Jesus, who is what makes heaven heavenly. If Jesus were not there, heaven would be boring. But if Jesus is there, we will happily rest in him until he returns and restores all things. Then Jesus's presence will bring heaven to earth. John wrote, "I also saw the holy city, the new Jerusalem, coming down out of heaven from God, prepared like a bride adorned for her husband. Then I heard a loud voice from the throne: Look, God's dwelling is with humanity, and he will live with them" (Rev 21:2–3). Heaven—the abode of God—literally

---

world" is because the "earth is not our ultimate home" (48–49). This is wrong. We experience trouble because of the fall, not because of our location.

descends to earth. Why? Because "This is my Father's world! The battle is not done; Jesus who died shall be satisfied, and earth and heav'n be one."[7]

Application

I was speaking to a group of seminary professors, and one mentioned how he had enjoyed his walk to school that morning. The sun was rising, birds were chirping, and he felt a sudden thrill of being alive. He thanked God for creating such a beautiful world, then he thought "Uh-oh. Have I just crossed the line? Have I enjoyed creation a little bit too much?"

I suspect many godly people suffer from such low-grade residual guilt. We enjoy earthly pleasures while in the back of our minds we worry we might have gone too far. I told the man that God "richly provides us with all things to enjoy" (1 Tim 6:17). God invented music and colors and peaches. Every wholesome pleasure was his idea first. He created every pleasure receptacle in our body, then flooded the zone with triggers. He does not fear that we might have too much fun. Neither should we.

We cannot enjoy wholesome pleasures too much, though we can enjoy them in the wrong way. I told the worried professor the Greek term *adiaphora* can help us. It usually appears in discussions of Christian freedom and means "things indifferent" or "things neither here nor there." Adiaphora are things we may use but do not need. We can take them or leave them. Any good, non-sinful pleasure may be enjoyed as long as it remains adiaphora. We are glad for it, but we receive it with an open hand. Because it is adiaphora, we willingly share it with others. Selfishly grasping for pleasure is a sign it has become an idol, and if God loves us, he will wrench it from us.[8]

Christians may be called to suffer, but we are not masochists. We do not score extra spiritual points if we choose the vacation, car, or pie that we like least. Do not waste energy wondering whether you are enjoying creation too much. Receive wholesome pleasures with gratitude and invite others to join you. Not only will you show the world how wonderful it can be to follow Jesus, but also you will bring joy to your heavenly Father. He takes pleasure when you find pleasure in this, your Father's world.[9]

---

[7] Maltbie D. Babcock, "This Is My Father's World," lyrics from his poem "My Father's World," in *Thoughts for Everyday Living* (New York: Charles Scribner's Sons, 1901), 180–82; hymn tune *Terra Beata*, arranged for Babcock's lyrics by Franklin L. Sheppard in *Alleluia* (Philadelphia: Presbyterian Board of Publication and Sabbath School Work, 1915).

[8] The discipline of fasting trains us to enjoy the many pleasures of creation without worshiping them, as it points us to the all-surpassing pleasure of intimacy with the Giver of all good things.

[9] For more on this topic, see Michael E. Wittmer, *Becoming Worldly Saints* (Grand Rapids: Zondervan, 2015) and *Heaven Is a Place on Earth* (Grand Rapids: Zondervan, 2004).

CHAPTER 13

You Shouldn't Waste Your Life on Temporal Things

The Legendary Belief

In its chapter titled "Life Is a Temporary Assignment," *The Purpose Driven Life* says the earth is not our home and then elaborates on what this means for us now. "God warns us to not get too attached to what's around us because it is temporary." And "Realizing that life on earth is just a temporary assignment should radically alter your values. Eternal values, not temporal ones, should become the deciding factors for your decisions." And "You will not be in heaven two seconds before you cry out, *'Why did I place so much importance on things that were so temporary? What was I thinking? Why did I waste so much time, energy, and concern on what wasn't going to last?'"*[1]

Evangelical sermons frequently urge us not to waste our lives on temporal things. Have you heard this warning in church? "There are two things that last forever—the Word of God and souls. Everything else is going to burn. So, live for what matters most."

Unraveling the Legend

You will get no argument from me that the Word of God and souls matter most. Though, as I will emphasize in the next chapter, our bodies matter too! I do question whether a thing's longevity is the deciding factor in its importance. The lake of fire lasts forever, but no Christian argues we should live for it!

And other things do not last forever yet remain important. Meals are not everlasting. They are meant to be eaten. Yet my mother never questioned her life choices after she prepared a scrumptious dinner. "Why do I even bother? I worked so hard and now it's gone!" Many men eventually go bald, yet they do

---

[1] Warren, *Purpose Driven Life*, 49–51 (see chap. 12, n. 4; emphasis his).

not regret wasting so much time washing and styling their hair in high school. Soccer games do not last forever—they only seem to go on and on—yet Christians around the world still enjoy playing and watching the sport.

So I wonder, will we really not be in heaven two seconds before we lament the time on earth spent mowing the lawn, washing our car, reading a book, walking our dog, drawing a picture, or weeding a garden? Almost nothing we do lasts forever. Including this sentence. We are temporal creatures who inevitably do temporary things. Does that mean we waste our lives when we do them? The answer depends on where meaning and value come from.

God Determines Value

Finite creatures like us cannot produce anything of lasting, permanent value. Sports pretends. Television broadcasts introduce championship games with epic music and dramatic flourishes that announce that someone will leave the field as an eternal hero. If the quarterback has already won several championships, we may hear that this one game is for the ages. Win this one, and he will always be remembered. But of course, he will be forgotten. His name may be written in the record books, but these will be thrown out when a future generation loses interest in his sport. His football cards may be the first things to go when the kids clean out their grandparents' attic. He may be the GOAT, the Greatest of All Time in football, basketball, or baseball, but these sports themselves are fewer than 200 years old. Does anyone remember the GOAT of the ancient Olympic games? Does anyone care?

The only value that lasts comes from God. This is the point of Ecclesiastes. The book begins and ends the same way: life under the sun is "absolute futility. Everything is futile" (Eccl 1:2; 12:8). So, what's the point? The book tells us in its final verse: "God will bring every act to judgment, including every hidden thing, whether good or evil" (12:14). This could not be worse. Everything about my life is absolutely futile, and I am going to be judged for it too? Well, that's a bummer.

Unless. What if God's judgment is the only thing that gives ultimate meaning to my life? What is the value of anything I do? Whatever God says. If God declares my work to be evil, then it will burn like chaff, no matter how impressive it seems right now. If God declares my work to be good and bestows a reward, then it is worth doing now and worth doing well, even if no one else seems to care.

The only question that matters, then, is, What does God reward? Certainly, he rewards grand, sacrificial gestures. Of course, he rewards leading someone to Jesus. What could be more important? This is what evangelical pastors get right when they encourage us to not waste our lives on temporal things. But God also rewards everything, no matter how seemingly trivial, that is done for him. Jesus said the smallest thing given to the smallest person still counts. "And whoever gives even a cup of cold water to one of these little ones because he is a disciple, truly I tell you, he will never lose his reward" (Matt 10:42).

On an average day, taking my dog for a walk is one of the least important things I do. He is a temporal creature that likely will go out of existence when he dies, never to be seen again. Yet God says, "The righteous cares about his animal's health" (Prov 12:10). Taking care of Sammy matters to God, so it should matter to me too. Gerard Manley Hopkins expressed the possibility of doing all things to the glory of God: "To lift up the hands in prayer gives God glory, but a man with a dungfork in his hand, a woman with a slop-pail, give him glory too. He is so great that all things give him glory if you mean they should."[2] What's in your hand? A mop? A shovel? Wield it for Jesus, and you will not lose your reward.

Answer Your Call

The elevation of everyday life was one of the main takeaways of the Reformation. Martin Luther tried desperately to not waste his life on temporal things, to live for what matters most. He left the temporal rewards of law school and his father's copper mining business to enter a monastery. But it was never enough. He deprived himself of his temporal need for food, warm clothing, and sleep. Yet he could never know for sure that God was pleased with him.

Because God was not. Luther realized his extreme spiritual efforts were thinly veiled selfishness and pride. He was desperately trying to satisfy God's holy requirements and save himself. Only, he couldn't. Then he discovered that was the point. Salvation comes from God to us, not from us climbing the ladder to God. Forgiveness of sin is something we receive, not something we achieve. Luther put his faith in Jesus and for the first time in years felt he could breathe. Now that his salvation was secure in Jesus, he found he had time on his hands. He no longer spent every waking moment trying to save himself. He was free to serve his neighbor.

Luther followed the apostle Paul, who said serving our neighbors is the Christian's calling. "For you were called to be free, brothers and sisters; only don't use this freedom as an opportunity for the flesh, but serve one another through love" (Gal 5:13). God's call to salvation is not one and done. It continues throughout our lives, supplying meaningful opportunities to serve others in frequently temporal ways. Before the Reformation, only monks, priests, and nuns had callings. Everyone else muddled through a lesser, temporal existence. The Reformation leveled the field. Luther taught that everyone is secure

---

[2] Gerard Manley Hopkins, "The Principle or Foundation," in *Gerard Manley Hopkins: The Major Works,* ed. Catherine Phillips (New York: Oxford University Press, 2002), 292.

only in Jesus, so everyone who believes in Jesus is free to serve God equally. Pastors and missionaries serve God by preaching the gospel, and mechanics, nurses, and waiters serve God by serving their neighbors for the glory of God (Col 3:17). Where today will you serve a child, a spouse, a customer? Do it for the Lord Jesus, and it counts (vv. 23–24).

The Tension of Life

The "Don't waste your life on temporal things" motto aptly reminds us that some things matter more than others. Jesus said, "For what will it benefit someone if he gains the whole world yet loses his life?" (Matt 16:26). What can compare with not going to hell? Yet our Lord himself spent much of his life in his father's shop, and none of that work survives. Whatever else Jesus did during the first thirty years of his earthly life, it wasn't professional ministry. Did Jesus waste 90 percent of his time on earth?

The "Don't waste your life on temporal things" motto reminds us that it might be wise to downsize to a smaller house so we have more time and money for the people and ministries that matter most. It doesn't seem wise to waste our whole retirement combing beaches, casting into lily pads, or chipping onto greens. Yet the resurrected Christ made breakfast on the beach, immediately after giving fishing instructions (John 21:4–14). Temporal things all.

Here is the tension of life: All things matter, but some things matter more. Some things matter more, but everything still matters. We should not worry about how important our callings seem to be in the kingdom. We should simply do whatever comes before us, do it with all our might, then go to bed. One day we will rise to receive our reward. Because Jesus rose from the dead, we must "be steadfast, immovable, always excelling in the Lord's work, because you know that your labor in the Lord is not in vain" (1 Cor 15:58).

This tension of life belies broad generalizations such as we must "not get too attached to what's around us because it is temporary." Good luck with that! How would we become unattached? We will eat something, read something, and wear something (hopefully!). We are finite, temporal creatures living in a finite, temporal world. Temporal things are the furniture of our lives. The Bible nowhere tells us to avoid things that are temporary, simply because they are temporary. Remember last chapter's ontological-ethical distinction? God commands us to avoid sin (ethics), not what is temporal (ontology). Avoid the temporal and you will miss many of God's gifts, which often come in temporal form. Check your prayer list. Much of what we ask for are temporary blessings—a clean scan, passing grades in chemistry, and daily bread. Thank God for these temporary gifts and ask him for the same things tomorrow.

Application

It had been a tough year for pastors, so one of us stood to encourage the others. "Let's remember how blessed we are to be pastors. Every day we get to do something of eternal significance." The man meant well, yet I cringed when he said it. What did his encouragement imply about the people in his church with ordinary jobs? Plumbers, janitors, and salesclerks. Wouldn't his implied comparison demoralize them? These ordinary saints may never get on the church platform, but they need to know they are not second-class Christians. God wants all of us doing all our callings for the Lord Jesus.

This is particularly obvious now. As Western culture becomes more hostile to Christianity, one of the best advertisements for Jesus is his followers doing everyday, temporal tasks for his glory. What if our neighbors said, "We don't much care for what these Christians believe, but we've got to say, they are the best at whatever they do. Need a carpenter, doctor, or tutor? Find a Christian. They do fine work for a fair price."

Paul knew this, so he commanded Christian slaves to serve their masters well. Slaves were on the low rungs of Roman society, yet their faithful service would "adorn the teaching of God our Savior" and attract others to Jesus (Titus 2:9–10). Slaves spent all day, every day, on temporal things. Their lives were not wasted. God said their ordinary callings were opportunities to serve others and point them to Jesus.

CHAPTER 14

_____

My Body Is a Temporary Residence for My Immortal Soul

The Legendary Belief

The last two chapters cited urban legends from *The Purpose Driven Life*. That may seem a bit much, but what better way to establish these statements are urban legends? Rick Warren's classic book has sold more than 50 million copies in eighty-five languages. It has its own Wikipedia page. It will survive my critique. So here is one more. *The Purpose Driven Life* rightly says death will not end our existence. Then it adds, "Your earthly body is just a temporary residence for your spirit." The book's accompanying calendar confirms, "You are a soul who inhabits a body."[1]

Funeral sermons sometimes celebrate this point, especially if the deceased was elderly. The preacher might say, "Mitch's body was just a shell for the real him. He is no longer here, as he has left behind his temporary home and gone to heaven. Monday was Mitch's moving day, when he traded in his crumbling, run-down body for a celestial palace. We miss him, but we wouldn't be so mean as to wish him back to his old shack."

Unraveling the Legend

Before I unravel this urban legend, let me share a story in which it seemed useful. I cannot imagine the horror of the friends sent to retrieve the bodies of Jim Elliot and his fellow missionaries killed by the Ecuadorian tribe. They found Nate Saint floating in a river, and one of them tried to tie a string to Nate's exposed arm. He could not bring himself to touch Nate's body, so he told himself that he was not touching his friend but only his body. He said, "A

---

[1]   Warren, *Purpose Driven Life*, 37 (see chap. 12, n. 4).

body is only a house and these fellows had left their house and, after the soul leaves, the body isn't much after all."[2]

I am entirely sympathetic. If I had his horrific task, I would be tempted to tell myself the same thing. But it is still wrong. Our bodies are not merely shells for the real us. We are humans, not hermit crabs.

Plato versus Paul

The idea that humans are souls temporarily living in bodies does not come from the Bible but from Greek philosophy. Plato taught we are souls who once lived among the heavenly forms—the eternal, unchanging, rational ideals—and unfortunately have now become trapped in earthly, physical bodies. The goal of life is to lounge around like philosophers, contemplating the forms until the day we die and are released from this lower, material world. Then we will return to the heavens, where we will twinkle and shine forever. Cue the "Countdown Song" from chapter 12.

Platonic thought was unwittingly smuggled into the church through the second-century Greek apologists who sought to win their Platonic culture to Christ, and most importantly through its two most influential theologians, Origen in the East and Augustine in the West. If Platonism was holes, Origen's theology would be Swiss cheese. He believed our material world was created as a punishment and probation for fallen souls to make their way back to God. Our souls would be reincarnated through a succession of worlds until we were sufficiently purified to be reunited with God. Then the physical world would be no more.[3] Augustine had converted to Neo-Platonism before he converted to Christianity, and he credited Neo-Platonism with helping him appreciate the truth and beauty of the Christian faith. He checked the extremes of Neo-Platonic thought—he disagreed with its view that bodies were evil—but he did concede that bodies were inferior to the higher spiritual life.[4] He passed this Platonic dualism on to the rest of the Western church, which intensified the error. Even a Reformed giant like John Calvin repeatedly claimed that bodies are "the prison houses" for souls.[5]

The apostle Paul never talks this way. He implies that we consist of two separable parts, body and soul, because some aspect of us survives our death.

---

[2]   Elisabeth Elliot, *Through Gates of Splendor* (1956; repr., Wheaton, IL: Tyndale, 1981), 237.

[3]   Origen, *On First Principles,* 1.8–2.3, trans. G. W. Butterworth (New York: Harper & Row, 1966), 66–94; and Joseph Wilson Trigg, *Origen* (Atlanta: John Knox Press, 1983), 103–15.

[4]   Augustine, *Confessions,* VII–X, trans. Henry Chadwick (New York: Oxford University Press, 1992), 111–220; *City of God,* XIII.16, XXII.4, trans. Henry Bettenson (New York: Penguin, 2003), 524–25, 1,026–27; and Allan D. Fitzgerald, "Body," in *Augustine Through the Ages,* ed. Allan D. Fitzgerald (Grand Rapids: Eerdmans, 1999), 105–7.

[5]   Calvin says this several times in his *Institutes of the Christian Religion.* For instance, see 1:186 (1.15.2), "unless souls survive when freed from the prison houses of their bodies."

Our bodies are buried or cremated, and some part of us goes to be with the Lord (2 Cor 5:1–10; Phil 1:22–24). But we only know this because of death, and we only die because of Adam's fall. We were never supposed to know we have two parts that can be divided. Our separation is unnatural, not the way we are supposed to be.

In his book on the body and soul, philosopher John Cooper describes our composition as "holistic dualism."[6] We have two parts, but they are meant to function inextricably together. No one can explain exactly how our body and soul intertwine, yet we know they do. Go ahead, raise your right arm. You have no idea how you did that. Your mind is the immaterial aspect of your brain. Together they sent a material, electrical-chemical signal to your arm that contained nonmaterial information that told your arm to physically raise and then lower. You did this amazing feat with barely a thought, and you do not know how. No one does. But look, you can do it again!

Souls can exist without bodies, but they won't for long. We believe that when Jesus returns, he will resurrect our bodies and put us back together, this time forever. Far from being merely temporary houses for our souls, our bodies are the targets of the Christian hope! Christians don't believe in reincarnation—that our souls can inhabit any body and still be us. We believe in the resurrection! Paul said our resurrection bodies will be spiritual, patterned on the resurrection body of Jesus (1 Cor 15:44–49). But they will still be physical, as Jesus pointedly showed that his resurrection body remained fully physical (Luke 24:36–43). And they will still be us. If our resurrection body is too different from our present body, we will not have been redeemed. We will have been replaced. This is not what God promises!

Thankful Creatures

A "too-low" view of our body correlates with a "too-high" view of our soul. Both moves pressure us to forget our place as grateful creatures in God's world.

I will start by saying something that may strike you as heresy, but only if you are thinking like a heretic. I believe your dog has a soul. He is more than a bundle of neuro-chemical impulses firing in a material body. He has an immaterial part as well. You see his spirit when he wags his tail, snarls at pedestrians, or lowers his head and whimpers in shame.

You may object that your dog does not have a soul because you do not believe he will live forever. I don't believe that either, and I didn't say that. You may think I implied it because you mistakenly think souls are inherently

---

[6] John Cooper, *Body, Soul, & Life Everlasting* (Grand Rapids: Eerdmans, 1989), 252–53. In a second edition (2000), Cooper acknowledges that "dualistic holism" might be a better description because its emphasis falls on the unity of body and soul (pp. xxvii–xxviii).

immortal, so whatever has a soul must live forever. As if God would be powerless to stop a soul's existence! Worse, some Christians think since God is spirit and they have a spirit, then they possess a Godlike substance. No wonder they think their pet doesn't have a soul! But all these assumptions are pagan thoughts. They come from Plato, not Paul.

Both my body and soul were created by God. Before I was conceived in 1966, no part of me existed anywhere (though God has always known that I would; Ps 139:16: "All my days were written in your book and planned before a single one of them began"). The God who created my body and soul is strong enough to snuff out both. I know he won't because he has promised I will live forever. And that's the point. My continued existence depends entirely on God's Word, not because some part of me is inherently immortal or indestructible.

Are you glad to be alive? Thank God, for your existence was all his idea. We did not get to vote on whether to be born. God wanted us here, and so here we are. As we were powerless to bring ourselves into existence, so we are powerless to take ourselves out. We may commit suicide, yet we will continue to exist somewhere so long as God chooses to keep us alive. Our existence is entirely contingent on God's desires. We get no say. We can only offer gratitude for our life.

The elevation of the soul and the corresponding denigration of the body are particularly prevalent in the LGBTQ+ movement. Here the danger of our urban legend becomes readily apparent. If we insist our bodies are merely temporary residences for our souls, what will we say to people who claim to be transgender? That is precisely the LGBTQ+ point. They argue that their bodies may be male, but their souls are female, so they must change their bodies to match their souls. I appreciate how difficult this is for some, but we must all recognize that God has given us our bodies and we should contentedly thank him for them. Our bodies are not shells, to be surgically altered to suit our feelings. Our bodies are a vital piece of who we are. We are our souls, and we are our bodies too. They matter so much that God has hung all our hopes on their future resurrection.

Application

The resurrection of Jesus is proof that he is Lord, but it was also a problem to the Greek mind. The philosophers in Athens listened attentively to Paul's message until he came to Jesus's resurrection. Then they "began to ridicule him" (Acts 17:32). Paul realized his message of a crucified and risen Lord was "foolishness to the Gentiles" (1 Cor 1:23). Bad enough that Jesus was killed in the most humiliating way, how stupid was he to rise from the dead? His soul had been freed to return to the heavens. What kind of silly god goes back for his body?

Followers of Jesus must embrace the scandal of his resurrection. If Jesus bodily arose from the dead, the firstfruits of our resurrection, then our bodies will rise too (1 Cor 15:20). We will enjoy our glorified bodies forever. In the meantime, there may be things we wish we could change about our bodies, from the lay of our hair to the shape of our thighs to the gnarly curl of our third toe. We may not like everything about our bodies, but we must love them. Not for their own sake, but for the One who made and gave his life for them.

Mini Myth

Humans consist of a body, soul, and spirit.

Many Christians think we consist of three parts: a body that relates to the physical world, a soul that relates to others, and a spirit that relates to God (this part is either dead or missing until the person is born again). They find biblical support in 1 Thess 5:23, "And may your whole spirit, soul, and body be kept sound and blameless at the coming of our Lord Jesus Christ," and Heb 4:12, which says the word of God is "sharper than any double-edged sword, penetrating as far as the separation of soul and spirit, joints and marrow."

However, these Scriptures are not giving an ontological description of the human being. They are speaking hyperbolically. The first passage encourages us to love God with all we have, like Jesus's command to "love the Lord your God with all your heart, with all your soul, with all your strength, and with all your mind" (Luke 10:27). Jesus was not saying we have four different parts to love God with; he was stringing synonyms for the same thing. And the second text says that God's Word powerfully penetrates the deepest part of our heart, dividing things, such as soul and spirit, that are indivisible (Heb 4:12).

Separating soul and spirit creates theological problems as it separates our higher, spiritual life from our lower, soulish and bodily lives. It implies we might be in tip-top spiritual shape while disobeying God in lesser social and physical areas. Conversely, we might be barely saved, a "carnal Christian" who has put his faith in Jesus yet has not cultivated the higher, spiritual walk. But what kind of Christian doesn't integrate his spiritual life with every other dimension? Can someone be in fine spiritual shape if he is gluttonously ruining his physical shape? Can he be right with God if he is not right with others?

We avoid this sacred-secular divide when we recognize that soul and spirit are two names for our same immaterial part. We have a material side, called our body; and we have an immaterial side, called our soul or spirit. Both sides are united in us, forgiven in Christ, and meant to be gratefully given to him.

CHAPTER 15

I Am Enough

The Legendary Belief

Lauren Daigle's hit song "You Say" was named Christian song of the year at the 2019 Billboard Music awards. It spent more weeks at number one than any other song on Hot Christian Songs, and Billboard ranked it as the second biggest Christian song of the 2010s. It is a very popular song![1]

Copyright rules prohibit me from quoting its lyrics, though the song is easy to find online or in the playlist of many teenagers. It begins with Daigle saying she resists the lies that tell her she is not enough. The chorus is a love ballad from God, who tells Daigle she is loved even when she doesn't feel it and she is strong even though she thinks she is weak.

These themes are increasingly common among Christians. One church advertisement contrasted a woman's previous self-talk with her new identity. Her old name was "Lacking." Her new identity is "Enough." Which raises the question, *Enough for what?*

Unraveling the Legend

When I first heard "You Say" in church, I stumbled over its opening lines. The congregation sang that they were fighting the lies that they were not enough and would never measure up. Wait. What? Is it a lie to think I will never be enough? Is it wrong to believe I will never meet the standard? Aren't these the truth? If I am or can be enough, why do I need Jesus?

Some readers may think I am missing the point. "You Say" has blessed people, many of them young and female, who have been wounded by others.

---

[1] Paul Mabury, Lauren Daigle, and Jason Ingram, "You Say," track 5 on Lauren Daigle, *Look Up Child* (Centricity Music, 2018).

These dear souls suffer from anxiety, depression, and low self-esteem, and they are pleasantly surprised to hear a Christian song about their worth. Isn't it wonderful to learn they belong and they are loved and held and strong?

Creation

Let's think about this through the biblical lens of creation, fall, and redemption. The story of creation assures us that we have incalculable value as human beings. If this is what we mean by "I am enough," that my worth is settled because I am the image of God, then I say "Amen! Exactly right." We cannot—and must not try to—do anything to increase our value. We should never apologize for who we are. We should never believe the lies of those who slander us. We should never feel worthless because we have been abused. We may not be tall or slim or the best at anything, but we bear the image of Almighty God. That is enough to cement our worth.

"You Say" is not entirely clear on this point. It rightly says I discover my value in You, assuming that the "You" is God. But it seems focused on performance—my falling down, my highs and lows, and my failures and triumphs. Perhaps the song brings up performance to remind us not to seek our value there but in the God who loves us. That would be terrific if the song consistently said that. The chorus channels God comforting my broken heart by praising the strength I possess. He says I am strong when I feel that I am weak. But God would never say this. In fact, he says the opposite!

When the apostle Paul begged God to remove his "thorn in the flesh," God replied, "My grace is sufficient for you, for my power is perfected in weakness." God did not assure Paul that he was much stronger than he thought. God confirmed that Paul was weak and would remain weak in himself so Jesus would receive more glory from his life. Paul understood and declared, "I will most gladly boast all the more about my weaknesses, so that Christ's power may reside in me. . . . For when I am weak, then I am strong" (2 Cor 12:7–10).

Others have noticed the message of "You Say" is to believe in yourself. The trade magazine *Billboard* summarized the song as "Lauren Daigle beats her inner negative voices to believe in her own strength." This perceived theme is why the song appears on secular, inspirational shows like *America's Got Talent*. It's the perfect fit. *Billboard* continues, "Daigle's worth, according to the song's lyrics, is found in God and whatever He says about her strength and ability to be loved."[2] This is confusing: How can our worth come from both God and our own strength? Isn't it better to say our worth lies wholly in Jesus, our Creator and Redeemer? Our worth does not lie in our strength and

---

    [2] Heran Mamo, "Here Are the Lyrics to Lauren Daigle's 'You Say,'" *Billboard*, July 30, 2018, https://www.billboard.com/articles/news/lyrics/8467747/lauren-daigle-you-say-lyrics.

openness to love that Jesus happens to notice. "You Say" does not focus on our belief in Jesus. It emphasizes what Jesus believes about us. Daigle sings that the only thing that matters is how highly God thinks of me. No. Jesus's identity is infinitely more important than mine. We are turning worship on its head. Rather than praising God, full stop, we are praising God to bolster our self-esteem. We are singing to God that we hear him saying to us, "You are amazing! You can do it! You've got this!"

Fall

Here is the bottom line: What is our deepest problem? Why did Jesus die? The "I am enough" meme suggests our main problem is low self-esteem. Jesus died to bind our emotional wounds and fill us with self-confidence so we might feel better about ourselves.

I know from counseling experience that anxiety, depression, and low self-image are significant problems for many people. I will never minimize their anguish as they struggle to get through day after excruciating day. I know their burdens can seem unbearable, and songs like "You Say" may feel like a ray of light in their gloom.

Anxiety and depression are real, but you don't need Jesus to beat them. You can learn to cope and feel better through counseling, pharmaceuticals, and therapeutic techniques. Thousands have. God says our deepest problem, and the reason Jesus came, is not for what we feel but for our sin. The angel told Joseph to name his Son "Jesus, because he will save his people from their sins" (Matt 1:21). You can feel like a million bucks and die without Jesus and go to hell. And you can be paralyzed by panic attacks and still know Jesus and his forgiveness. We want all people to know Jesus and to feel their worth, but if you ask God why Jesus died, he would say what he already told us, "to reconcile us to himself" (2 Cor 5:17–21). Our feelings may follow, and we pray they do. But they are not what matters most.

What if you are counseling non-Christians who battle anxiety and low self-esteem? I doubt it is wise to start with their sin and why they deserve hell. That may push them over the edge. Consider a cancer patient who needs lifesaving surgery but also has contracted pneumonia. If you operate now to remove his cancer, he will not survive. You first must treat the pneumonia, then wait until his body is strong enough to endure the surgery. You must do both, in the right order, or he will die. Similarly, we may need to spend some time helping our friend understand her identity as an image bearer of God. We may need to help her understand why the abuse she suffered was not her fault and why it does not define her. We may need to strengthen her appreciation for creation so she can endure the brutal truth of the fall. Perhaps it would sound something like this: "Remember when we said you were not responsible for what happened to you and that you must reject what was said about you? That is all true. You are not that person. Yet you are not without problems. Your deepest need is my deepest need, the forgiveness of sin." Our friend may be too distressed for us to begin with the truth of her sin. But if we do not get there eventually, she cannot be saved.

Redemption

The most distressing aspect of "I am enough" is how it distracts from Jesus. The point of worship is to boast in Jesus, to praise him for his great love and rest in his grace. This seems impossible to do when we are singing about ourselves—how we struggle with feeling unloved and not belonging and how God helps me feel better about all that. Can you imagine your grandparents' generation singing such self-focused lyrics in church? If we lose Jesus or the reason he died, we lose everything. We may be a spiritual gathering with a religious veneer, but we are no longer Christian.

Here is a helpful test for any song or testimony: Does it boast in Jesus? Paul said that true Christians "boast in Christ Jesus, and do not put confidence in the flesh." Paul was proud of his religious identity, yet he considered all of it "to be a loss in view of the surpassing value of knowing Christ Jesus my Lord." And not just a loss, but "dung, so that I may gain Christ" (Phil 3:3–8). Let's follow Paul's lead. Let's sing and talk in ways that make much of Jesus and avoid songs and sermons that make much of us.

To be fair, some may claim they are boasting in Jesus when they say, "I am enough." They say what they mean is "in Christ, I am enough." I have three responses. First, then say that. Especially given our therapeutic culture's obsession with self-esteem, you cannot say "I am enough" and expect our biblically illiterate, self-focused audience to fill in the blank with "but only in Jesus, right?" Second, it seems more biblical, and it is Paul's point in 2 Cor 12:1–10, to say "Jesus is enough." If the point is that I am only enough in Christ, then cut to the chase and say, "Jesus is enough." "He must increase, but I must decrease" (John 3:30). Third, why are we skating so close to the edge, saying things that *Billboard* magazine and *America's Got Talent* interpret in decidedly non-Christian, damning ways? Don't Jesus and his good news demand our best efforts at clarity? Jesus did not sacrifice his life only for us to mumble the reason and fumble it out-of-bounds. We speak clearly when something matters to us. What matters more than Jesus and the lost who desperately need his salvation?[3]

In summary, this is how the biblical story recasts this urban legend:

---

[3]   Here is an example from a devotional of the sloppy confusion this chapter seeks to correct: "Let go of the lies that you are not enough and take hold of the truth that you are more than enough with Jesus and

Creation: I am enough (I am the image of God)
Fall: I am not enough (I have rebelled against God and deserve hell)
Redemption: Only Jesus is enough (I rest in Christ)

The lie we must reject is not "I am not enough." The lie is that "I am by myself." Satan and his demons do not want me to think I am not enough, because that thought will drive me to Jesus. They want me to believe that I am alone. Left to myself I deserve hell, and there is nothing I can do about it. But the good news of Jesus is I am not by myself. I am in Christ, and that is enough.

Application

When I graduated from high school, I passed out my senior picture to friends, signing the back with "Phil 4:13." You may have seen this reference etched in the eye black of outfielders and quarterbacks before a big game. The verse reads, "I am able to do all things through him who strengthens me." The "him" is Jesus, but the part I wanted my friends to hear was "I am able to do all things." It was my early version of "In Christ, *I am enough*."

If I had read the surrounding verses, I would have realized that my boasting was the opposite of what God was saying. Have you seen the Phil 4:13 T-shirt, "I can do all things through a verse taken out of context"? In this passage Paul is thanking the Philippians for their gift and explaining that he does not need much because he has learned how to be content with a lot or a little. He can be "well fed or hungry," having "abundance or in need. I am able to do all things through him who strengthens me" (Phil 4:12–13). So, athletes who sport "Phil 4:13" are unknowingly saying they are content whether they hit home runs or strike out, whether they throw touchdown passes or interceptions. And I was signaling that I was okay with either success or failure in college and my career. Not what any of us had in mind.

The good news of Jesus is so radically different than our natural goals that sometimes we miss it entirely. We get it exactly backwards and upside down. But Jesus's good news is better than our best news. Jesus did not die to make all our dreams come true. He died and rose again to replace our dreams with himself. As we mature, we learn that is more than enough.

His power at work in you!" If I am only enough in Jesus, then "I am not enough" is not a lie. It must be the truth.

CHAPTER 16

Freedom Explains the Problem of Evil

The Legendary Belief

The Christian apologist conceded to his university audience that the most difficult question to answer is why an all good and all-powerful God allows evil to exist. He said we cannot exhaustively answer this question, but we can explain how evil is possible. God created us to enjoy a loving relationship with him. He knew that love requires freedom—you can't force someone to love you—so he decided to give us free will. But that required risk. God cannot guarantee what we do with our freedom, otherwise we would not be free. He knew we would use our freedom to rebel, but he gave us freedom anyway, in the hope that we might later return and genuinely love him.

This popular argument for the problem of evil is known as the free will defense. No one has expounded it more forcefully than Alvin Plantinga, who added that it is possible humans possess transworld depravity. Although this sounds like the world's worst airline—you know Transworld Depravity would charge extra for seats and never depart on time—it simply means humans would eventually rebel in every possible world God might create. If transworld depravity is possibly true, it explains how evil may not be God's fault. God gave us freedom, we possess transworld depravity, and so we went bad and brought evil into the world. Our sin is entirely on us; we may still believe God is good.[1]

Unraveling the Legend

The free will defense says something important. God did give us freedom and we did use that freedom to rebel. Yet the defense only works within an Arminian

---

[1] Alvin Plantinga, *God, Freedom, and Evil* (Grand Rapids: Eerdmans, 1974), 48–53.

theology. Calvinists disagree with the premise that God cannot guarantee what free creatures freely choose. They believe that regeneration and glorification are two instances when God guarantees our choices without violating our freedom. At regeneration God changes our hearts so we freely repent and believe, and when we are glorified, we will be fully free yet unable to sin. Calvinists reason that if God can guarantee our free choices on the new earth, he easily could have done so in the garden of Eden. If at the end, why not at the start?

Nevertheless, the free will defense initially sounds more palatable than the Calvinist emphasis on divine sovereignty. If everything that occurs belongs somehow to God's decree, how is God not responsible for evil?

Extreme Calvinists may respond that God decrees evil, deal with it. More nuanced Calvinists think it is important not to make God the author of evil, and they carefully express God's relation to evil negatively. They say God is asymmetrically related to evil, or that evil is not outside God's decree. This seems to have been John Calvin's view. He wrote, "Men act perversely, not without God's ordination that it be done."[2] The onus is on us. We are the agents who sin, and our transgression is mysteriously "not without God's ordination."

Arminians reply that either Calvinist view is a problem. How can a good God either directly or indirectly decree the horrific evils of our world? It is much easier to believe God is good if he merely gave us the freedom to choose good or evil.

Love Limits Freedom

But things are not so simple. It is obvious why Calvinists struggle to defend God's goodness, but Arminians have the very same problem. It just takes an extra step or two to see it. For example, consider the difficult truth that only some people are saved. Calvinists say this is ultimately God's decision. He elects some to life and reprobates others, either by actively damning (double predestination) or merely passing by those he did not choose (single predestination).[3] Both forms of Calvinism say the deciding factor in salvation is God's decree. He chooses whom he saves.

Arminians counter that the cause of God's election is not his will but his foreknowledge. God looks down through time to see what people will do with the freedom he gives them. If he sees they will repent and believe, then he chooses to elect them. If he sees they will not repent and believe, then he

---

[2]   John Calvin, *Concerning the Eternal Predestination of God,* trans. J. K. S. Reid (London: James Clarke, 1961), 175.

[3]   Double predestination means God actively elects some to life and others to damnation, while single predestination means God elects some to life and merely ignores the rest, permitting them to continue on the road to hell.

chooses to pass them by. The deciding factor is not God's will but their free choice. He gives them freedom. What they do with it is up to them.

This would seem to exonerate God, except he knows whether a person will repent or rebel, and he knows before he created her. Why would he create someone knowing that she will reject him and suffer forever in hell? Wouldn't it be more loving for him not to create her at all? Or if he did create her, wouldn't it be more loving to limit her freedom so she could not choose hell?

Good parents only give their children freedom the parents can live with. When my children were small, we lived on a busy street. Semitrucks shook the house as they rumbled by, so we built a fence in the backyard to limit our kids' freedom and save their lives. What kind of parent would give their child freedom to play near a busy road? What kind of God would give his children freedom to wander into hell? Especially the ones he knows would go there? Why give a shot at love to those he knows will shoot themselves?

The point is not to deny God's goodness, only to say the free will defense does not fully exonerate God. Anyone who believes in God's foreknowledge and the reality of hell will be unable to solve the problem of evil.[4] Arminians and Calvinists are in the same boat. But this is no cause for despair. Neither group can solve the problem, but no one can say more about evil than Christians.

The Cross

Christians cannot explain the mystery of evil, and that is okay. No one can. Our advantage is that this mystery lies at the center of our faith. Evil is an important part of the Christian story. Our religion makes no sense without it.

What is the greatest evil that has ever occurred? What is the greatest evil that could ever occur? Wouldn't it be the cross? The cross is the greatest injustice; the innocent Son of God bearing the guilt and shame of the world. No one can suffer more undeservedly. The cross is also the greatest possible suffering. Who can begin to comprehend the anguish in Jesus's cry, "My God, my God, why have you abandoned me?" (Mark 15:34). Jesus sweat blood as he braced for that impossible moment. But there was no way to prepare. When it happened, it crushed his soul to hell.

Do you know why Jesus died? This is not a trick question. Jesus died and rose again "so that everyone who believes in him will not perish but have eternal life" (John 3:16). Consider this: you know the reason for the greatest evil that has ever and could ever occur. That means you do not need to know the

---

4   The only Arminians who escape this problem are open theists, but their denial of God's exhaustive foreknowledge raises devastating doubts about God's power. Can we trust a God who is surprised by future events?

reason for the tragedies and injustices that fall on you. Your sufferings are real; please do not spritz them with Christian clichés to make them seem better than they are. Your loved one's death is not okay. Your daughter's funeral is not her wedding to Jesus. Cancer and strokes are not gifts from God. The abuse you suffered is not merely one of the "all things" that "work together for good" (Rom 8:28).

Accept that your tragedy is terrible. Feel its weight. Admit your spirit is crushed, then bring your pain to Jesus. He beckons, "Come to me, all of you who are weary and burdened, and I will give you rest. . . . I am lowly and humble in heart, and you will find rest for your souls" (Matt 11:28–29). Jesus wept at Lazarus's tomb, and he sympathizes with your pain. He feels it more, as his divine nature supplies infinite capacity for his emotions. You can trust the Son of God who suffered more than you will ever know so that you might live forever with him. You may not understand why your immense suffering happened and you may never know—God has not promised to explain everything to us in the sweet by and by. But the cross assures us that we can trust God with whatever evil we are suffering. If God was God at the cross, he remains God in whatever evil we endure. Run to him.

Application

When it comes to the problem of evil, we are all hypocrites. Political leaders cry over the evils of a school shooting yet celebrate when children are killed in the womb. Celebrities lament sexism and rape culture yet laugh at pornography. We all claim to agonize over evil that we still happily choose.

If evil is as bad as we say, we must hate sin. Every time we sin, we are voting for a fallen world. Give me more slander, racism, and murder! Three cheers for cancer, traffic deaths, and birth defects! Does evil trouble you? Does it deeply disturb your soul? Then stop celebrating the fall! Recognize that sin is not your friend. It will take away from you everyone and everything you ever cared about. You will die alone, with only Jesus to carry you home. Rest in him and hate the sin that required his crucifixion.

The most disturbing problem of evil is not why God allows it. The greater mystery is why we, who are offended that God permits it, gladly choose it. We are not wrong to raise the problem of evil. But we are hypocrites.

Mini Myth

"Why do bad things happen to good people?"

Someone told Jesus the tragic news that Pilate had killed some Galileans as they were offering sacrifices. Jesus said these Galileans were not worse than others, "but unless you repent, you will all perish as well." Then Jesus mentioned the eighteen who died when the tower in Siloam fell on them. They were not more sinful than others either, "but unless you repent, you will all perish as well" (Luke 13:1–5).

Jesus threaded the needle between two extremes. We should not think tragedy means someone was a greater sinner than others. This was the mistake of Job's comforters, who assumed he must be concealing some heinous sin. Yet we should not think the victims were not sinners. Jesus assumes everyone is sinful, both those who died and those who survived. Our universal depravity is why he came, "to seek and to save the lost" (Luke 19:10). Rather than ask why bad things happen to good people, a better question is, Why do good things happen to bad people?

This perspective frees us to thankfully receive every gift God sends our way. And it steels our spine when life is hard. We will not hastily charge God with injustice but recognize that he continues to give us more joys than we deserve. As my mentor used to say when he suffered another blow, "Oh well. I deserve hell. Everything else is bonus."

CHAPTER 17

———

Satan Is Tempting Me

The Legendary Belief

The actress joked with the talk show host about her experience that morning. I think she had dropped her toast with jelly facedown on the carpet. As the audience groaned in commiseration, she smiled and shook her finger. "I said, 'Oh no you don't. Not today, Satan!'" The audience laughed to think of Satan stooping to silly pranks and to think there is a real, personal devil. Satan is comedic gold, from Flip Wilson's "The devil made me do it" to Dana Carvey's histrionic Church Lady. *"Or could it beeeee . . . Satan?!"* In what must be the most audaciously successful marketing campaign in history, the prince of darkness has packaged himself for our secular age as a harmless, humorous catchphrase.

Some Christians are on to him, and they go hard the other way. They believe not only that Satan is real but that he has a personal interest in them. When considering a particularly attractive temptation, they are apt to say, "Satan is tempting me." Is he?

Unraveling the Legend

Satan is perhaps the highest creature God ever made. But he is only a creature. He is not omnipresent. He can only be in one place at a time. Where do you think he is today?

In the early days of the church, Satan was surely hounding the disciples, probing for cracks in their devotion to Jesus and each other. He likely had a hand in the dispute between the Hellenistic and Hebraic Jews (Acts 6:1), Jewish and Gentile believers (15:1–35), and Paul and Barnabas (15:36–41). Peter caught him meddling in the first Christians' gifts of charity. Peter pressed a conniving Ananias. "Why has Satan filled your heart to lie to the Holy Spirit and keep back part of the proceeds of the land?" (5:3).

Peter knew why. Satan sought to destroy the unity, integrity, and reputation of the young church with one blow. If their Jerusalem neighbors could not trust the Christians to tell the truth about money, they would never believe their story that Jesus rose from the dead. So Satan enticed Ananias and Sapphira to keep part of their sale for themselves and pretend they gave all.

In the days of the Reformation, Satan was probably pestering the courageous leaders of the Protestant church. Martin Luther said he sometimes heard the devil bumping around in his monastery as he studied or tried to sleep, and he allegedly threw an inkwell at the devil when he felt his presence in the room. Some might chalk this up to medieval superstition—Luther's mother thought demons stole eggs, milk, and butter—but if you were the devil, wouldn't Luther's study be a likely place for you to haunt?

Prince of the Air

Where is Satan today? Not where the average person assumes. Too many people derive their doctrine from cartoons, and they imagine Satan huddled with his henchmen in hell, plotting how to lure more unsuspecting souls their way. But Satan does not wear red spandex and carry a pitchfork. He does not have horns and he has never been to hell. Yet. Hell is not his headquarters. Hell is his punishment. When Satan's forces are routed at the last battle, God will throw the devil "into the lake of fire and sulfur where the beast and the false prophet are, and they will be tormented day and night forever and ever" (Rev 20:10). Until then Satan is "the ruler of the power of the air, the spirit now working in the disobedient" (Eph 2:2). He is somewhere on this planet, organizing his legions of demons and scheming against the church and Jesus's most devoted disciples.

Satan may be hard to spot, for he "disguises himself as an angel of light" (2 Cor 11:14). He does not announce his presence except to his most ardent supporters, as most people do not like to think of themselves as fighting on his side. Satan operates in the shadows, sowing distrust and division among Christians (2:5–11) and enticing church and world leaders to pursue money and power most. He is the father of pragmatism and the "just this once" defense. As in, "I am still a good person because my heart is in the right place. But just this once, so I can keep my position and do good in the future, I will give the people what they want" (see Pilate, Matt 27:11–26).

Satan may be hard to spot because he cloaks his work in what is often attributed to circumstances or natural causes. Paul said the devil had blocked his travel plans. He and his team desired to return to Thessalonica and encourage the disciples' faith, "but Satan hindered us" (1 Thess 2:17–18). It makes sense that Satan would fight against the greatest missionary who ever lived, preventing him from reaching the Thessalonians, so that Satan might tempt them into leaving the faith (1 Thess 3:5). But the church has grown exponentially since Paul's day. Now there are millions of Christians. What are the odds that Satan himself has noticed any one of us? I would not be so arrogant to suppose I have drawn fire from the prince of darkness himself. I am not that important.

On the other hand, I would be disappointed to learn in the next life that I was assigned to some bush-league demon who flunked out of temptation school. A demon so dumb he confused exorcise with exercise and avoided both. A demon who whined when assigned anything more demanding than enticing people to check their likes on social media. A demon who could not possess a cat, even if the cat was black and walking under a ladder in front of a broken mirror in the séance room of a haunted house. In New Orleans. Wouldn't it be humiliating to learn that this lazy, dim-witted demon was able to limit my damage to the kingdom of darkness? Worse, what if this knucklehead managed not only me but also five hundred thousand others just like me? I want to love Jesus so much and follow him so closely that this mouth breather must beg for reinforcements. I want to become a pain in the neck for a whole company of higher-up demons, to force their attention so they have to deal with me. I want weekend seminars devoted to one question: *How do we stop Wittmer?*

Personal Enemy

You and I are in a battle with spirit beings that seek to destroy us. These demons intend to drag us to hell where we will be tormented forever with them. Does that make you angry? Angry enough to stop falling for their tricks? Paul explains, "For our struggle is not against flesh and blood, but against the rulers, against the authorities, against the cosmic powers of this darkness, against evil, spiritual forces in the heavens" (Eph 6:12). Our real enemies are not who we think. Paul's layers of synonyms describe our opponents, though none of us know how high in the chain we are fighting.

That is okay. Writers employ a figure of speech called *synecdoche*, in which a part stands in for the whole. They might say "thirty head" when they mean "thirty cattle" or "Biden" to represent his entire administration. Similarly, the authors of Scripture may use "Satan" for the entire realm of fallen angels. When Peter says, "Your adversary the devil is prowling around like a roaring lion, looking for anyone he can devour," he means both Satan and his demons are looking for victims (1 Pet 5:8). When Paul tells married people to sleep together lest "Satan may tempt you because of your lack of self-control," he is probably using the head devil to represent them all (1 Cor 7:5). With all that is on his plate, it seems unlikely that Satan himself would mess with any given marriage in Corinth. Yet Paul tells husbands and wives to have lots of sex because of Satan.

I think it is permissible to say, "Satan is tempting me" as long as we know we are using a figure of speech, taking a part, in this case the head, to refer to the whole. But if we aim for literal precision, we might have to say that "idiot demon intern" is tempting me again. He must be a newbie because his temptations are clumsily transparent. Trade my integrity for a couple of bucks? A lifetime of regret for a moment of pleasure? My reputation for a crude joke? If we are going to fight our way into the higher echelons, we must defeat the flunkies first.

Application

It is scary to think that powerful spirit beings are working overtime to damn us to hell. Yet Peter assumed that Ananias and Sapphira could have resisted Satan himself, and he commands us to "resist him, firm in the faith, knowing that the same kind of sufferings are being experienced by your fellow believers throughout the world" (1 Pet 5:9).

How do we resist Satan? By hiding in Jesus.

How do we hide in Jesus? By running to him in prayer.

Prayer draws us close to Jesus, which makes us a larger target for spiritual attack. Satan and his demons do not worry about Christians who sideline themselves. But if we mean business, so do they. So we must pray. The more we love Jesus, the more the Spirit uses us, the more we must pray for God's protection for ourselves and those closest to us. We should not fear, for "the one who is in you is greater than the one who is in the world" (1 John 4:4). Satan can do nothing but what God allows. Paul suffered "a thorn in the flesh" that he called "a messenger of Satan." Yet he recognized that God was firmly in control and that he permitted Satan's assault so Paul's heavenly vision would not inflate him with pride (2 Cor 12:6–10).

Martin Luther said the devil is God's devil, whom he compared to a chained dog. He can "bark, run here and there, and tear at the chain. But because it is tied and you avoid it, it cannot bite you." As long as we "continue in the fear of God and in prayer; then the chained dog cannot harm us."[1] Rather than cower in fear before the prince of darkness, Luther mocked the devil for being powerless before Jesus. Germans are comfortable with salty language, and Luther relentlessly used it to pull Satan's pants down and laugh. He ran to Jesus for safety, turned to face the devil and said, "But if that is not enough for you,

---

[1]   Martin Luther, "Sermon on John 16:5–15," *Weimar Edition* vol. 52, 296, quoted in *What Luther Says,* compiled by Ewald M. Plass (St. Louis: Concordia, 1959), 1:402.

you Devil, I have also [pooped and peed]; wipe your mouth on that and take a hearty bite."[2]

Such language is not for me, but I admire Luther's spirit of ridicule. It is hard to give in to someone we are mocking, so pantsing Satan is a great way to resist him. We display utter contempt for Satan, not from our own strength but because we are hiding in Christ. God promises, "Resist the devil, and he will flee from you. Draw near to God, and he will draw near to you" (Jas 4:7–8). Satan looks silly next to Jesus. His program is ridiculous. He knows it, and we should let him know that we know it too. Let's run to Jesus with Satan's britches. Turn around, point, and laugh.

---

[2] *D. Martin Luthers Werke: Kritische Gesamtausgabe, Tischreden* [Table Talk] (Weimar, 1912–21), vol. 6, no. 6827; 216, 9–11, quoted in Heiko A. Oberman, *Luther: Man between God and the Devil* (New York: Image, 1992) 107.

CHAPTER 18

All Sin Is the Same before God

The Legendary Belief

Sam was upset to learn his practicing homosexual friend would not be allowed to join his church. "We welcome him to attend our services and events and participate in a small group," said the pastor, "but he cannot become a member of the body of Christ unless he repents and turns to Jesus. None of us are perfect. We all may fall as we battle various temptations. But he must agree with God about his sin."

Sam was unimpressed. "I concede that homosexual acts are sinful, but so are gossip and gluttony. Yet you allow these sinners to join our church. Why do we only take a stand against certain sins? Isn't all sin the same before God?"

Unraveling the Legend

Sam is right that gossip and gluttony are sins that should be confronted. The latter may be awkward and difficult to prove, as obesity has more than one cause. Not all fat people are gluttons, and not all gluttons are fat. Yet gluttony is one of the seven deadly sins, for gluttons simultaneously care too much and too little for creation. They care too much by turning their food into idols, thinking one more Snickers bar will finally satisfy. They care too little by gulping down food as if neither it nor their bodies matter to God. They do not enjoy God's gifts or maintain their temple of the Holy Spirit (1 Cor 6:15). Like cows of Bashan on ladies' night at the Golden Corral, gluttony has received a free pass for too long (Amos 4:1).

Still, Sam seems to be doing the same thing that he accuses his pastor of doing. He wants to give a free pass to some sins; he simply disagrees about which ones. He seeks to use his church's silence on gluttony to leverage its silence on homosexuality. If his church doesn't stand publicly against all sins, they cannot stand publicly against any.

Sam forgets that Western culture does not treat all sins the same. There are no pride parades for gluttons. No months that celebrate them; no media stories that tout their virtues; no flags flown in their honor. Few people who struggle with food insist they be allowed to live their truth.[1] Many gluttons pray for change. They confess their sin, receive Jesus's forgiveness, and continue their struggle. The church must always include anyone—gay or glutton—who struggles with sin. We must draw the membership line, however, with those who do *not* struggle, with those who insist that we accept their sin. God accepts us all just as we are, but he loves us too much to allow us to stay that way.

Sam's church is not discriminating against homosexuals. It merely insists that faith and repentance are inseparably linked, describing the same turn from opposite directions. As we turn toward Jesus in faith, we must turn away from sin in repentance. We cannot do one without the other. Anyone who tries will pull a muscle.

What about Sam's claim that all sin is the same? As with most complex questions, that requires a nuanced, yes/no response.

How All Sins Are the Same

All sin is the same in that it shares the same twisted root and the same final fruit.

First, all sin shares the same twisted root. God told Adam not to eat from the tree of the knowledge of good and evil or he would die. The serpent contradicted God's Word, whispering to Eve that she would not die but instead would become wise "like God, knowing good and evil" (Gen 3:5). What should Eve have done? Picked up a stick and beat the serpent's brains in. *Who are you? And how dare you? I owe my life, with all its pleasures and joys, to God. What have you ever done for me? Now scram!*

But she didn't. Rather than immediately submit to God's Word, Eve elevated herself above both God and the serpent and judged between them. She used her empirical ability—she "saw that the tree was good for food and delightful to look at," and her rational capacity—"that it was desirable for obtaining wisdom" (Gen 3:6). Eve used all that she had to make her best decision. She had to get this right. And because she relied on herself, she made the worst possible decision in the history of the world.

---

[1] This may be changing, as more husky folks seek to participate in Western culture's victimhood Olympics. Some quickly take offense at "fat shaming" and boldly insist that "big is beautiful." No one should be embarrassed or teased for who they are, but neither should they promote a condition that causes health problems.

Eve thought she was being impartial; she could not have been prouder. Who did she think she was? The audacity to think she had the right and the ability to stand over God's Word! All sin begins with this root of autonomy. Autonomy comes from two Greek terms, *auto*, which means "self," and *nomos*, which means "law." Autonomous people become their own law. They know what God says about this or that. They simply do not care. They want what they want because they want it. No one, especially God, may cramp their style.

Pick any sin that you noticed today. Can you trace it back to this poisonous root? How does cutting in line, watching inappropriate movies, or discussing the dating habits of Susie in accounting demonstrate the sin of autonomy? We rarely sin out of ignorance. We know what God expects from us. We sin when we want to do what we want to do, just because we want to do it. Some sins have more disastrous immediate effects than others, but all sprout from the same autonomous root.

Second, all sin shares the same final fruit. There are no cute sins, white lies, or harmless infractions. Eve's sin was outwardly as mild as can be. She took a bite from a piece of fruit. But because her sin sprang from autonomy—the desire to play God in her life—she must die. And not only her. If God was going to save her, his perfect Son must die in her place. Until then, animals would do. Creatures who had always felt safe in the presence of God were suddenly grabbed by the neck, slit, and skinned. All sin ends in a horror show. The path to the cross is strewn with carcasses and drenched with blood, culminating in the sacrifice of God's perfect Lamb. Every sin deserves death and hell. The forgiveness of any sin requires the crucifixion of the Son of God.

How Some Sins Are Worse

All sin has the same root, but some roots go deeper than others. Cain was more self-obsessed than his mother, and he killed his brother in a fit of jealous rage. Cain's descendant Lamech was more autonomous yet, and he bragged that "I killed a man for wounding me, a young man for striking me" (Gen 4:23). By the time of Noah, "the LORD saw that human wickedness was widespread on the earth and that every inclination of the human mind was nothing but evil all the time" (Gen 6:5). Sinful autonomy had made the world unlivable, so God hit reset, drowning everyone in a flood and starting over with eight people.

All sin has the same final fruit, but some intermediate fruits are worse than others. Jesus said anger and insults are in the same line as murder and lust is adultery of the heart. But though it is shameful to commit adultery with someone in our heart, it is worse to commit adultery with our body. I would rather you insult me than shoot me, assassinate my character than murder me. I would rather you covet my stuff than steal my stuff.

The Roman Catholic Church distinguishes between venial and mortal sins. I disagree with the implication that only some sins are deadly and with the church's use of this distinction in its penitential system.[2] Yet the idea that some sins are worse has biblical support. The Catholic Church says a sin is mortal when it meets three criteria: (1) it is serious and weighty, (2) we know it is serious, and (3) we do it freely.

(1) Jesus agreed that some sins are more serious than others. Some amount to splinters while others comprise a whole "beam of wood" (Matt 7:3). Some amount to gnats while others are as large as camels (23:24). Jesus saved his fiercest denunciations for religious hypocrisy and destroying the faith of children. The latter is so weighty that the culprit would be better off with a heavy millstone tied around his neck and "drowned in the depths of the sea" (18:6).

(2) Jesus agreed that knowledge increases culpability. He told a parable in which the servant who did not know his master's will received a lighter beating than one who flagrantly disobeyed. He said the damned in Capernaum would be punished more severely than the people of Sodom, as they had been privileged to hear Jesus and see his miracles (Matt 11:23–24). And he told Pilate "the one who handed me over to you has the greater sin" (John 19:11).

(3) The Mosaic law agreed that intent matters. Anyone who purposefully struck and killed another must be put to death, yet if someone "pushes a person without hostility or throws any object at him without malicious intent or without looking drops a stone that could kill a person and he dies," this person must be allowed to flee to a city of refuge (Num 35:22–25).

All sin is the same in that it shares the same root and fruit; some sin is worse because its roots are more selfish and its fruit more damaging to others.

Application

All sin is the same, so we must never look down on others who struggle with temptations we do not face. "Thank God I'm not a tax collector or a racist or a child molester" has no place in our church. Some sins make us shake our heads. I know that "there but for the grace of God, go I" is true, yet some sins are hard to imagine doing. Doesn't matter. All of us sinners are in the same sinking boat. We need the same sacrifice of Jesus for our sin.

Some sins are worse. God hates all sexual immorality, yet he adds that homosexual acts are particularly unnatural (Rom 1:24–27). They are

---

[2]   The Catholic Church says that venial sins lengthen one's penance and time in purgatory while mortal sins damn to hell if one dies before confessing them to a priest. The big three mortal sins are apostasy, adultery, and murder; but other sins, such as malicious slander, may meet the criteria and be considered damnable offenses.

"detestable" (Lev 18:22; 20:13). Parents sin when they fail to teach God's commands to their children (Deut 6:4–7); they outrageously offend when they sacrifice their children to Baal. Some sins are so heinous they surprise even God (Jer 19:5).[3]

All sin is the same and some sins are worse. This tension calls for discernment and humility. We need discernment to appropriately discipline and repent of sin. We should fire a pastor who cheats on his wife. We do not fire him for taking a third slice of peach pie at the church potluck, though we may hold an intervention. Some sins, such as embezzlement and abuse, require long periods of mourning. Other sins, such as a curt comment in a hurried moment, require only a quick apology and then move on with your life. We need humility to understand our sins are not better than another's. Better implies good, and no sin is good. How can anything be good that required the crucifixion of the Son of God?

Go ahead and rank sin. List them in order. Then draw a red cross through them all.

Mini Myth

"The only sin anyone will be held accountable for is the sin of unbelief."

This myth confuses the rescue from damnation with the reason for damnation. Faith in Jesus is the only way to avoid the penalty of sin. The damned would have escaped hell if they had turned from their sin and believed in Jesus. Their failure to turn is why they are not rescued, but it is not the reason they need rescue.

Refusing to believe in Jesus is one of those sins that deserves damnation. Paul wrote, "If anyone does not love the Lord, a curse be on him" (1 Cor 16:22). Yet if this is the only sin that God holds us accountable for, we may mistakenly assume that those who never heard of Jesus will receive a free pass at the last judgment. But Paul says the suppression of general revelation is enough to convict those who have never heard of Jesus, so that "people are without excuse" (Rom 1:18–21). Elsewhere Paul lists sins, including moral impurity, promiscuity, jealousy, anger, and drunkenness, and declares that "those who practice such things will not inherit the kingdom of God" (Gal 5:19–21; cf. 1 Cor 6:9–10; Eph 5:3–5).

The only sin anyone will be held accountable for is all of them. Every sin must be judged. Make sure that yours are judged in Jesus. Cling to him.

---

[3]   Our omniscient God knew all the sins his people would commit. God said he "never entertained the thought" of child sacrifice to impress how outrageously cruel the Israelites had become.

CHAPTER 19

Jesus Never Spoke about Homosexuality

The Legendary Belief

The reporter leaned in to ask his gotcha question, "What does God think about homosexuality?" The pastor replied, "I believe Jesus is God in the flesh, so the best way to know what God thinks about any subject is to look at Jesus and listen to him. Jesus spoke often about caring for the poor and outcast. He condemned many sins, most notably the scorn the religious leaders of his day heaped on tax collectors and prostitutes. Yet, unlike many who claim to follow him today, Jesus never spoke about homosexuality."

The reporter nodded his head. Just as he suspected. So many spiteful Christians out of step with the Lord they claim to follow. How important could homosexuality be if Jesus never spoke about it?

Unraveling the Legend

This popular urban legend makes two mistakes. First, it forgets that it wouldn't matter if Jesus did not condemn homosexual practice. The rest of the Bible clearly does. The Bible begins by denouncing homosexual acts in the strongest possible terms. The law of Moses says, "You are not to sleep with a man as with a woman; it is detestable" (Lev 18:22). And "if a man sleeps with a man as with a woman, they have both committed a detestable act" (20:13).

And the Bible never lets up. When Paul lists the kinds of people who "will not inherit God's kingdom," he includes "males who have sex with males" (1 Cor 6:9). The first "males" translates Paul's Greek term *arsenokoitai*, literally "male bedders," which Paul creates by combining the Greek words *arsenos* and *koitēn* from the Septuagint translation of Lev 18:22. This shows that Paul thought the Law's prohibition against homosexual practice still applied in his day. The second "males" translates the Greek term *malakoi*, which describes the soft, effeminate partner who plays the role of the woman in the sexual act. Paul believed both the male aggressor and receiver in the homosexual act were guilty of sin that precluded them from the kingdom of God.

Paul is even more explicit in Rom 1:18–32. He declares God's wrath is currently falling on those idolaters whose suppression of general revelation leads them to sexual immorality, homosexual practice, and "envy, murder, quarrels, deceit," and so forth (v. 29). Regarding homosexual activity, Paul includes lesbians who "exchanged natural sexual relations for unnatural ones" (v. 26) and men who "left natural relations with women and were inflamed in their lust for one another. Men committed shameless acts with men and received in their own persons the appropriate penalty of their error" (v. 27).

Progressive commentators attempt to evade Paul's words by saying he only opposes (1) pedophilia, in which men abuse boys; (2) the excessive, out-of-control lust found among some homosexuals; or (3) heterosexuals who act against their own sexual nature and commit homosexual acts. They say Paul had no concept of sexual orientation and was unaware of committed, same-sex unions; we cannot know what he might have thought about men marrying men or lesbians committing to monogamous lifelong relationships.

In response, (1) Paul includes more than pedophilia, as he mentions women having sex with women and men having sex with men. (2) Paul vehemently denounces homosexual acts and declares they arise from out-of-control lust. This does not mean he only opposes the out-of-control part and would accept homosexual acts that are ordered and natural. Consider how two men or two women attempt sexual union. What could be natural, proper, or orderly about that? In sum, if someone strongly condemns something, we should not take that as an invitation to attempt a milder version. If someone burglarizes my house, sets it on fire, paints profanity on my driveway, chops down my trees, turfs my lawn, kicks my dog, and smashes my Precious Moments figurine, I will not say, "Well, that was excessive!" It would be, but that is not the main problem. All of it is bad.

(3) Paul lived before Freud articulated the category of sexual orientation, yet the ancient Greeks understood the concept. Plato's *Symposium* noted some men were only attracted to other men. Paul would have known this and would have met effeminate *malakoi* who looked the part. Furthermore, the ancient world did have some committed, adult same-sex relationships. Plato mentions Agathon and Pausanias in his *Symposium* and Ctesippus and Cleinias in *Euthydemus*. Xenophon said the sacred band of Thebes consisted of men who lived together "like married people." Juvenal mentioned a man who was given in marriage to another man and said the day may soon come when the state recognizes male-to-male marriages. In the fourth century, Roman emperors Constantius II and Constans passed a law that prohibited a man from marrying

another man "as if he were a woman." Would such a law need to be passed if gay marriage was not on some people's minds?[1]

Paul's first-century world is not so different from ours today. His words map directly onto our cultural moment. For those who nevertheless believe God blesses same-sex marriage, please answer this question: If God wanted to say homosexual activity was sin, how could he do it in a way you would accept? If there is nothing God could say against homosexual practice that you would not dismiss as a vestige of an ancient, out-of-date culture, then why bother to read the Bible on this subject? You already know God's mind, independently of what he says in Scripture. There is no way God can change your mind. You have made sure of that.

Please heed the warning of Rom 1:32. Paul says God's wrath is being revealed against not only those who commit the sins listed in Rom 1:18–32, but also those who "applaud others who practice them." If we encourage any of the sins in this passage, we are placing ourselves in the target zone of God's wrath. Do not let the sins of others damn you.

Those who say Jesus never spoke about homosexuality forget that the red letters in their Bible do not count more. The black letters are equally God's Word. The red letters matter and the black letters matter. All the letters matter because they all reveal God's will. They all express Jesus's view on whatever topic they address. But for argument's sake, let's follow the urban legend's limited focus on the red letters. There the legend makes a second mistake. It misses that the red letters also speak about homosexual practice.

What Jesus Said

When Jesus was asked about divorce, he told his listeners they must start with God's plan for marriage in creation. In Matt 19:4–5, he quoted Gen 1:27, God made us "male and female," and Gen 2:24, "This is why a man leaves his father and mother and bonds with his wife, and they become one flesh." Jesus limited marriage to male and female unions. Only one man and one woman have the compatible body parts to become one flesh. Same-sex couples are unable to achieve sexual union, and it is degrading to try.

On another occasion Jesus learned the Pharisees were offended by his statement that what comes out of the mouth is more defiling than what goes in. In response, he listed various sins that come out of the mouth and defile a person. "For from the heart come evil thoughts, murders, adulteries, sexual immoralities, thefts, false testimonies, slander" (Matt 15:19). Did you catch that "sexual immoralities" is plural? This catchall term (*porneia* in Greek)

---

[1]   Branson Parler, "Worlds Apart?: James Brownson and the Sexual Diversity of the Greco-Roman World," *Trinity Journal* 38 (2017): 183–200.

included every sexual sin denounced in the Old Testament: adultery, forni-
cation, incest, bestiality, and homosexual acts. The New Testament does not
record Jesus explicitly saying the last three in this list, but he covers them
all in his disgust for every kind of sexual immorality. If he meant to exclude
something from this list, he would have said so. The New Testament's silence
indicates Jesus agreed with the Old Testament's teaching that homosexual acts
were wrong. And he said so.

Agree to Disagree?

Some Christians concede homosexual practice may not be God's best but
lament that this issue is dividing families, churches, and denominations. Why
cannot the followers of Jesus agree to disagree? They say we should retain
fellowship with everyone who believes the articles of faith in the Apostles'
Creed. The church must unite around core doctrines, not whether this act or
that lifestyle is right or wrong.

It is true the Apostles' Creed focuses exclusively on doctrine. It does not
mention sins to avoid. However, approval of homosexual practice is a belief,
and this belief jumbles most lines of the Creed. Same-sex activity shatters our
understanding of God as Father and we as his creatures. How should we think
about and use our bodies? It redefines sin, what our Lord Jesus died to save us
from and what he will judge when he comes again. He has ascended to heaven
where he rules the world. How must we now submit to his authority? It confuses the work of the Holy Spirit and the church as the bride of Christ, divides
the communion of saints, limits the forgiveness of sins, and muddles the resurrection of the body and the life everlasting—how will our present bodies be
restored sexually? So pretty much everything.

We should not be surprised that homosexual activity messes with doctrine,
because God says as much in Paul's letter to Timothy. Paul explains God's
law was written to convict sinful people: "The law is not meant for a righteous person, but for the lawless and rebellious, for the ungodly and sinful,
for the unholy and irreverent, for those who kill their fathers and mothers, for
murderers, for the sexually immoral and males who have sex with males, for
slave traders, liars, perjurers, and for whatever else is contrary to the sound
teaching that conforms to the gospel concerning the glory of the blessed God,
which was entrusted to me" (1 Tim 1:9–11). God explicitly says homosexuality opposes sound teaching. It is heresy that must be denounced by all ministers of the gospel. Homosexual practice is a gospel issue because it mislabels
sin and so misconstrues salvation. It is divisive—how can it not be? Anyone
who agrees to disagree about this important doctrine is fighting God, who does
not make peace with any sin, including this one.

Suburban Legend

"Christians who denounce homosexual acts yet eat bacon and shrimp are hypocrites."

A recent line of attack against traditional Christians argues that "Christians who denounce homosexual acts yet eat bacon and shrimp are hypocrites." How can we quote the Old Testament's commands against homosexual practice yet ignore what the Law says about eating unclean things?

The Bible is not a flat, static book. It has a plot, and its plot centers on Jesus. Some of the Law's commands anticipated Jesus fulfilling them, such as its prohibitions against bacon and shrimp (these rules intended to teach the concept of holiness and prevent the Israelites from dining with pagans and adopting their idols); others remain and were reinforced by Jesus, such as its opposition to homosexual acts. The commands that prepared people for the coming of Jesus were fulfilled with his arrival. Paul explains, "These are a shadow of what was to come; the substance is Christ" (Col 2:17). Jesus fulfilled the Law's holiness code. If today we refrain from unclean food for religious reasons, we deny the reality of Jesus. Good Christians eat bacon and shrimp, unless they are vegans or their doctor tells them not to. Good Christians still avoid homosexual acts because Jesus and the whole Bible tell them to.

Application

Jesus said homosexual acts are sinful, and he loved sinners. This is difficult to pull off in a culture that settles for nothing less than applause for the LGBTQ+ movement, but we must extravagantly embrace all sinners while courageously exposing the lies that are ruining lives. We must never joke about LGBTQ+ issues. We must always speak as if an LGBTQ+ person is in the room. How will they perceive our attitude? A mocking tone might score points, but it will lose the person. Have you ever agreed with someone who disrespected you? Even if you suspected they were right, you would never give them the satisfaction.

Let's tell people struggling with same-sex attraction that we all are sexual sinners. None of us have the moral high ground. Let's assure them of our love. No matter what, we will always be here for them. And because we love them, let's damn to hell the lies our culture constantly preaches at them. Let's encourage us all to love our bodies, to gratefully receive them as God's precious gifts. Let's confess how the fall has ravaged our desires, including our sexual appetites and identities, and plead the blood of Jesus. He may or may not heal our gender dysphoria, same-sex attraction, and sexual lust in this life, but he forgives us every time we fail. So let's choose to keep fighting, and to accept into church membership all who struggle, and to lovingly serve all who disagree.

CHAPTER 20

You're Not Supposed to Judge

The Legendary Belief

The most popular verse in the Bible, the one everyone knows Jesus said but are deeply confused about what he meant, is "Do not judge, so that you won't be judged" (Matt 7:1). To many minds, a soft and indulgent Jesus gave them both a license to do as they please and the moral high ground. Did someone criticize your behavior? Did they suggest you did wrong? Gasp and look down at them with righteous indignation, "Don't you know that Jesus said not to judge?"

This audacious turning-of-the-tables is surprisingly effective. As Western culture invents new ways of sinning, many Christians are afraid even to mildly express their disagreement. Were you invited to a same-sex wedding? Then you must attend and congratulate the happy couple. Yes, God calls such unions "detestable" (Lev 18:22; 20:13), but isn't it a bigger sin to judge those who are sinning? How will we win people to Jesus with that attitude? Worse, why would you think that practicing homosexuals must be won to Jesus? Many of them exude love and the fruit of the Spirit. They are the finest Christians we know. Unlike you, and your haughty, judgmental spirit.[1]

And just like that, those who believe what God says about sin are considered bad Christians, on the strength of one flagrantly misread verse.

---

[1] I understand the pressure to attend the sinful ceremony of a close friend or family member, and I realize Christians may disagree about what to do in any particular case. We must express our love to the participants while also not condoning what God vigorously condemns. One option is to kindly decline to attend the wedding but invite the couple to your home for dinner. Make it hard for them to deny your love for them.

Unraveling the Legend

Do you know who violated our culture's understanding of Jesus's command not to judge?

Jesus!

In Matt 7:1 he says, "Do not judge," yet in John 7:24 he tells us to "judge according to righteous judgment." Both instances use the same Greek term, *krinō*. Apparently, there is a type of judgment that Jesus demands us to make.

This would be obvious to anyone who reads the verses immediately following Jesus's command to not judge. He contrasts "the beam of wood in your own eye" with "the splinter in your brother's eye" (Matt 7:3). Jesus's point is that we should be more vexed by our own shortcomings than our brother's, but he assumes we possess the good judgment to see both our beam and our brother's splinter. Next, he warns us not to "give what is holy to dogs or toss your pearls before pigs," which requires us to judge who are dogs and who are pigs (v. 6). A few verses later Jesus commands, "Be on your guard against false prophets who come to you in sheep's clothing but inwardly are ravaging wolves. You'll recognize them by their fruit" (vv. 15–16). Such fruit inspection requires continual judgment and running off every wolf we find. Surely Jesus expects us to judge the wolves we catch eating sheep!

Judgmentalism

So, what did Jesus mean when he said, "Do not judge, so that you won't be judged"? He did not mean we should lower our standards, avoiding critiques of others so we might avoid God's judgment. We "must all appear before the judgment seat of Christ," whether we speak out against evil and injustice or hide our heads in the sand (2 Cor 5:10). In fact, since not judging sin is itself a sin, expect the final judgment to be worse for those who silently acquiesced.

The context of Matthew 7 indicates Jesus is criticizing a critical, judgmental spirit. He mocks those whose keen eye can discern a small speck in their brother's eye while remaining oblivious to the wooden beam protruding from their own. How can they see anything, let alone something so small in their brother? Eyes so sensitive to their brother's fault should be red and watery from their own sin. Jesus's point is that we must not give ourselves a pass. Repentance starts at home. We should help our brother with his splinter, but only after we have confessed and removed our own log.

Those who criticize others while letting themselves off the hook will receive equal criticism in return, from others now and from God at their last judgment. Jesus cautions, "For you will be judged by the same standard with which you judge others, and you will be measured by the same measure you use" (Matt 7:2). He did not mean that nonjudgmental people will escape judgment, but that condescending, critical people will have it worse, for they will be judged by their own words.

In sum, many contemporary readers misunderstand the blindness of Matthew 7. They assume "Do not judge" means turning a blind eye to the sins of others, and they think this is well and good. But Jesus speaks of a blindness that comes from allowing unconfessed sin to cloud our vision. Jesus hates both kinds of blindness, and he commands us to fix each, in the right sequence. "First take the beam of wood out of your eye, and then you will see clearly to take the splinter out of your brother's eye" (v. 5). We must feel more acutely our own sin, not so we can ignore the sin of others, but so we can better help them. When we extract the beam from our eye, we can see clearly the path home to Jesus.

Discernment

Jesus opposed a condemning, judgmental spirit, but he commands us to discerningly judge between truth and falsehood and between right and wrong. Hear what he said to the churches in Revelation.

Jesus praised the church in Ephesus for not tolerating "evil people. You have tested those who call themselves apostles and are not, and you have found them to be liars" (Rev 2:2). Also, "You hate the practices of the Nicolaitans, which I also hate" (v. 6). Testing and hating require a lot of judging, and Jesus approves!

On the other hand, Jesus judged the church in Pergamum for not judging enough. In what should alarm Christians who have made peace with sexual sin, Jesus faults this church for tolerating some "who hold to the teaching of Balaam . . . to eat meat sacrificed to idols and to commit sexual immorality." Jesus commanded them, "Repent! Otherwise, I will come to you quickly and fight against them with the sword of my mouth" (vv. 14–16).

Similarly, Jesus judged the church in Thyatira because they "tolerate the woman Jezebel, who calls herself a prophetess and teaches and deceives my servants to commit sexual immorality and to eat meat sacrificed to idols. . . . Unless they repent of her works, I will strike her children dead. Then all the churches will know that I am the one who examines minds and hearts" (vv. 20–23). Jesus will judge them for not judging Jezebel.

Jesus's commands to judge belief and practice are echoed throughout Scripture. For instance, why does the first half of Paul's epistles tell us what to believe and the second half tell us how to behave? Paul deploys this pattern so we can discern Christian doctrine and ethics, judging what is true and false and right and wrong. Paul expected the church to forcefully judge both true doctrine ("If anyone is preaching to you a gospel contrary to what you received, a curse be on him!"; Gal 1:9) and right practice ("When you are assembled in the name of our Lord Jesus . . . hand that one over to Satan for the destruction of the flesh"; 1 Cor 5:4–5).

No one should be offended by Scripture's insistence that we judge belief and practice, because everyone already does. The question is not whether we will evaluate what people believe and do, but by which standard we will make the evaluation. *Not whether, but which.* Are we committed to God's Word as our authority, or will we succumb to a lesser standard? Those who reject the teaching of Scripture replace Jesus's authority with themselves. Have you noticed? Our most popular modern religion is the Self.

The religion of Self writes its own doctrine: *I must live my truth.*

The religion of Self sings its own praise choruses: *"This Is Me" from* The Greatest Showman.[2]

The religion of Self celebrates its own sacrament: *the selfie.*

The religion of Self establishes its own moral code: *Do not judge me.*

The religion of Self is enforced by its own priests: *cultural gatekeepers who cancel those "sinners" who judged someone from an underprivileged class (i.e., those whose sex, race, disability, gender identity, sexual orientation, or social status has hindered them from achieving their best life).*

Any religion that begins with us is bound to make an inconsistent mess, so we should not be shocked that the culture that preaches "Do not judge" is itself extremely judgmental. It cancels people for believing things that until recently were considered common sense. If we say a man cannot become a woman or that two women cannot marry, we are told our bigoted words inflict trauma on those determined to try. *Trauma!* To update an old poem, "Sticks and stones may break my bones but words, they really hurt me!" We are not even allowed to remain quiet, for now "silence is violence." Nothing short of applause will satisfy our inquisitors, and they watch to see who stops clapping first.

Our intolerant age thinks it acts from tolerance, and it is too blind to spot the irony. The worshipers of Self are oblivious to the judgmental beams in their own eyes as they inspect the speech and silence of others for specks of offense. The very words of Jesus that they love to cite, "Do not judge, so that you won't be judged," were spoken against them.

Application

A recent survey found that more than 60 percent of born-again Christians aged 18–55 believe Jesus is not the only way to God. When asked why they do not share their faith with others, respondents chose these top reasons: (1) They can

---

[2] Keala Settle and The Greatest Showman Ensemble, vocalists, "This Is Me," by Benj Pasek and Justin Pau, track 7 on *The Greatest Showman: Original Motion Picture Soundtrack*, Atlantic Records, 2017.

get to heaven through their different religious belief; (2) We shouldn't impose our ideas on others; and (3) The Bible tells us not to judge others.[3]

"Do not judge" has real-life consequences. This mistaken belief is not a religiously neutral, value-free proposition. It is the moral foundation of the religion of Self, and it is aggressively evangelizing the hearts and minds of evangelical Christians. If we are going to pass our faith on to the next generation, we must stand against the Self's soft totalitarianism and graciously discern truth from error and right from wrong.

No one can avoid making judgments, least of all those who assume they are not making them. But we do not have to make judgments on our own. We are relieved of that responsibility. We may freely submit to God's judgments and pass those along to others. When asked, "Who gives you the right?" we respond that we have no right. But God has every right. Do you want to know what he says?

---

[3] Leonardo Blair, "Nearly 70% of born-again Christians say other religions can lead to Heaven: Study," *The Christian Post,* October 21, 2021, https://www.christianpost.com/news/nearly-70-percent-of -born-again-christians-dont-see-jesus-as-only-way.html?utm_source=dlvr.it&utm_medium=facebook. For the original Probe Survey Report, see https://probe.org/introducing-probes-new-survey-religious -views-and-practices-2020/.

CHAPTER 21

———

I Should Never Feel Shame

The Legendary Belief

Brené Brown is a bestselling author, university professor, and popular speaker who inspires audiences to embrace vulnerability and imperfection on their way to becoming authentic people in caring friendships. Her TED Talks are like an old friend nudging us into our best selves.

In one celebrated talk, "Listening to Shame," Brown calls shame "the swampland of the soul." Shame drives two large and oppressive thoughts, "Never good enough" and "Who do you think you are?" Brown wants to ease our burden of shame, so she makes a key distinction between shame and guilt. She says guilt focuses on behavior, "I did something bad," while shame focuses on the self, "I am bad."

Guilt says, "I'm sorry. I made a mistake."

Shame says, "I'm sorry. I am a mistake."

Shame is "highly correlated with addiction, depression, violence, aggression, bullying, suicide, [and] eating disorders" while "guilt is inversely correlated with those things."

Brown concedes it is better to feel a little shame than to be a sociopath who destroys lives without remorse, but she does not attempt to reconcile this admission with her definition of shame. I doubt she thinks I should feel small twinges of "I am a mistake" that start me down the road to depression, bullying, and eating disorders. Elsewhere she writes, "There is nothing positive about shame. In any form, in any context and through any delivery system, shame is destructive. The idea that there are two types, healthy shame and toxic shame, did not bear out in any of my research."[1]

———

[1] Brené Brown, *I Thought It Was Just Me: Women Reclaiming Power and Courage in a Culture of Shame* (New York: Gotham, 2007), 62.

The thrust of Brown's talk, and the main takeaway for millions of satisfied viewers, is that shame is bad. Shame thrives in "secrecy, silence, and judgment." We relieve other people's shame when we empathetically say, "Me too," and we ease our own shame when we choose vulnerability and embrace the truth that we are not perfect. We must never yield to shame's lie that "I am a mistake."[2]

Unraveling the Legend

Brown's talk contains encouraging points, but her distinction between guilt and shame commits the logical fallacy of the false dualism. This fallacy occurs when we present two extremes, caricature one, and conclude that the one left standing must be correct. In this case, Brown presents two options, guilt and shame. But why should we think these are our only choices? Especially when guilt seems much too light—I made a mistake, and shame seems much too dark—I am a mistake. Brown rightly rejects the option that is too heavy but that leaves her with the option that is far too light.

Did Jesus suffer a horrifying death on the cross merely to fix our mistakes? Did he cry out in agony for an oops, a whoops, a flub? Brown is correct that we are not mistakes, but our condition is much worse than she allows. There is a third option that lies between her idiosyncratic extremes of guilt and shame. It's the biblical doctrine of sin, and it includes both guilt and shame, rightly understood.

Sin is much more than a mistake. It is treason against our Creator and Redeemer. We have rebelled against the One who loved us so much that he chose to bring us into existence and then sent his Son to die for us. And we did it on purpose, with our eyes wide open. Even those who have never heard of Jesus "suppress the truth" they know about God (Rom 1:18). No one gratefully worships God rightly on their own. We all twist his revelation to make him into a slightly larger version of us. We have "exchanged the glory of the immortal God for images resembling mortal man, birds, four-footed animals, and reptiles" (v. 23). And then we assault his image bearers, dominating others for our own advantage. Having turned away from God, our "mouth is full of cursing and bitterness" and our "feet are swift to shed blood" (3:14–15). Paul concludes, "There is no one righteous, not even one" (v. 10). "For all have sinned and fall short of the glory of God" (v. 23).

Our sin makes us guilty before God. Guilt is our legal status for suppressing the truth about God so we can take his place. It is much more than "I made a mistake." Guilt is the just declaration that we are in the wrong. We cannot

---

[2] Brené Brown, "Listening to Shame," TED Talk, 2012, https://www.ted.com/talks/brene_brown_listening_to_shame.

defend what we did. We deserve to die and go to hell. So, we hang our heads in shame.

Shame is that feeling of humiliation that accompanies our guilt. It is much less than "I am a mistake," which only makes our pain of regret more intense. We know we are enormously valuable and somewhat gifted, the furthest thing from a mistake. We had so much promise. *How could we? What were we thinking?* One theologian defines shame as "the painful emotion that arises from an awareness that one has fallen short of some standard, ideal, or goal."[3] This is a good start, but the shame we rightly feel is more intense. We didn't merely fall short of a goal, like a gymnast who slips off a balance beam. We are like the gymnast who trained her whole life for the Olympics, then kicked over the apparatus and cursed the judges before stomping off the floor. When we cool down, we realize we would have been better off to have never trained at all. We wish we had not been so gifted (i.e., we are not a mistake). Our talents provided a platform, and now the whole world knows not only what we have done but what we have become. We are ashamed for our fit of rage and for what it reveals about our character. We are the sort of person who does this sort of thing. We are mortified.

The Value of Shame

The opposite of shame is not self-esteem. The opposite of shame is shamelessness. People who lack the capacity to feel shame are psychopaths. Lacking a moral compass and impervious to criticism, they must be stopped before they harm others.

God never tries to talk sinners out of their shame. When he found Adam and Eve hiding behind trees and covering their private parts with fig leaves, he did not say, "You should not be hiding from me and from each other. How inappropriate! My children should never feel shame!" God agreed with their disgrace and made larger, more permanent clothing to conceal their shame (Gen 3:7–8, 21).

God tells sinners they must feel shame. Listen to his frustration with the wayward children of Israel, "You have the brazen look of a prostitute and refuse to be ashamed" (Jer 3:3). "Were they ashamed when they acted so detestably? They weren't at all ashamed. They can no longer feel humiliation. Therefore, they will fall among the fallen. When I punish them, they will collapse, says the Lord" (6:15; cf. 8:12, Zeph 3:5).

The first step toward salvation is to acknowledge our deserved guilt and shame. True repentance says, "Here we are, coming to you, for you are the

---

[3]   Te-Li Lau, *Defending Shame* (Grand Rapids: Baker, 2020), 29. This is an insightful book on the necessary theological and pastoral role of shame.

LORD our God. . . . Let us lie down in our shame; let our disgrace cover us. We have sinned against the LORD our God" (Jer 3:22–25). Shame does make us hide from God and from each other, but the solution is not to talk ourselves out of it. The solution is to come to Jesus. Jesus died in the most shameful way possible, a naked, despised outcast nailed high on a pole as a warning to others. Crucifixions were supposed to be shameful. That was the whole point. Our crucified Lord dragged our shame down with him to his grave, and when he arose, he left it in the dust.

We must feel our guilt and shame so we can give both to Jesus. If we continually tell ourselves we should never feel shame, that is one important thing we cannot give to our Lord. Our shame becomes a crushing burden that we stagger beneath, alone. But if we own our shame, we are free to unload it on Jesus and live joyfully in his resurrection power.

Do you see the malpractice of attempting to talk people out of their shame? Christian counselors who incorporate Brown's false dualism between guilt and shame ultimately harm their clients. This can only go one of two ways; either is a disaster. A client might follow Brown's direction, eliminating "I am a mistake," which leaves her with the much too weak "I made a mistake." But someone who believes she is basically a good person who makes mistakes will not understand why Jesus died. How can a person repent if she thinks she is not a sinner?

A client may just as easily go in the other direction. He may be aware of his moral failures, knowing his condition is much worse than "Oops, I did it again." But if his only other option is "I am a mistake," he may tragically conclude he is too far gone and of no value. Now what?

The Christian doctrine of sin may not be popular, but can you see how people are much worse off without it? Only the biblical story of creation, fall, and redemption supplies real hope.

Creation: I am not a mistake. I am God's noble, valuable creature.

Fall: I have made more than mistakes. I deserve guilt and shame for my sins and depraved character.

Redemption: I give my guilt and shame to Jesus who bore them on Calvary. His Spirit transforms me into a new creation in Christ.

Application

Guilt and shame are inextricably united, as shame is the humiliation that accompanies severe guilt. The more serious the offense, the more shame we feel. This chapter has argued against modern psychology's separation between guilt and shame. We are much better off to take both together and distinguish between true guilt and shame and false guilt and shame.

Many people wrongly feel guilt and shame for who they are or what has happened to them. For instance, consider a girl who carries the horrific burden of being molested by her father. I am not saying this is easy. It may require years of counseling, and even then she may never repair the pieces of her shattered life. But she must strive to believe the guilt and shame she feels are false. She is not to blame. We must never take responsibility for sins inflicted on us.

No one should ever feel "creation shame." God made us in his image. We are his kings and queens on earth. But we all should feel "fall shame." In other words, we should not feel shame for our created, valuable essence, but we should feel shame for our fallen, bent characters. We have thought and done things that we hope no one ever finds out about. How devastating if they knew our deepest, most twisted sins! Embrace that shame. Own it. It's yours. Now run to Jesus. Give it to him. He buries it in the deepest pit of a bottomless sea. You are free!

Mini Myth

"I should not be motivated by guilt."

Guilt is not the highest motive. It is much better to love others from hope and gratitude. We hope for the grace to be revealed when Jesus returns, and we are thankful for that promise and for the grace we have already received. Guilt and shame are not the highest motives, but they are appropriate for those who have sinned, especially when their self-absorption leaves them cold to healthier motivations. "Have you no shame?" can be an effective last-ditch effort to turn someone around.

Paul used guilt and shame when he chastised the Corinthians for suing each other in court. Their selfishness was foolishly shortsighted: "I say this to your shame!" (1 Cor 6:5; cf. 15:34). His second letter rejoiced that the Corinthians had been filled with remorse for their many sins and repented. Guilt and shame had done their work (2 Cor 7:9–10). Paul was not satisfied, and he prayed that they would "become fully mature," but guilt and shame had stopped the bleeding (13:9). The Corinthians had turned around. They were headed in the right direction, growing in the grace of their Lord.

CHAPTER 22

The Safest Place to Be Is in the Center of God's Will

The Legendary Belief

The commencement speaker shared personal stories of harrowing danger and risky ventures that stretched his faith in God. As he reflected on his lifetime of obedience, the one thing that stood out was how his predicaments always seemed to work out when he sought the Lord first. He assured the Christian college graduates: "Your future may be uncertain. You may not know whom to marry or what ministry opportunity to pursue. But fear not. Bathe every decision in prayer. Ask God what he wants you to do, then step forward with confidence. The safest place you can ever be is in the center of God's will."

Unraveling the Legend

I appreciate the speaker's emphasis on prayer, but God has not promised to give us personal, specific instructions about whom to marry or what job offers to accept. That is not how the will of God works. I also question whether God has promised to keep us safe. Two millennia of Christian martyrs may want to have a word! Let's take both issues, in order.

Knowing God's Will

The will of God exists in two forms: his moral will, revealed in the Bible (1 Thess 4:3–8); and his sovereign, decretive will, seen only in life's rearview mirror (Eph 1:11). God's sovereign will includes every event that has ever occurred. If God did not sign off in some way, either by directly decreeing or choosing to allow, the event would not have happened. As John Calvin said, "unless he [God] willed it, we would not do it."[1]

We cannot explain the apparent conflict between God's sovereign will, which contains evil events like the Holocaust, and God's moral will, which abhors such tragedies. And we must not try. Calvin said we cannot fathom this seeming contradiction because we are creatures. We must remember our place: God is up there, and we are down here. Why should we suppose that we could comprehend his ways? God alone understands how his two distinct wills coalesce into one seamless and perfect will.[2]

Some worry that a God whose sovereign will includes horrors cannot be good. Doesn't evil implicate God? See chapter 16 for a brief discussion of evil, and how the cross eases much of the sting from this problem. For now, consider that the relation between God's sovereign will and evil may also be read from the opposite direction. If suffering only occurs within God's plan, then we can take great comfort. No matter what happens, God is not surprised. He is in total control. He holds us and our world in his grip.

God's sovereign will is hidden. We cannot know his decree before it happens, and we should not try. We should be content to focus on the moral will God has revealed and for which he holds us accountable. Augustine imagined a good son who prayed for his father to live and an evil son who prayed for his father to die. Neither knew that in God's sovereign plan their father would soon die. So, the evil son prayed according to God's sovereign will but not according to his moral will, and the good son prayed according to God's moral will but not according to his sovereign will. The evil son gets no credit for guessing right, while the good son is good because he prayed as he ought. Augustine's point is that we should not evaluate our prayers by whether they come true. We should focus on what God wants us to pray for, trusting that God will use even evil acts for his good ends.[3]

How do we find the center of God's will? If you mean God's sovereign will, we are already there. Everyone and every event lies smack in the middle of God's hidden decree. If you mean God's moral will, we find the center by reading the Bible and obeying it. Paul explains, "For this is God's will, your sanctification: that you keep away from sexual immorality. . . . For God has not called us to impurity but to live in holiness" (1 Thess 4:3, 7).

When it comes to major life decisions, we have more freedom than we might think. God's moral will is not a bull's-eye we must hit but a vast ocean

---

[1]   Calvin, *Institutes* 1:217 (1.17.5) (see chap. 2, n. 3).

[2]   Calvin, *Institutes* 1:233–34 (1.18.3) and *The Secret Providence of God*, ed. Paul Helm, trans. Keith Goad (Wheaton, IL: Crossway, 2010), 93–98.

[3]   Augustine, *Faith, Hope and Charity (Enchiridion)*, chap. 26, trans. Bernard Peebles, in *The Fathers of the Church, Writings of Saint Augustine*, vol. 4 (Washington, DC: The Catholic University of America Press), 454–55.

we may sail. We are free to go anywhere that does not dash us on the rocks of sin. A Christian is not permitted to marry an unbeliever or someone who already has a spouse. But we are free to marry any unattached, opposite-sex believer in the Lord. A Christian should not take jobs that increase the amount of evil and suffering in the world. It would be hard to justify working as a telemarketer for a strip club in an Appalachian casino, to use one suspiciously precise example. But we may accept any wholesome task that serves our neighbor and develops culture for the glory of Christ. God's sovereign will supplies peace of mind as we choose; we rest in the confidence that he remains in charge regardless how our decision turns out. And God's moral will compels us to give our best, doing whatever we choose "in the name of the Lord Jesus, giving thanks to God the Father through him" (Col 3:17).

We should pray for wisdom and consult with others as we decide whom to marry, what job to pursue, and how to spend our time and money. But in the end, we are free to step up and make our choice. We may do any number of things and remain in the center of God's will.

Staying Safe

The good news is that we who strive to obey Scripture are already near the center of God's will. The uncomfortable news is that because of the idols in our culture and our own hearts, this is a most dangerous place.

Jesus told his disciples, "If anyone wants to follow after me, let him deny himself, take up his cross, and follow me. For whoever wants to save his life will lose it, but whoever loses his life because of me will find it" (Matt 16:24–25). This is crazy talk. Assuming the disciples were like most people, they wanted happiness, freedom, 2.4 kids, and enough money to live. These commonsense goals weren't wrong, except their goals were mostly about them. Jesus said his disciples must willingly lose everything—crucifixion stole every comfort and shred of dignity from a man before it snuffed him out—so they might rise to a new life centered on him.

Paul confessed, "I have been crucified with Christ, and I no longer live, but Christ lives in me" (Gal 2: 20). Paul listed his impressive credentials—a Jew's Jew, full of zeal and righteousness—then noted that "everything that was a gain to me, I have considered to be a loss because of Christ. . . . I also consider everything to be a loss in view of the surpassing value of knowing Christ Jesus my Lord. Because of him I have suffered the loss of all things and consider them as dung, so that I may gain Christ" (Phil 3:7–8). The Greek word for dung is *skubala*, which sounds more fun than it is. Scuba diving is great. Skubala, not so much.

Paul said his many reasons for self-confidence kept him from knowing and boasting in Jesus. So he died to his career, connections, and prestige. He lost his freedom and soon his head. Paul nailed his accomplishments and dreams to the cross so he might know Jesus "and the power of his resurrection and the fellowship of his sufferings" (Phil 3:10). Trading our lives for Jesus requires faith. It is the best deal we can ever make, but it still hurts. The center of God's will is not safe. It crucifies all who wander near.

Dying to ourselves is the best way to prepare for our second, external danger. King David noticed that "the wicked person schemes against the righteous and gnashes his teeth at him" (Ps 37:12). Those who worship false gods are threatened by the authority of the Lord Jesus, and they are liable to lash out at his followers. A first-century Jewish mob stoned Stephen (Acts 7:54–60), and a second-century Roman stadium erupted at Polycarp, the bishop of Smyrna. They yelled that he must die because "this is the teacher of Asia, the father of the Christians, the destroyer of our gods."[4] They were not wrong. If Jesus is Lord, then Caesar can't be. The followers of Jesus seek to destroy all other gods. Consequently, "all who want to live a godly life in Christ Jesus will be persecuted" (2 Tim 3:12).

Our suffering is not the end of the world. Literally. Asaph was bothered by his troubles, especially when compared to the wicked, who seemed to "have an easy time until they die, and their bodies are well fed" (Ps 73:4). Yet, he said, "I am afflicted all day long and punished every morning" (v. 14). Then Asaph "entered God's sanctuary" and remembered the wicked will come to ruin while he will be taken up into glory (vv. 17–24). He exulted, "My flesh and my heart may fail, but God is the strength of my heart, my portion forever" (v. 26). We may suffer for Jesus now, but if we do this right we will be drawn into closer intimacy with him, which makes it worth it.

Peter would soon be crucified upside down, yet he told his friends, "Don't be surprised when the fiery ordeal comes among you to test you, as if something unusual were happening to you. Instead, rejoice as you share in the sufferings of Christ, so that you may also rejoice with great joy when his glory is revealed. If you are ridiculed for the name of Christ, you are blessed, because the Spirit of glory and of God rests on you" (1 Pet 4:12–14). No persecution is wasted that publicly identifies us with Jesus.

The center of God's will is not safe. The Bible's Hall of Fame chapter ends with martyrs who "were sawed in two" or "died by the sword." They "wandered about in sheepskins, in goatskins, destitute, afflicted, and mistreated. . . . They wandered in deserts and on mountains, hiding in caves and holes in the ground." These all died in faith; "the world was not worthy of them" (Heb 11:37–39). Hebrews' next chapter applies their suffering and the suffering of Jesus to us. If the Son of God and the holiest saints suffered in this way, what

---

[4] "Martyrdom of Polycarp, 22 February 156 (or 155)," in *A New Eusebius,* ed. J. Stevenson, rev. W. H. C. Frend (Grand Rapids: Baker, 2013), 29.

should we expect? We should "endure suffering as discipline." Our Father uses trials "for our benefit, so that we can share his holiness" (Heb 12:7, 10). The center of God's will can never be safe because God believes our sanctification is more important than our success.[5]

Application

This chapter does not need a separate application. It is loaded with practical takeaways—obey God's moral will, trust his sovereign will, and celebrate your freedom in Christ. The mini myth closes with a final one, based on the life of Jesus.

Mini Myth

"God blesses in proportion to our faith."

This statement has a ring of truth. God's ultimate blessing is salvation, and that comes through faith in Jesus. Lesser blessings may also depend on how much we believe. When two blind men told Jesus they believed he could heal them, he touched their eyes and said, "Let it be done for you according to your faith" (Matt 9:27–29).

But this periodically true statement can have a false focus. When the healed blind men leaped for joy, what do you suppose they shouted? "Jesus said it would happen according to our faith! Wow! We must be fantastic believers! Has anyone seen such faith in Israel?" No, no, and no. If the blind men had droned on about themselves, friends and family would have rolled their eyes. *Shouldn't you be more excited about Jesus?*

This is the main problem with this mini myth. It oversells us and undersells God. If we only believed harder, if we squeezed out a little more faith, then God would certainly bless. As if his kindness was at the mercy of our frail faith. But as we learned in chapters 1 and 3, faith has one job: to respond to God's Word by claiming his promises and obeying his commands. If we do not have a divine promise or command, it does not matter how much we believe. We have no guarantee.

God freely blesses those who lack faith: his rain and sunshine fall on the fields of the unrighteous too (Matt 5:45). And he may sometimes withhold blessing from those who trust with all their heart. Many fervent followers of Christ did not receive the blessings they requested. Neither did Jesus. "During his earthly

---

5   Fallen people in a fallen world will not be safe until we are home with Jesus. But we can be secure in our salvation, even now. Jesus said he gives his followers "eternal life, and they will never perish. No one will snatch them out of my hand. My Father, who has given them to me, is greater than all. No one is able to snatch them out of the Father's hand" (John 10:28–29).

life, he [Jesus] offered prayers and appeals with loud cries and tears to the one who was able to save him from death, and he was heard because of his reverence" (Heb 5:7). Jesus was heard, but he did not get the answer he was looking for. Thank God for unanswered prayer. Our salvation depends on it!

Jesus calls us to follow his faithful example. We must believe in Jesus; nothing is more important. Do this, and it will not matter whether and to what extent God blesses us now. We will trust our heavenly Father, come what may.

CHAPTER 23

———

God Won't Give You More Than You Can Handle

The Legendary Belief

Tig Notaro is an affable comedian whose stand-up routine satirized a popular urban legend. Tig had endured a brutal year. It began with pneumonia that shed half a pound per day from her already thin frame. Then her mother died from a fall. Then Tig was diagnosed with breast cancer.[1]

Tig smiled at her nightclub audience and said:

> But you know what's nice about all of this is that you can always rest assured that God never gives you more than you can handle. Never. Never. When you've had it, God goes, all right, that's it. I just keep picturing God going, you know what? I think she can take a little more.
>
> And then the angels are standing back going, God, what are you doing? You are out of your mind. And God was like, no, no, no. I really think she can handle this. But why, God? Like, why? Why? I don't know. I just, you know. Just trust me on this.

Unraveling the Legend

I don't think Tig Notaro claims to be a follower of Jesus. Consequently, she may not be aware that God agrees with her sardonic point. He gave the apostle Paul far more than he could handle. Paul said that while he was in Asia "we were completely overwhelmed—beyond our strength—so that we even despaired of life itself" (2 Cor 1:8). Paul wanted to die? How encouraging!

---

[1]   Vanessa Grigoriadis, "Survival of the Funniest," *Vanity Fair*, December 18, 2012, https://www.vanityfair.com/culture/2013/01/tig-notaro-breast-cancer-dont-connect-with-jokes; "What Doesn't Kill You," transcript, episode 476 of *This American Life*, hosted by Ira Glass, originally broadcast on WBEZ Chicago, distributed by Public Radio International, https://www.thisamericanlife.org/476/transcript.

If Paul and his companions fell into deep despair, we need not think there is something wrong with us when we sink beneath icy gales of gloom. Sometimes the storms of life swamp our little boat, and there is not much we can do about it.

Tig's poignant set is powerful, but it does not rise above gallows humor. Life stinks, but what can you do about it? I'm a comedian, so I'll soothe my soul with dark jokes about a sadistic, tentative deity. Turn my lemons into comedic lemonade.

Tig's set works, but it's as far as she can go. If she puts her faith in Jesus, she will learn that God may allow the circumstances of life to overwhelm us, and that is a good thing. God never promises not to give us more than we can handle. Here's why.

More Than We Can Handle

Most people seem able to manage the stress and demands of life most of the time. They may not enjoy their work, families, or what's for dinner, but they more or less muddle through. As long as their teams are competitive and win a championship once in their lifetime (I'm looking at you, Cleveland), they find enough joy to keep going. Life is not great, but it's okay. They don't have time for church. Their weekends are already full of travel, sports, binge watching television, and checking updates on their phone. They are comfortable as they coast into hell.

What do you pray for such people? Disruption. You beg God to grab their attention. To do something that shoves them to the ground so they are forced to look up. This week one of these people that our church has been praying for learned she has a tumor. We prayed that God would heal her, but more importantly that God would use this health scare to draw her heart to him. Thank God that she has more than she can handle. What a perfect moment to turn to Jesus!

Consider why you came to Christ. Wasn't it because you realized your sin was more than you could handle? You needed God's forgiveness, or you were through. You were headed for hell and there was nothing you could do about it. What keeps you close to Jesus? Isn't it the continual awareness that your sin is more than you can handle? We never outgrow the gospel. We never get beyond our complete and utter dependence on Jesus.

We may easily forget this in the rush of life—our hearts are "prone to wander, Lord, I feel it, prone to leave the God I love"[2]—so our Father may lovingly allow us to be overwhelmed by relational stress, work demands, or financial hardship. This was Paul's takeaway from his affliction in Asia. He

---

[2]   Robert Robertson, "Come, Thou Fount of Every Blessing," verse 3, Hymnary.org, accessed September 26, 2022, https://hymnary.org/text/come_thou_fount_of_every_blessing.

said the benefit of despairing of life was that he and his friends knew they had to depend on God. "Indeed, we felt that we had received the sentence of death, so that we would not trust in ourselves but in God who raises the dead" (2 Cor 1:9). He learned this lesson again when he struggled with his thorn in the flesh. God knew Paul's visit to heaven might inflate him with pride, so he gave Paul a painful, perhaps humiliating trial to break him and throw him on the grace of God. Paul learned to "take pleasure in weaknesses, insults, hardships, persecutions, and in difficulties, for the sake of Christ. For when I am weak, then I am strong" (12:10). He realized it was beneficial to suffer beyond what he could endure. If he could handle whatever life threw at him, he might conclude he didn't need Jesus. And he would be infinitely worse for it.

Bottom line: if God never gives you more than you can handle—if you never feel overwhelmed by relationships, work, or money—that might be evidence that God does not care about you. So take your stress as a sign of your Father's love. When you have reached the end of your rope, do not tie a knot and hang on, as if your survival depended on you. Instead cry out to your Father, begging him to pull you hand over hand to himself. Then your trial will turn out for your good, regardless of what happens in the short run. When life is too much, your Father's arms are enough. He never gives you more than *he* can handle.

Manageable Temptations

How does this explanation that God gives us more than we can handle square with 1 Cor 10:13, which says God "will not allow you to be tempted beyond what you are able, but with the temptation he will also provide a way out so that you may be able to bear it"? The answer depends on what Paul means by the Greek term *peirasmos,* which can mean either "trial" or "temptation." Is Paul saying we can handle every trial God sends our way or that God will help us through every temptation? To answer that question, let's see what Paul is saying in context.

The temples of ancient Corinth had banquet halls where worshipers gathered to enjoy the meat that was offered to the god or goddess. Some Christians thought they might continue attending these temple feasts because they liked going out with friends and they knew that "an idol is nothing in the world" (8:4). There was no chance they would slip into idolatry.

Paul's response slowly builds over three chapters. He begins by addressing the Corinthians' attitude. They were proud of their superior knowledge that kept them pure as they dined at the temple. But what about others who were not as well-informed? These weaker Christians might miss the stronger Christians' subtle distinction and conclude that idolatry was compatible with following Jesus. "So the weak person, the brother or sister for whom Christ died, is ruined by your knowledge" (v. 11). Is that what you want?

Paul explains a better use of Christian freedom—we should use our knowledge and rights to build up rather than destroy—before turning his attention to the meat itself. He warns that the knowledgeable Corinthians were not as safe as they supposed. Some were already committing the idolatry they thought they would never do. They should heed the example of Israel. God's people had been delivered from Egypt and witnessed God's miraculous provision, yet many soon succumbed to (1) idolatry, (2) sexual immorality, (3) testing the Lord, and (4) complaining (1 Cor 10:6–11).

The Corinthians were slipping into the same sins. (1) They were committing idolatry: Anyone who eats meat in the temple participates in the idolatry of the temple. Behind every idol is a demon, so congratulations, Corinthians, you are in league with demons (1 Cor 10:18–20). (2) They were participating in sexual immorality—temple feasts in the Greco-Roman world often included prostitution. A night of wine and laughter climaxed in other sensual pleasures. (3) Their sin tested Jesus, "provoking the Lord to jealousy" (v. 22). (4) And they would be tempted to complain now that Paul was onto them.

Paul concludes this section by commanding the Corinthians to stop attending the idolatrous and immoral temple feasts. They could buy meat in the marketplace without asking whether it was leftovers from a temple sacrifice, but they should not eat meat in a friend's home if someone said it had been offered to idols. They must always eat and drink "for the glory of God" (vv. 14–31).

Our passage, God "will not allow you to be tempted beyond what you are able," forms the hinge between the miserable example of Israel and Paul's command to stop dining in temples (v. 13). Paul realizes his Corinthian Christians are in a tough spot. Their friends may not understand why they no longer come to the temple. They might be offended when the Christians put down their fork at a meal in their home. Relationships might break from the strain, taking business opportunities down with them. How many deals are cut among friends over dinner? Paul appreciates the sacrifice that is required yet assures the Corinthians their situation is not unique. They are not the first to be tempted to fudge their commitment to God for the sake of family, friendships, and business deals, and they will not be the last. When they feel the pressure to go along to get along, remember their faithful God will "provide the way out" of the temptation so that they "may be able to bear it" (1 Cor 10:13).

With this background, here is how to integrate this passage with the biblical truth, and our practical need, to face more stress than we can handle. Paul is clearly speaking about temptation to sin. The Corinthians need not succumb to the sin of idolatry, immorality, complaining, and testing the Lord. They may face situations of unbearable stress, but they will never encounter a situation that forces them to sin. Similarly, we may face trials that crush our spirits beyond all ability to cope. But we will never suffer a trial in which the only way out is to sin. God will always supply a way of escape from sin, even as we stumble beneath the pressure of the moment.

In case you haven't noticed, the answer to both trials and temptations is God. His grace will carry us when the trial is more than we can handle, and his gracious Word will open a door to avoid sin. Sometimes walking through this door will seem more than we can humanly do. That means our temptation has become a trial, which we meet by resting in his sustaining grace.

Application

The key difference between people who rejoice in Jesus and those who muddle through life is perspective. Where we look determines what we see, so it is crucial that we look to Jesus rather than to ourselves. The urban legend "God won't give you more than you can handle" puts the focus squarely on us and how much we can handle. This is not helpful. We would be better off in every way if we put our focus on Jesus. The point is not "God won't give me more than I can handle," but "My grace is sufficient for you" (2 Cor 12:9).

You are not equipped to handle the pressures of this day. Thank God. Rest in Jesus—let him carry you—and find he is enough.

PART III

Jesus and Salvation

CHAPTER 24

The Son of God Put on Skin

The Legendary Belief

The Christian recording artist paused between songs to share a gospel message. He explained our sin had compelled the Son of God to identify with us. "He left heaven and took on flesh because that is the only way we could be saved. God put on skin so he might keep the law on our behalf and die in our place."

Unraveling the Legend

The singer had the right idea but did not go nearly far enough. He said the Son identified with us by coming to earth in a human body. That's half of it. But we also possess a human soul, or mind. Shouldn't the Son also have a soul/mind like ours? The early church said yes. Here is why.

Orthodox Christology

The fourth- and fifth-century church settled the central themes of the Christian doctrine of Jesus. Jesus must be both divine and human to save us; he must be human to be our representative, and he must be divine to escape Adam's corruption and bridge the ethical gap between us and God. This raised the question: How might one person possess a full divine nature that is infinite and a full human nature that is finite?

The church could not explain how but it did state what. The Council of Nicea (325) emphasized the Son is fully equal, or *homoousios* with the Father. The Council of Constantinople (381) clarified the Son is also distinct from the Father and Spirit, who are equally and entirely divine. The Council of Ephesus (431) stressed that Jesus's two natures must not be divided, as if here he acts from his deity and there he acts from his humanity. Jesus did not suffer from multi-personality dissociative disorder. The Council of Chalcedon (451) added that Jesus's two natures must not be merged. His deity and humanity are not blended into some heavenly man-Jesus smoothie.

Chalcedon summarized the church's conclusions by drawing a circle around the person of Jesus. We cannot state positively how Jesus's two natures interact while remaining intact in his one person, but we can state what beliefs lie outside the circle. We can only say what we must not say. The four fences of Chalcedon say Jesus's two natures exist "without confusion, without change," and "without division, without separation." We must neither separate Jesus's two natures so that he becomes two persons nor emphasize the unity of his two natures until we cannot tell them apart. This is minimal Christian orthodoxy.

Besides keeping Jesus's two natures distinct yet united, the early church also emphasized the integrity of each. It rejected heresies that diminished Jesus's deity, such as Arianism. Condemned at the Council of Nicea and found today among Mormons and Jehovah's Witnesses, this false teaching said the Son is a second-string deity, less divine than the Father. The church also opposed heresies that minimized Jesus's humanity by denying either his body or soul. The heresy of the first kind was Docetism. This Greek philosophical perversion said Jesus was a divine phantom. He appeared to have a human body but didn't really, because God would not lower himself to become sullied by our icky physical world. The heresy of the second kind was Apollinarianism. This fourth-century teaching joined Docetism in denying Jesus's full humanity but emphasized the other part. Jesus had a human body but not a human mind.

Apollinarianism

Apollinarius of Laodicea joined his friend Athanasius in defending the conclusions of the Council of Nicea. He agreed the Son must be *homoousios* (same nature) with the Father but struggled to say how a Son that high could become *homoousios* with us. How could the infinite divine Word unite with a finite human soul? One or the other would have to give. Apollinarius figured it should be the human mind that is displaced, because it is changeable and thus liable to sin. And we know Jesus could not sin. So Apollinarius concluded the divine Word plugged into Jesus's human body, filling the spot where his human mind would have been. He wrote, "We confess . . . that the Word himself has become flesh without having assumed a human mind, i.e., a mind changeable and enslaved to filthy thoughts, but existing as a divine mind immutable and heavenly."[1]

Apollinarianism is sometimes called "spacesuit Christology" or "God in a bod." The Son put on a human body much like an astronaut wears an outer shell to move about in alien space. Jesus did not have a human mind, so he could not sin. But he had a human body, so he could die for the sins of the world. His outer shell might be human, but his core was pure God.

Gregory of Nazianzus was not impressed. He turned on his Nicene teammate with two scathing letters that earned him the posthumous title, "Gregory the Theologian," at the Council of Constantinople (381). Gregory sarcastically warned that if anyone trusts in Jesus "as a man without a human mind, he is really bereft of mind and quite unworthy of salvation." Then he added this clincher: "For that which he has not assumed, he has not healed."[2] Jesus can only restore the parts of us that he possesses. If we want Jesus to redeem our bodies so that they rise again, then he must possess a human body. If we want Jesus to redeem our minds so they are reconciled to God, then he must possess a human mind. Jesus cannot heal what he does not have. A halfway human Jesus can only be a halfway Savior. The half of us that he does not share will be lost forever.

Worse, by omitting Jesus's human mind, Apollinarius had damned what is arguably our most important part. Gregory asked, If "the Godhead took the place of the human intellect," then "how does this touch me? For Godhead joined to flesh alone is not man, nor to soul alone, nor to both apart from intellect, *which is the most essential part of man*. Keep then the whole man, and mingle Godhead therewith, that you may benefit me in my completeness."[3]

What about Apollinarius's fear that giving Jesus a human mind might open the door to sin, since the human mind is corruptible and able to sin? Gregory responded that human bodies are equally corruptible and subject to condemnation. If the possibility of sin and damnation is reason for Jesus not to have a human mind, then he had better not have a human body either. Now no part of us can be saved! The answer is not to protect Jesus from contamination with our lower, potentially sinful parts but to remember that Jesus became each so

---

[1] Apollinarius, Letter to the Bishops at Diocaesarea, 2, in J. Stevenson, ed., *Creeds, Councils and Controversies*, rev. W. H. C. Frend (Grand Rapids: Baker, 2012), 103.

[2] Gregory of Nazianzus, Epistle CI.184A, in *Creeds, Councils and Controversies*, 105.

[3] Gregory of Nazianzus, 105 (emphasis mine). In this quote Gregory distinguishes between the intellect and soul. Both he and Apollinarius followed Plato's anthropology which distinguished between body, soul, and spirit. Apollinarius said the Logos took the place of Jesus's spirit or intellect while Jesus retained a human body and soul. However, since contemporary theology rightly equates soul and spirit, and since Gregory countered Apollinarius by saying Jesus had both a human mind and soul, this chapter follows other early church historians in claiming that Apollinarius denied Jesus's human mind or soul (which I take to be the same).

he might sanctify both. Jesus lowered himself to where we are so he might lift us up to where he is.[4]

Reading Scripture Rightly

It is dangerous to talk about our different parts, because, as chapter 14 explained, humans are meant to be integrated wholes. Gregory distinguished between the human body and mind to answer Apollinarius, whose argument depended on their separation. But our unity of body and soul is essential for properly interpreting Scriptures that might be used to support Apollinarianism.

The first is John 1:14, "The Word became flesh and dwelt among us." Doesn't this imply the Son only took a human body? It would be shocking if this is what John meant, since he wrote this line against Cerinthus, the incipient Gnostic whose Docetism denied the full humanity of Jesus. Once John spotted Cerinthus in a bathhouse in Ephesus. He said to his disciples, "Let us fly, lest even the bathhouse fall down, because Cerinthus, the enemy of truth, is within." We learn from this story that John did not mind public nudity, except with heretics. Interesting place to draw the line![5] John recognized the danger in denying Jesus's full humanity, and he passed this resolve on to his disciples. When one of them, Polycarp, met another Docetic teacher named Marcion, he was asked by Marcion if he recognized him. Polycarp replied, "I do recognize you, the first-born of Satan."[6] So again, not a fan.

Gregory knew these stories and insisted that John 1:14 was not referring to Jesus's human body at the exclusion of his human soul. John was using synecdoche, a figure of speech that means the whole by mentioning one part. As "shots in arms" refers to entire people who are vaccinated, so "the Word became flesh" means the Son became every last part of us. If this were not true, Gregory notes that John 17:2, "you have given him authority over all flesh" (ESV); Ps 65:2, "to you shall all flesh come" (ESV); and Ps 145:21, "let all flesh bless his holy name forever and ever" (ESV) would mean that "God is God only of flesh, and not of souls."[7] But "flesh" is shorthand for the whole person, leading the Christian Standard Bible to translate Ps 65:2, "All humanity will come to you," and Ps 145:21, "let every living thing bless his holy name forever and ever."[8]

---

[4]   Gregory of Nazianzus, 106.

[5]   Irenaeus, *Against Heresies* III.4, in J. Stevenson, ed., *A New Eusebius,* rev. W.H.C. Frend (Grand Rapids:, Baker, 2013), 128.

[6]   Irenaeus, 128–29.

[7]   Gregory of Nazianzus, *Creeds, Councils and Controversies,* 107.

[8]   The CSB does retain the term "flesh" in John 17:2, yet it means the whole being of every person. The whole verse reads, "since you gave him authority over all flesh, so that he may give eternal life to everyone you have given him."

Synecdoche also explains Heb 10:5, which quotes Ps 40:6 in the Septuagint, the Greek version of the Old Testament. It reads, "Therefore, as he [the Son] was coming into the world, he said: **You did not desire sacrifice and offering, but you prepared a body for me.**" Does this imply that Jesus came in a human body and not a human soul? No. Hebrews emphasizes Jesus's body because it is speaking of temple sacrifices, which required the physical "blood of bulls and goats" (10:4). It would be hard to slit the throat of a spirit. I wouldn't try. Jesus came to sacrifice himself for our sins, and since his body is the only part the soldiers could kill, we read that "we have been sanctified through the offering of the body of Jesus Christ once for all time" (v. 10). But Jesus's human soul was inextricably involved in his sacrifice. His last words from the cross were "Father, *into your hands I entrust my spirit*" (Luke 23:46, emphasis added).

Application

When someone is caught doing something bad and there is no way to excuse their behavior, they may try to get by with the shrug, "I'm only human." This is a category mistake. Apollinarius assumed that some aspect of our humanity was too frail for Jesus to assume without falling into sin. But Jesus is not dragged down by the weight of our weakness. Rather he joins our humanity to elevate it.

Humans do not have to sin.[9] We know this because the Son of God who became human can "sympathize with our weaknesses." He was "tempted in every way as we are, yet without sin" (Heb 4:15). Sin is not a necessary part of being human. Sin eats away at our humanity. Fully actualized humans—Jesus now and we at our resurrection—do not sin ever. Until that day, we have a fully divine and fully human High Priest interceding for us in heaven. So, "let us approach the throne of grace with boldness, so that we may receive mercy and find grace to help us in time of need" (v. 16).

---

[9] Following Augustine's lead, theologians describe humanity's relation to sin through the story of creation, fall, and redemption. At creation, humans were *posse peccare, posse non peccare* (able to sin, able not to sin). After the fall, we were *non posse non peccare* (not able not to sin). At regeneration, we become *posse non peccare* (able not to sin). And when we are glorified, we will be *non posse peccare* (not able to sin).

CHAPTER 25

———

Jesus Loves Sinners and Dislikes Religious People

The Legendary Belief

The guest preacher hummed a high fastball at the conservative congregation. "Some of us have spent our entire lives in church, immersed in Christian songs and sermons, and we may have become a little too satisfied with ourselves and our walk with Christ. How can I tell? By how quickly we condemn outsiders who struggle with temptations we do not face. Watch out! Jesus saved his fiercest denunciations for people like us. He hated the religious establishment, but he loved sinners. If Jesus was on earth today, where would you find him? Sure, he'd come to church on Sunday mornings, if only to flip over a few tables. But on Saturday nights? He'd visit a gay bar. If that offends you, you do not know the heart of Jesus. Your smug, superior spirit fills him with disgust."

Unraveling the Legend

It is nearly a truism today that Jesus loves sinners and dislikes religious people. This axiom is often mentioned by those seeking to excuse sexual sin. If you say a particular immoral act is wrong, you will be accused of judging, which is much worse than the act you are opposing. You have outed yourself as a devoutly religious person, the kind Jesus disdained.

What an odd thing to believe about a person who spent much of his earthly life in synagogues and making triannual religious pilgrimages to the temple in Jerusalem! The religious leaders noticed that Jesus ate and drank with "tax collectors and sinners" because that was remarkable (Luke 5:29–30). The tax collectors and sinners did not mention Jesus dining with religious leaders because of course he did.

Jesus spent time with religious people because he loved them. When a rich young ruler confidently said he had kept every command since childhood,

"Jesus loved him" and told him what else he must do to live forever. Jesus did not tell him to get lost because he was rich and religious. He told him to give his wealth away and "then come, follow me" (Mark 10:17–21).

Jesus was kind to prostitutes, and they loved him back. And he did excoriate the Pharisees and teachers of the law, who loathed him in return. But why? Did Jesus have a soft spot for sinners because of their sin and animosity for religious people because they were religious? Or does something else better account for his interactions with each? We might spot the difference if they all gathered in one room, which is exactly what they did.

Dinner with Sinners

Once Jesus was eating dinner at a Pharisee's house when "a woman in the town who was a sinner" (read: lady of the night) showed up with "an alabastar jar of perfume." As was the custom of his day, Jesus and his disciples were reclining on couches around a low table. They lay on their left sides and took their food with their right hands, their feet sticking out behind them. The promiscuous woman "stood behind [Jesus] at his feet, weeping." She wept so much she "began to wash his feet with her tears." She "wiped his feet with her hair, kissing them and anointing them with the perfume" (Luke 7:36–38).

What a noisy, fragrant, scandalous scene! Religious leaders typically avoid interaction with promiscuous women. What kind of fraud allows a prostitute to fondle him in public! That's what the host wanted to know. He looked away in disgust, embarrassed for Jesus. "This man, if he were a prophet, would know who is touching him—she's a sinner!" (v. 39). Jesus's cover was blown. He was not what many thought he was.

Jesus looked across the table and locked eyes with his host. "Simon, I have something to say to you." Jesus told him about a creditor who forgave the entire debt of two people. One owed 500 denarii and the other only 50. Which of them will love the creditor more? Simon said the one who was forgiven more. Jesus said "exactly," then compared Simon with the sinful woman. Simon had not washed or kissed Jesus's feet or anointed his head with oil, yet the woman washed Jesus's feet with her tears then kissed and bathed them in perfume. She loved Jesus much because "her many sins have been forgiven." It's likely Jesus had met her earlier that day or week and forgiven her sins. The grateful woman returned home and then went looking for Jesus to express her appreciation. Jesus propped himself on his elbow, twisted to the right, and looked at the woman caressing his feet. He reaffirmed his love. "Your sins are forgiven" (vv. 40–48).

The creditor in Jesus's story loved both debtors equally. He forgave all there was to forgive. He could not have loved either more than he did. But the debtors loved back unequally, because "the one who is forgiven little, loves little" (Luke 7:47). The difference lies in us, not in Jesus. He loves both the Pharisee and the prostitute, but the latter tends to love him more. The Pharisee would have loved more if he had realized there were more sinners at dinner than the sketchy lady who came in late and made a scene. We all are bankrupt sinners. Some of us just don't realize it yet.

Save the Lost

Jesus had a standard comeback to the Pharisees who were offended that he ate with tax collectors and sinners. Whether it was Matthew's party with his tax collector friends or Jesus inviting himself over to Zacchaeus's house, Jesus's response to the perplexed was the same. "I have not come to call the righteous, but sinners to repentance" (Luke 5:32). "For the Son of Man has come to seek and to save the lost" (19:10).

Jesus came to save the lost, not the found. Those already in the sheepfold do not need rescue. This explains why Jesus was so hard on the religious leaders. They were not only assumed to be in the sheepfold; they were the shepherds! They gave their lives to holiness and religious ritual and urged others to follow their example. No way they were lost.

But they were. Jesus called them every name but what their mamas gave them because he had to shake them loose from their false security. He said they were "whitewashed tombs, which appear beautiful on the outside, but inside are full of the bones of the dead and every kind of impurity" (Matt 23:27). "Snakes! Brood of vipers! How can you escape being condemned to hell?" (v. 33). Jesus was angry because he loved them so much. He needed them to admit they were lost so he could save them.

This strategy worked with the greatest Pharisee of them all, the apostle Paul. If Jesus disliked religious people because they were religious, he would have hated Paul before his conversion. Paul was the most religious, the most devout, the most holy and zealous Pharisee in his world (Phil 3:4–6). Yet Jesus loved him enough to knock him off his high horse. He blinded Paul with the light of his love. He showed him he was lost so he could be found (Acts 9:1–9). Paul realized the cross of Christ destroyed all his religious accomplishments. If Jesus had to be crucified for Paul, what did that say about his righteous deeds? They were nothing but "dung" compared to "the surpassing value of knowing Christ Jesus my Lord" (Phil 3:8). Paul concluded, "'Christ Jesus came into the world to save sinners'—and I am the worst of them" (1 Tim 1:15).

Jesus used tough love on the righteous and religious to reveal their sin. He was soft on the tax collectors and prostitutes who already knew they were sinners. No need to beat them over the head with it. They freely admitted it. Everybody knew it. Their guilt and shame were exposed for all to see.

The story of the woman caught in adultery does not appear in our earliest manuscripts, yet it rings true with the Jesus we see in the rest of the Gospels. The self-righteous Pharisees thrust a woman caught in adultery before the Lord. *Should we stone her?* Jesus said, *Sure, and start with the person who is perfectly holy. He gets to throw first.* The Pharisees slunk away, silently conceding they were not as holy as they presented. Now that they admitted they were lost, they had a chance to be saved. The woman lingered before the Lord, ashamed of her sin. Jesus spoke kindly to her because she knew she was lost. She was ready to be found. "'Neither do I condemn you,' said Jesus. 'Go, and from now on do not sin anymore'" (John 8:2–11).

Application

Understanding how lost we are is an essential step of conversion and an important motivation for our Christian life. Paul wrote, "For the grace of God has appeared, bringing salvation for all people, instructing us to deny godlessness and worldly lusts and to live in a sensible, righteous, and godly way in the present age" (Titus 2:11–12).

How does the grace of God teach us to "deny godlessness and worldly lusts"? Wouldn't it teach us instead to embrace these sins? If every sin can be forgiven in Christ, why should we stop sinning? If God loves me no matter what I do, what does it matter what I do? Sin away! It's covered!

Grace teaches us to stop sinning by pointing to our future. In the next verse, Paul says we will live rightly as "we wait for the blessed hope, the appearing of the glory of our great God and Savior, Jesus Christ" (v. 13). We live as those who will give an account of our lives to the Lord. We want him to find us watching for him when he returns.

Grace teaches us to stop sinning by pointing to our past and present.[1] The grace of God has already come, "bringing salvation for all people." The Heidelberg Catechism explains this motivation.

Question one asks, "What is your only comfort in life and in death?"

Answer: "That I am not my own, but belong—body and soul, in life and in death—to my faithful Savior Jesus Christ."

Question two asks, "What must you know to live and die in the joy of this comfort?"

---

[1]   We who grew up in church may not have a sordid past, but we do have a present sinful nature and potentially sordid future that we are saved from. We live in gratitude for God's grace that delivers us from our sin and misery of the past, present, and future.

Answer: "Three things: first, how great my sin and misery are; second, how I am set free from all my sins and misery; third, how I am to thank God for such deliverance."[2]

The rest of the catechism follows this outline: my sin and misery, God's salvation, and my gratitude for God's deliverance. Sin, grace, gratitude. This is the Christian order. Only if I understand the depths of my depravity can I begin to appreciate the power of grace. And if I understand grace I will automatically be filled with gratitude. The Greek term for grace is *charis* and the term for gratitude is *eucharistia*. Gratitude has grace within it. Gratitude is built on grace because it is our response to grace. But we cannot understand grace unless we first understand how lost we are.

The Pharisees believed they were the holy ones (their name means "separated ones"). They kept the law blamelessly. They did not need Jesus. They judged Jesus to see if he measured up. There's at least a little Pharisee within us all. We can scarcely believe that someone well-intentioned like us deserves hell. Hell exists for wicked people, not we who are trying our best.

We must become lost so we can be found. We may not be sexually immoral like the woman who anointed Jesus's feet, but our sin also deserves the hell of God's wrath. Admit that, and we will be filled with gratitude for Jesus's love. We will love much because we have been forgiven much.

---

[2] A modern translation of the Heidelberg Catechism is available online at https://www.crcna.org /welcome/beliefs/confessions/heidelberg-catechism.

CHAPTER 26

Jesus Is More Loving and Compassionate Than the God of the Old Testament

The Legendary Belief

Old Testament scholar Peter Enns asks how to reconcile the New Testament portrayal of Jesus with the God he finds in his area of expertise. The Old Testament God told Israel to enter the Promised Land and exterminate the nations that were living there. They must "make no treaty with them and show them no mercy" (Deut 7:2). Conversely, Jesus commands his followers to love all their neighbors, including their enemies. Enns concludes, "Jesus' teaching is a reversal of the Old Testament's dominant tone of exclusivism. You do not hate your enemies; you love them. You do not kill them; you evangelize them."[1] Jesus is far more loving and compassionate than the petulant Jehovah who drowns the world in a flood, slays Egyptian firstborn sons in their sleep, opens the ground to swallow Korah's family, and incinerates stubborn folks with fire from heaven.

Unraveling the Legend

Pitting Jesus against Jehovah is so common today that it is nearly a truism. When someone angrily plots revenge, he or she may say, "I'm about to go Old Testament" on the person who committed the offense. Such folks are not inclined to follow Jesus, the meek and mild Savior who urges them to turn the other cheek. Of course, they do want Jesus around for their sins, which they hope will find a kind and sympathetic judge, while reserving the right to imitate Jehovah for the sins of others.

Pitting Jesus against Jehovah may be common, but it is not new. It was possibly the first heresy in the history of the church. In the second century, Justin Martyr wrote *Syntagma against All Heresies*, which may be the first time the term "heresy" was invoked to describe false teaching that left unchecked

---

[1] Peter Enns, "Inerrancy, However Defined, Does Not Describe What the Bible Does," in *Five Views on Biblical Inerrancy*, ed. J. Merrick and Stephen M. Garrett (Grand Rapids: Zondervan, 2013), 112.

would destroy the Christian faith. Justin aimed much of his fire at Marcion (c. 85–160), a contemporary who denied that Jesus and the Old Testament God were the same deity. Tertullian soon followed with *Against Marcion,* and the rout was on.

Marcion

Marcion entitled his most important book *Antithesis* because it showed the many ways Jesus and the New Testament opposed the Old Testament and its god. Marcion believed the latter was too weak and vile to be the supreme God. He was a lesser god, or demiurge, who created a lower, physical world and limited his salvation to the Jewish people. He enforced retributive justice— an eye for an eye—and ruthlessly wiped out Israel's enemies. His take-no-prisoners approach reflected his deep insecurities. He was neither omnipotent nor omniscient, losing track of humanity when it was only two people. After the fall, this bumbling god came looking for Adam, plaintively calling out, "Where are you?" (Gen 3:9).

Marcion said this Old Testament god planned to send a messiah to collect the Jews and rule the world by punishing the heathen. At this point the supreme God intervened. He sent his Messiah, who only pretended to be born and live a normal, bodily existence to avoid arousing suspicion from the demiurge. But when Jesus began his ministry, he immediately showed he was altogether different from the Old Testament god. That god commanded war and taking captives as slaves; Jesus said to love our enemies. The demiurge demanded righteousness, and he despised lepers; Jesus embraced sinners and touched and healed lepers. The demiurge sent bears to maul children; Jesus welcomed children into his arms. The demiurge was a Jewish tribal deity who threatened damnation; Jesus came for all people and offered love and forgiveness. The demiurge obsessed over an earthly kingdom; Jesus brought a heavenly reign.

The Old Testament god caught on to Jesus and inspired his followers to crucify him. But he did not realize Jesus wasn't mortal and that his death permitted Jesus to descend to Hades and find many takers for his gospel of unconditional forgiveness. Marcion said Jesus judges no one, though he does allow us to choose the exclusive, judgmental ways of the demiurge and burn in the fires of his hatred. We can go to hell if we want. Marcion believed the Old Testament god would someday send his messiah to establish a millennial kingdom, but this earthly reign will be defeated by Jesus's heavenly realm, the final, celestial abode for all who choose Jesus and his love.

Marcion's disdain for the Old Testament prompted him to eliminate that entire section from his Bible. He also cut out any references to the Old Testament in the New Testament, including any suggestion that Jesus fulfilled Old Testament prophecy. He was left with the Gospel of Luke and some of Paul's epistles (he thought Paul's separation of law and grace showed he understood the radical difference between the testaments), with every allusion to the Old Testament removed. Marcion's heresy compelled the church to affirm the Old Testament and the goodness of the physical world. The bits of the Bible he had left also prompted the church to begin the process of establishing our canon, determining which books belong in our Bible and why.

Dangerous Division

Modern-day Marcionites do not advocate cutting chunks out of Scripture, but they do insist that much of the Old Testament message is neither true nor good. Brian McLaren believes the Old Testament contains "violent images, cruel images, [and] un-Christlike images" of God. Most troubling is the God who appears in the Noah narrative. McLaren complains that "a god who mandates an intentional supernatural disaster leading to unparalleled genocide is hardly worthy of belief, much less worship. How can you ask your children—or non-church colleagues and neighbors—to honor a deity so uncreative, overreactive, and utterly capricious regarding life?"[2] Professor Eric Seibert argues the Old Testament stories of violence indicate "not everything in the 'good book' is either good, or good for us." He writes, "At times the Bible endorses values we should reject, praises acts we must condemn, and portrays God in ways we cannot accept."[3]

These modern Marcionites try various strategies to handle such Old Testament horrors. Seibert suggests using Old Testament texts of violence as conversation starters. Christians cannot agree with what the Israelites did, but we can read these stories from the perspective of the victims and raise our own sympathetic awareness of those who suffer in our world.[4] McLaren adds that we should read the Old Testament books as a "community library" rather than an authoritative constitution. As a library presents competing perspectives on perennial questions, so the books of the Bible present different answers to the big questions of life. We should not expect our Bible to be internally consistent but should take its messy conversation as our cue to join its great debates. Even God, when he appears in the biblical text, does not give the final answer on anything, because he does not want to oppressively "shut down any conversation."[5] Ultimately, Seibert, McLaren, and Enns agree that the Old Testament

---

[2]   Brian McLaren, *A New Kind of Christianity* (San Francisco: HarperOne, 2010), 98, 109.

[3]   Eric Seibert, "When the 'Good Book' is Bad: Challenging the Bible's Violent Portrayals of God," February 1, 2013, *Peter Enns* (blog), https://www.patheos.com/blogs/peterenns/2013/02/when-the-good -book-is-bad-challenging-the-bibles-violent-portrayals-of-god/.

[4]   Eric A. Seibert, *The Violence of Scripture: Overcoming the Old Testament's Troubling Legacy* (Minneapolis: Fortress, 2012), 81–89.

[5]   McLaren, *A New Kind of Christianity,* 78–97.

describes God from the perspective of a warring, tribal people. Enns says this shows "how God is willing to meet his people where they are and allow them to tell the story in ways that reflect their own cultural context."[6]

Besides noting the irony that both Seibert and Enns teach Old Testament in Christian colleges—why devote your life to a subject that gets so much wrong?—the view that Scripture is a collection of books that invites our critique disregards what the Bible claims to be, the authoritative and true Word of God. Why even bother with the Bible? These Marcionites already know what is right and wrong, independently of what they read there. If the Bible is merely a library, why not pick a different one? And if the Old Testament is simply God meeting people where they are, how do you know that your understanding of God is not him doing the same with you? Chronological snobbery comes with an expiration date. Someday, and with any luck before you die, someone new will pull the same trick on you.

The Marcionite road does not stop with the New Testament. The same hermeneutic that replaces the Old Testament god with the New Testament Jesus will eventually replace Jesus with us. Today we hear that yes, Jesus did call God his "Father" and he did choose men to be his twelve disciples, but that was only because he was a product of his patriarchal culture. Our egalitarian world is more advanced, and we know better than Jesus how to incorporate women into leadership and how to speak about God with more inclusive names. I am not saying these two issues bear the same theological weight or that egalitarians are Marcionites. I am saying Marcionism inevitably elevates us over the Son of God.[7]

Role Reversal

You may concede Marcionism is a heresy with a bad track record. But what about its foundational claim that Jesus is more loving and compassionate than the God revealed in the Old Testament? Isn't that true?

No. In fact, it would be easy to argue for the opposite. The Old Testament God leads with grace and compassion. When he revealed himself to Moses, he passed in front of Moses and proclaimed his name: "The LORD—the LORD is a compassionate and gracious God, slow to anger and abounding in faithful love and truth, maintaining faithful love to a thousand generations, forgiving iniquity, rebellion, and sin" (Exod 34:5–7). But didn't this compassionate God destroy the world with a great flood? Yes, and the New Testament says he will

---

6   Enns, "Inerrancy," 109.

7   For example, William Webb's redemptive movement hermeneutic implies that our ethical understanding and treatment of women has advanced beyond what was revealed in the New Testament. See Webb, *Slaves, Women & Homosexuals* (Downers Grove, IL: InterVarsity, 2001).

do it again with fire. The New Testament adds that the flood was a sign of God's patience, who put up with human wickedness "while the ark was being prepared" (1 Pet 3:20). The long-suffering God of the Old Testament did not destroy the heathen living in Canaan until their sin had "reached its full measure" (Gen 15:16). He tolerated years of child sacrifice, even among his own people (2 Kgs 16:3; Jer 19:4–5). Given the West's practice of abortion, a better question than why did God kill sinners in the Old Testament is why hasn't he yet judged us?

The New Testament warns that day is fast approaching. The next time the world sees Jesus, he will be riding a white horse leading armies from heaven. He will slay his enemies and rule the world "with an iron rod. He will also trample the winepress of the fierce anger of God, the Almighty" (Rev 19:15). An angel will beckon birds to dine on the flesh of the fallen, and the beast and the false prophet will be "thrown alive into the lake of fire that burns with sulfur" (vv. 17–21). This passage occurs two chapters from the end of the New Testament, as far removed canonically from the Old Testament as you can get. And it gets worse: "And anyone whose name was not found written in the book of life was thrown into the lake of fire" (20:15). The loving Jesus casts sinners into hell, a fate far worse than anything depicted in the Old Testament.

If someone wants to distinguish the Old Testament God from the New Testament God, it is an open argument which God is more compassionate and which is more wrathful. That is as it should be. Because the Old Testament and New Testament God are the same God, we should not be able to separate them. Jesus is Jehovah, the holy and loving God who justly punishes sinners and justly saves those who repent and trust in him. Old and New Testaments meet at the cross, where God's justice is satisfied and his love is unleashed. Separate Old and New Testaments, Jehovah and Jesus, and you cannot be saved.

Application

The Bible is a continuous, developing story that must not be pitted against itself. The New Testament flows organically from the Old Testament, as a river from its spring. The God of the Jews is the Head of the Church. God reveals more of himself as the story develops—we learn the one God is triune because of the incarnation and Pentecost—but his new revelation never contradicts what came before. The Alpha and Omega is the same God from beginning to end. You can trust the One who is the same yesterday, today, and forever (Heb 13:8).

Mini Myth

"The Holy Spirit is an energy force."

A recent survey found 58 percent of self-identified American Christians believe the Third Person of the Trinity is not a real, living person but merely a symbol of God's presence, purity, or power.[8] He is an impersonal force, an "it" rather than a "Thou." Wolfhart Pannenberg suggests a sophisticated version of this, wondering whether it might be more faithful to Scripture and modern science to think of the Spirit as a divine "force field" in which we all live and move.[9]

Jesus does compare the Spirit to a wind that blows where it pleases (John 3:8), yet other passages inform this metaphor by implying the Spirit is a person. The Spirit exhibits personal characteristics:

- intelligence (John 14:26: he "will teach you all things and remind you of everything I have told you"),
- will (1 Cor 12:11: the Spirit distributes gifts "as he wills"),
- emotions (Eph 4:30: "don't grieve God's Holy Spirit").

Like other persons, the Spirit can be lied to (Acts 5:3–4) and blasphemed (Matt 12:31). And like other persons, the Spirit ministers (Rom 8:26) and convicts (John 16:8). The Spirit is a powerful force in us and in our world, but only because he is a divine person.

---

[8] George Barna, "What Does It Mean When People Say They Are 'Christian'?" *American Worldview Inventory 2021*, Cultural Research Center, Arizona Christian University, August 31, 2021, https://www.arizonachristian.edu/wp-content/uploads/2021/08/CRC_AWVI2021_Release06_Digital_01_20210831.pdf.

[9] Wolfhart Pannenberg, *Systematic Theology*, vol. 1 (Grand Rapids: Eerdmans, 1991), 382–84.

CHAPTER 27

We Are All God's Children

The Legendary Belief

Martin Luther King Jr.'s iconic "I Have a Dream" speech on the steps of the Lincoln Memorial rivals Lincoln's Gettysburg Address as the most important speech in American political discourse. King said he had a dream that one day America would live up to its founding ideal that "all men are created equal."[1] He dreamed the children of slaves and the children of slave owners might live together in unity. He dreamed that his own four children would grow up in a world where their character counted far more than their skin color. He dreamed the words of "My Country 'Tis of Thee" would come true, and freedom would ring for all Americans throughout the land. We are all God's children, King believed, whether white or black, Jew or Gentile, Protestant or Catholic, and we must join hands and together bask in freedom's glory.[2]

King's powerful speech challenges us to live up to God's righteous standard for race relations. But what about his assumption that we all are God's children: white and black, Jew and Gentile, Protestant and Catholic? Today it is common to include other religions too—Islam, Buddhist, Hindu, and what have you. Is it true that every human is God's child?[3]

---

[1]   United States Declaration of Independence.

[2]   See Martin Luther King Jr., "I Have a Dream" (speech, Lincoln Memorial, Washington, DC, August 28, 1963), American Rhetoric Top 100 Speeches, https://www.americanrhetoric.com/speeches/mlkihaveadream.htm.

[3]   King did not speak as inclusively as we might today, referring only to black and white "men." I assume he meant all people and did not intend to exclude women.

Unraveling the Legend

We must answer this question in both a broad and narrow sense. In a wide, generic sense every human person is a child of God. Luke called Adam, the father of the human race, a "son of God" (Luke 3:38), and Paul approvingly cited a pagan poet who said, "We are God's offspring" (Acts 17:28–29). Paul confirmed, "I kneel before the Father from whom every family in heaven and on earth is named" (Eph 3:14–15). Our Christian God is not a local, tribal deity. He is the God and Father of the whole world. We assure all people that they are loved and valuable. We all bear God's image and may proudly take our place in his noble, human family.

However, there is a narrower, more intimate meaning of God's child that matters most. The Pharisees told Jesus they were not bastards like him because they knew who their father was. "'We weren't born of sexual immorality,' they said. 'We have one Father—God.'" Jesus replied, "If God were your Father, you would love me, because I came from God and I am here. . . . Why don't you understand what I say? Because . . . you are of your father the devil, and you want to carry out your father's desires. He was a murderer from the beginning" (John 8:41–44). The Pharisees promptly proved Jesus's point, for they "picked up stones to throw at him" (v. 59).

Jesus knew his religious opponents were God's children in that they belonged to the human family. But in the way that mattered most they were children of the devil. There is only one way to become God's child in the deepest, most intimate sense—through faith in Jesus. His closest disciple exclaimed, "See what great love the Father has given us that we should be called God's children—and we are! . . . Dear friends, we are God's children now, and what we will be has not yet been revealed. We know that when he appears, we will be like him because we will see him as he is" (1 John 3:1–2).

Adoption

Can you hear the amazement in John's voice? He was an ordinary fisherman, waiting for the Messiah to come and deliver Israel from the oppression of Rome.

Then he met the Messiah! That would have been enough.

Then the Messiah selected him to be his disciple! That is far more than John could have dreamed.

Then they became best friends! Okay, this is getting ridiculous.

Then Jesus died on the cross to forgive John's sins and save him from hell! Are you kidding me? John wasn't sure how many more blessings he could stand, yet they were still coming. Could it be true? He was also God's child?

We praise philanthropists who build orphanages in poor and war-ravaged countries, rescuing children from life on the streets. They are rightly admired for giving hundreds of kids a fresh start. Now imagine a philanthropist who does even more. Say he has a son who becomes friends with one of the orphans. They form such a tight bond that the son cannot bear to leave his friend and return to his home country. He begs his dad, "Can't we adopt him? Can't he come live with us?" If the father follows through, that one fortunate orphan will spend a lifetime trying to process the exhilarating truth that the humanitarian did not merely want to *save* him—that would have been enough. The father wanted more. The father wanted *him*.

Our heavenly Father has only one natural begotten Son, that is, one Son of the same nature. On the night before his crucifixion, this Son spoke tenderly to his disciples. He said he had chosen them to be his friends and to remain in his Father's love. His Father would also be their Father! (John 15:9–16). Then Jesus gave his life to make that happen. John can hardly believe it: "See what great love the Father has given us that we should be called God's children—and we are!" (1 John 3:1). It would have been enough for God to save us from hell. Who could complain? But God did not merely want to *save* us. He wanted *us*. So, before the world began, "he predestined us to be adopted as sons through Jesus Christ for himself" (Eph 1:5). "God sent his Son . . . to redeem those under the law, so that we might receive adoption as sons. And because you are sons, God sent the Spirit of his Son into our hearts, crying, *Abba,* Father!" (Gal 4:4–5; cf. Rom 8:15–17).

The truth of our adoption must transform how we think about ourselves. What if this Thanksgiving, your mother has a little too much wine and lets slip that you were adopted? You never suspected this, and you are blindsided by the news. You might be an accomplished, well-adjusted adult with a family of your own, but your world would be rocked. Wouldn't you wake up in the middle of the night and wonder, *Who am I? Where do I belong?* We never need to ask this with God, though his adoption of us could not be more dramatic. We were born in sin, children of Adam bound for hell. Then he "rescued us from the domain of darkness and transferred us into the kingdom of the Son he loves" (Col 1:13).

Who are we? The children of God.

Where do we belong? In our Father's house.

Grace and Works

Our Father's adoption does important theological work. A perennial problem in the Christian life is how to avoid the opposite errors of legalism and license. Legalism emphasizes works in a way that minimizes grace, and license emphasizes grace in a way that minimizes works. The former says we must work to earn our salvation while the latter says works play no part in our salvation. God says these extremes are a false choice. We are "saved by grace through faith," and we are saved "for good works, which God prepared ahead of time for us to do" (Eph 2:8–10).

How may we responsibly talk about grace and works that puts each in its proper place? The answer requires both internal and external truths. Internally, chapter 25 explained how a heart full of gratitude for grace motivates us to joyfully keep God's commands. We must not think for a second that obedience earns our right standing with God; neither must we abuse forgiveness as a Get Out of Jail Free card to sin as we please.

Externally, the objective truth of adoption safely steers our boats between the opposite shoals of legalism and license. Salvation includes justification— God's legal declaration that we are righteous before him; sanctification—our moral change that progressively grows in righteousness; and glorification— our future perfection in righteousness. Adoption directs our hearts toward our final glorification, for we know that as God's children we are "heirs of God and coheirs with Christ—if indeed we suffer with him so that we may also be glorified with him" (Rom 8:17). Adoption also unites justification and sanctification. Justification alone would lead to license: we may sin freely because our right standing depends entirely on Jesus and nothing we do. Sanctification alone would lead to legalism: we must work hard to become righteous and prove ourselves worthy of Jesus. Adoption explains why justification and sanctification are both necessary for salvation, and in this order.

A successful adoption requires both a legal and moral change. Legally, the child assumes the last name of his father and enjoys the privileges of belonging to his family. Morally, the child begins to behave as one of the family. The legal change must come first. You do not get the benefits of being my child unless you are my child. My children may contact me day or night, whenever they need help. If the neighbor kid comes into my bedroom at 2:00 a.m., complaining that he's having bad dreams and can't sleep, I'll say, "Go home and tell *your* parents!" Adoption explains why only those who are justified—who have legally been declared righteous through faith in his Son—have the right to the privileges of the children of God.

Adoption also explains why sanctification must come next. What would we make of an adopted child who never comes down for dinner, never goes on family vacations, and does not appear in any family photos? He prefers to stay in his room, playing video games. Wouldn't we say, "That is not how this works? If you are part of our family, we expect you to participate with the rest of us. You are not just some kid. You are our child now." In the same way, adoption tells us why good works do not earn our standing with God and why good works are necessary. We are not God's children because of our actions, but all God's children should act like it.

Application

God calls us his servants (Phil 1:1) and he calls us his sons (Gal 4:5–7). The term "son" is not sexist, as it might sound to twenty-first-century ears. It is quite inclusive. In the first century a father's wealth was only inherited by sons. When God declares that all his children are sons, he is saying that everyone who puts their faith in Jesus, whether man or woman, becomes a "son" of God with equal and full rights of inheritance.

God calls us servants because we owe him our allegiance and very best work (Col 3:23–24). God calls us sons because we have privileges that servants do not enjoy. A servant labors in part out of fear. If he spills paint on the Persian rug or concocts a gender-reveal explosive that spews blue powder before igniting nearby brush that torches his master's garage of antique cars, he may be out of a job. A son, on the other hand, knows there is no mistake he can make that will get him evicted from the family. He may accidentally burn down the house, but he will still be welcomed into the family's new home, though closely monitored.

The freedom of a son inspires him to do his best. His number one goal is not to avoid mistakes but to make something great for his father. He works free and loose, willing to think creatively and take responsible risks because he labors from a secure base. If you have put your faith in Jesus, you are both God's servant and his son. Give him your best out of gratitude for your adoption, knowing that no matter what happens, it is going to be okay.

CHAPTER 28

All Children Who Die before the Age of Accountability Will Be Saved

The Legendary Belief

A week and a half after the September 11, 2001, terrorist attack, pastor John MacArthur was a guest on *The Larry King Show*. America was reeling, trying to make sense of what happened and wondering when the next attack might come. Perhaps because the terrorists claimed to be soldiers for God, King chose to probe the dark side of religion. He wondered where babies go when they die. He asked, "What about a two-year-old baby crushed at the bottom of the World Trade Center?"

MacArthur answered, "Instant heaven."

King shot back. "Wasn't [he] a sinner?"

MacArthur was just as fast. "Instant heaven."

Unraveling the Legend

MacArthur was stating the popular evangelical view that all babies who die before they are old enough to understand and respond to the gospel are taken to be with Jesus. We all should wish this is the case, and we have reason to think it is. This chapter's urban legend is not simply that all children who die before the age of accountability will be saved. The legend is that Scripture says this. It does not, and for good reason.

The Need to Believe

The Scriptures consistently teach that salvation comes "by grace through faith" (Eph 2:8). This "faith comes from what is heard, and what is heard comes through the message about Christ" (Rom 10:17). Simply put, we are saved when we put our faith in Jesus. Scripture's best-known verse says God "gave his one and only Son, so that everyone who *believes* in him will not perish but have eternal life" (John 3:16; emphasis mine). God immediately doubles down: "Anyone who *believes* in him is not condemned, but anyone who does not *believe* is already condemned, because he has not *believed* in the name of the one and only Son of God" (v. 18; emphasis mine). Paul and Silas got the point, and when a terrified prison guard cried, "What must I do to be saved?" they replied, "Believe in the Lord Jesus, and you will be saved" (Acts 16:30–31). Paul gave his life to spreading the good news about Jesus, and said the church needs more missionaries to do the same, because how can anyone "believe [in Jesus] without hearing about him? And how can they hear without a preacher?" (Rom 10:14).

Bottom line: those who believe in Jesus are saved; those who do not believe in Jesus are not saved. This raises the excruciating question about infants and the mentally disabled: What happens to those who live and die without developing the mental ability to believe in Jesus? How can they be saved?

Are the Kids All Right?

I cannot imagine a more painful and personal question. For the godly parents who have buried children or lovingly raised offspring whose minds will never be able to express faith in Jesus, it is essential to say first that God loves our kids far more than we do. He chose to bring them into this world, supervising their conception, gestation, and birth. He assures our broken hearts that "all [their] days were written in [my] book and planned before a single one of them began" (Ps 139:16). The song we learned in Sunday school is still true. "Jesus loves the little children, all the children of the world. Red and yellow, black and white, they are precious in his sight. Jesus loves the little children of the world." When "people were bringing infants to him so he might touch them," Jesus rebuked his disciples for rebuking the parents. He said, "Let the little children come to me, and don't stop them, because the kingdom of God belongs to such as these" (Luke 18:15–16). What an intriguingly suggestive consolation, just shy of a promise. When we lose a child, remember the kingdom belongs to people like her, and beg God to bring her home.

At the same time, and this is admittedly hard to accept, God would remain just if he did not permit deceased infants into his presence. The Scriptures teach that whole families and communities are bound together with the sin of their leaders. When God destroyed the world with the great flood, "he wiped out every living thing that was on the face of the earth," including the unknowing babes (Gen 7:23). When God rained fire on Sodom and Gomorrah, he burned up "all the inhabitants of the cities," including their kids (19:25). When Achan kept some of Jericho's spoils for himself, his children were stoned to death and cremated with him (Josh 7:20–26). When Korah led a rebellion against Moses, God opened the ground and swallowed his entire family down into Sheol (Num 16:28–34). When Israel settled in the Promised Land, God remembered how the Amalekites had attacked his people as they were leaving Egypt. He commanded King Saul to return the favor "and completely destroy everything they have. Do not spare them. Kill men and women, infants and nursing babies" (1 Sam 15:1–3). Children who had not personally sinned suffered along with the heads of their clan.

What is true of these families and nations is also true of humanity. Adam's original sin passes to each of his descendants (Rom 5:12–21). Theologians debate exactly how Adam's guilt and corruption are transferred to us, but parents soon discover something is wrong with their adorable bundle of joy. The second word every child learns, right after "Mama," is "No!" The third word is "Mine!" and somewhere down the line is "Dada," then "Dada, No! Mine!"

Some theologians distinguish between Adam's sin and our own, saying God does not hold children responsible for Adam's original sin until they are old enough to understand right from wrong and commit their own sin. They note God spared Israel's children from dying in the wilderness with their rebellious parents, perhaps because many of the kids were not old enough to "yet know good from evil" (Deut 1:39). They also point out that every person will be judged by Christ "for what he has done in the body, whether good or evil" (2 Cor 5:10). If we are only judged for what we have done, infants would seem to skate.[1]

However, the wilderness wandering may not be the best example for the age of accountability, as God spared every Israelite who was younger than twenty years old. Surely many of these teenagers were old enough to know right from wrong. And the demise of Achan's, Korah's, and Amalekite kids with their fathers suggests God would be just to include all children in the communal guilt of humanity. If we are paying attention, we notice it does not take long for infants to register their selfish bent. Augustine saw the shadow of depravity in nursing babes who jealousy refused to share their mother's abundant milk with a sibling. Wait a few months, and the child throws his first tantrum. We are born on a quest for control.[2]

Augustine reconciled God's justice and love for children in his doctrine of infant baptism. He believed the waters of baptism regenerated a child, so all baptized babies who died went immediately to heaven. This is comforting to

---

[1]   R. Albert Mohler and Daniel L. Akin, "The Salvation of the 'Little Ones,'" *Southern Seminary Magazine: The Tie* 74, no. 2 (Summer 2006): 4–5, https://albertmohler.com/2009/07/16/the-salvation-of-the-little-ones-do-infants-who-die-go-to-heaven. See also Ronald H. Nash, *When a Baby Dies* (Grand Rapids: Zondervan, 1999), 59–70; and John Piper, *Let the Nations Be Glad!* 3rd ed. (Grand Rapids: Baker Academic, 2010), 155–56.

[2]   Augustine, *Confessions* 1.vi (8)–vii (11), trans. Henry Chadwick (New York: Oxford, 1991), 7–9.

grieving parents—unless their babies died before receiving the water of life. Roman Catholic hospitals ease this problem by including holy water in their birthing rooms in case something goes wrong in delivery and emergency baptism is needed. The medieval church carved out a middle ground for deceased, unbaptized infants. They cannot go to heaven because of Adam's original sin, but they should not go to hell either, since their minds were not sufficiently developed to commit actual sin. The Western church popularly believed, though never proclaimed as official dogma, that these unfortunate babies went to *limbo infantum,* a sort of air-conditioned hell. Visit a medieval cemetery, and you will see infant graves lying in limbo, a middle space between the saved and the damned.

Covenant Kids?

Augustine's Roman Catholic solution does not work for me, a Baptist who believes in believer's baptism. Neither do I agree with some Reformed friends who variously suggest infant baptism presumes the child is born again or less, the child is elect and will someday be born again. I agree with my Reformed friends who say the child of a Christian parent belongs to the visible church, though I do not think baptism is necessary for this to be true.

I do appreciate Reformed theology's point about the special status of children who have a Christian parent. Peter told the very first Christians that "the promise is for you and for your children" (Acts 2:39), and Paul said the child of a believing parent is made holy because of that parent (1 Cor 7:14). We must not read too much into Paul's statement, as he also says a Christian makes his or her unbelieving spouse holy, and no responsible reader thinks this means the non-Christian spouse is saved. But we must not read too little into Paul's statement either. God sets the child of a Christian parent apart as holy and special to himself. This should instill confidence as we encourage grieving Christians that they will see their child someday.[3]

The Synod of Dort conveys a pitch-perfect note of cautious hope. This seventeenth-century council gave us the steely-eyed five points of Calvinism, so this was no sappy, tell-the-people-what-they-want-to-hear sort of gathering. And yet, when confronted with the difficult question of deceased infants, they said Christian parents "ought not to doubt" their child is resting in the arms of Jesus. Dort grounds its argument in the "gracious covenant" that includes Christian parents and their children.[4] While my Baptist convictions differ on

---

[3] We should not read too much into Peter's statement that "the promise is for you and for your children" (Acts 2:39). The promise is also "for all who are far off," presumably Gentiles who had not yet come to faith in Jesus. Peter is not guaranteeing that all Gentiles or every child of a believing parent will be saved, but only "as many as the Lord our God will call."

[4] *The Canons of Dort,* First Point, Article 17.

the covenant of grace (I baptize professing believers rather than children born into the covenant), Acts 2:39 and 1 Cor 7:14 give reason to think God extends his covenantal love to our children who die before they are able to express faith in Jesus. Regeneration normally coincides with saving faith, but God may take the extraordinary step of regenerating those who are unable to believe.

Where does this leave us? There is reason to think John MacArthur's position is correct. All babies who die go immediately to heaven. There is more reason to think the dying babies of a godly parent are instantly with our Lord. When David and Bathsheba's son died, he said, "I'll go to him, but he will never return to me" (2 Sam 12:23). David may only have meant his son had gone to Sheol, the realm of the dead, and someday David would die too. However, Second Temple Judaism believed Sheol had separate compartments for the saved and the damned, and perhaps this was already understood in David's time. He may have expected to join his son with the saved in Sheol, at "Abraham's side" (Luke 16:22).[5]

We do not have a slam dunk Bible verse that promises dead children are saved, and for good reason. Consider the horror that well-intentioned Christians would unleash on the world if God had promised that all babies who died went instantly to heaven. Wouldn't godly parents be tempted to kill their kids? Wouldn't some follow the iron logic to Hindu, Buddhist, and Muslim communities and kill other people's kids? Yes, that would be terrible, but why risk everlasting damnation? If we knew with certainty that every dead child would live forever on the new earth, how coldhearted must we be to let any of them live? This is why, when it comes to our children, God could not do more than drop encouraging hints. If he had promised what we have reason to suspect is true, not many of us would have lived to see our first birthday.

Application

This chapter's excruciating question wrestles our hearts to the ground, forcing us to treasure what we know while leaving open those questions God has not answered. As Moses was saying goodbye to the Israelites, he reminded them, "The hidden things belong to the LORD our God, but the revealed things belong to us and our children forever" (Deut 29:29). The question of where deceased babies go is partially hidden behind the love and justice of God. We must obediently leave this mystery with God, trusting the King of the world to do what is right. But what he has told us of his faithfulness and desire for our kids—these comforting truths belong to us and to our children, forever.

---

[5]   Matthew Y. Emerson, *He Descended to the Dead* (Downers Grove, IL: IVP, 2019), 30–33.

CHAPTER 29

———

Any Religion Will Save You as Long as You're Sincere

The Legendary Belief

Actor Will Smith suffered public backlash when he failed to heed Moses's lesson. Angered by a comedian's joke, Smith walked onto the Oscars stage and struck a Rock! His views on religion are equally concerning. Smith has said:

> I love the nature of humanity's search for meaning. For me I'm certain about my relationship with the model of perfection of human life that's laid out with the life of Jesus Christ. I'm certain of that. So I'm at home and not fearful when I sit in a mosque or a synagogue or a Buddhist temple, the same way that I'm home in the Church of Scientology. I like anywhere people are searching for the truth, and I respect their path and I'm intrigued by their path. . . . My grandmother raised me to be a do-gooder in the church, that it was about doing what you can to help your community. So whatever religion does that—Jewish, Muslim, Scientology—it's cool because the end result is the same.[1]

Smith's sentiment is popular in the West, even among professing Christians. Chapter 20 mentioned a recent survey that found more than 60 percent of born-again Christians believe others "can get to Heaven through their different religious belief." This tracks with other polls. The Pew Research Center discovered that 65 percent of American Christians believe other religions may provide salvation, and 80 percent of these could name one that did.[2] They

---

[1] Damian Romano, "The Gospel of Will Smith," *Christians in Context* (blog), December 18, 2008, http://www.christiansincontext.com/2008/12/gospel-of-will-smith.html; "Will Smith on Hollywood, Religion and Tom Cruise," interview with Allison Samuels, *Newsweek*, November 27, 2008, https://www.newsweek.com/will-smith-hollywood-religion-and-tom-cruise-85237.

[2] "Many Americans Say Other Faiths Can Lead to Eternal Life," Pew Research Center, December 18, 2008, https://www.pewforum.org/2008/12/18/many-americans-say-other-faiths-can-lead-to-eternal-life/.

apparently suppose that if you are sincere, more than one religion can save you.

Unraveling the Legend

When it comes to how and how many are saved, there are four general options. Here they are, from most permissive to most restrictive.

1. Universalism: Everyone will be saved in the end, regardless of what they believed or did during their lives on earth. Universalists fall into two camps: those who emphasize divine sovereignty and those who favor human freedom. The former suggest God will save everyone because his yes is stronger than our no (e.g., Karl Barth), while the latter say God will supply as many chances as needed in the afterlife until everyone returns to him (e.g., Origen). Universalism isn't as popular as you might think because most everyone can think of someone they expect to be in hell. At least Hitler.

2. Pluralism: Everyone who sincerely follows their religion will be saved by their religion, for each religion supplies its own path to God. Americans tend to prefer this option because it allows them to say no one is better than anyone else while still damning Hitleresque people to hell.

3. Inclusivism: Everyone who sincerely follows their religion will be saved by Jesus, whether they know and follow him or not. Many Christians prefer this option because it says Jesus is necessary for salvation while making room in the kingdom for people who live and die without hearing about him.

4. Exclusivism: Only those who knowingly follow Jesus are saved.[3] I believe this is what Scripture teaches. Before I say why, let's first break our urban legend into two parts: pluralism and its different but existentially similar neighbor, inclusivism.

Any Religion Will Save You

When people say any religion will save you, they might mean to include the tiny ones with a short shelf life, even the one your hippie uncle made up to evade the draft. But they usually have in mind the major world religions: Judaism, Christianity, Islam, Buddhism, Confucianism, Daoism, Shintoism, and Hinduism (sorry Wicca, not you). They say each of these religions contributes something important to our understanding of God, who is bigger than any one of them. Like blind people touching various parts of an elephant, each of us supplies a valuable piece of the whole. None of us should presume to understand the entire picture. And we definitely should not think our religion

---

[3]   This definition assumes mental ability. See the previous chapter for the exceptional cases of deceased infants and mentally disabled.

is better than another. And we most definitely should not say it. And we most, most definitely should not fight about it and seek to destroy the other religions so our God wins.

There is much that could be said in response to religious pluralism, but I will focus on four facts. First, the major world religions fall into three groups: (1) atheistic religions: Buddhism, Confucianism, Daoism, and Shintoism; (2) Hinduism; and (3) biblical religions: Judaism, Christianity, and Islam. The first category should eliminate itself for religious people. What kind of religion does not believe in God? How can that possibly lead to everlasting life? Atheistic religions are ultimately no better than modern secularism: we are alone in the world; no one is coming to save us. This leaves our choice between the second and third categories, the biblical religions and Hinduism.

Second, Hinduism is essentially the pluralist position. Pluralists are not high-minded idealists who rise above the religious fray. Their religious view is not bigger than all the rest but is in fact one of them. When *Newsweek* magazine covered religion in America, its writer recognized the United States as a nation of pluralists. She wrote, "We are slowly becoming more like Hindus and less like traditional Christians."[4] Religious pluralism is Hinduism, and Hinduism worships many gods. Which means none of them are God.

Third, this leaves the biblical religions as the only religions that claim to believe in a supreme, personal deity. If you believe in God, the only viable candidates are Judaism, Islam, and Christianity. You can choose Judaism, the religion fulfilled in Christianity; you can choose Islam, the latecomer that parodies and distorts Judeo-Christianity; or you can believe in the triune God who reveals himself in our Lord Jesus Christ. Christianity wins this hands down. As Peter told Jesus when asked if he would leave, "Lord, to whom will we go? You have the words of eternal life. We have come to believe and know that you are the Holy One of God" (John 6:68–69; see chapter 8 for a more detailed contrast of Christianity with Judaism and Islam).

Fourth, pluralism inevitably marginalizes Jesus. Pluralists assume they are being kind and generous to other people and their religious views. But here's the thing. It is impossible to open our arms to other faiths without pushing Jesus to the margins. If it is possible to be saved by any other way than Jesus, then Jesus and his death are not necessary. We might think it's nice that he gave his life for us, but if we can be saved by Krishna or Allah, then Jesus did not need to die. He gave his life for nothing.

---

[4] Lisa Miller, "U.S. Views on God and Life Are Turning Hindu," *Newsweek* (August 14, 2009), https://www.newsweek.com/us-views-god-and-life-are-turning-hindu-79073.

As Long as You're Sincere

So much for "other religions can save you." Christians cannot be religious pluralists, for Jesus said he is the only way to salvation (John 14:6). However, many Christians are inclusivists. They think they can stay true to Jesus's declaration while emphasizing the second part of the urban legend, "as long as you're sincere."

A notable example is the Roman Catholic Church. Its new catechism cites the church father Cyprian, "Outside the church there is no salvation." He continued that no one can have God as his Father who does not have the church as his mother, and he compared the church to Noah's Ark, the only place of safety in a world that was going to hell. Since the third century, the church has interpreted Cyprian as he intended: people must belong to the church to be saved. Contemporary Roman Catholicism does not like the exclusionary tone in Cyprian's words, so it puts a postmodern spin on his statement "Outside the church there is no salvation." The catechism explains, "Re-formulated positively, it means that all salvation comes from Christ the Head through the Church which is his Body. . . . This affirmation is not aimed at those who, through no fault of their own, do not know Christ and his Church."[5] The catechism quotes the Second Vatican Council: "Those who, through no fault of their own, do not know the Gospel of Christ or his Church, but who nevertheless seek God with a sincere heart, and, moved by grace, try in their actions to do his will as they know it through the dictates of their conscience—those too may achieve eternal salvation."[6]

The catechism gives examples. Jews, Muslims, and other religions are accepted by God if they are doing the best they can. Look how much we have in common! Jews have the Law and the Old Covenant and are waiting for the Messiah. Muslims "acknowledge the Creator," and other religions share in our common humanity and destiny with God. This looks suspiciously like pluralism, except for the church's insistence that Jesus is the only Savior. Everyone who is saved is saved by Jesus through his church, whether they know it or not.[7]

There is an important difference between pluralists and inclusivists. Pluralists say other religions can save you while inclusivists insist the only Savior is Jesus. But in the real world the line between these two views can become smudged and hard to make out. Both insist a good Muslim who does his religious best will be saved. Pluralists say he is saved by Allah while inclusivists say he is saved by Jesus. This is a significant difference, though it is easily lost

---

5   *Catechism of the Catholic Church,* §846–47, 224, website of the United States Conference of Catholic Bishops, https://www.usccb.org/sites/default/files/flipbooks/catechism/226/.

6   *Catechism,* §847, 224.

7   *Catechism,* §839–45, 222–24.

on the Muslim and those following his case. In both instances his devotion to Islam is what God rewards with salvation.

Immediately after insisting everyone is saved by doing their religious best, the Catholic catechism urges the church to send missionaries around the world. But why? If someone is saved because they worship the God who made the sun and the moon, why go and tell them more difficult information they might reject? Which is easier, to respond rightly to general revelation or to believe the specific historical facts about Jesus of Nazareth? I can imagine an islander saying he knows there is a God, but he is not convinced that Jesus is his Son. Now this man is going to hell. If inclusivism is correct, we should have left him alone. Some say he is better off to learn about Jesus now so he might enjoy his salvation before he dies. Sure, but is that worth risking everlasting damnation? Better to die in ignorance and rise to everlasting glory than to learn about Jesus, reject his story, and go to hell.

Our culture's pluralism has seeped into Roman Catholic and Protestant churches. Many lay Christians are functionally pluralists, while many priests and pastors stop one notch back, at inclusivism. Perhaps this double whammy explains why fewer Christians are compelled to evangelize or become missionaries. Why tell others about Jesus if belief in him is not necessary? Why tell others about Jesus if their rejection means they are now headed from heaven to hell? What kind of evil person would do that to somebody? Both pluralism and inclusivism ruin our missionary motivation.

Exclusivism

Exclusivism means that only those who believe in Jesus are saved. This label sounds negative, until you remember we are talking about a relationship. Intimate relationships must be exclusive to last. Husbands and wives who cheat will not stay married long. It is the same with Jesus. He demands our exclusive loyalty.

The last chapter cited biblical texts, such as John 3 and Rom 10:13–17, that state our need to know and believe in Jesus to be saved. The Spirit of God uses the Word of God to give birth to the children of God. Exclusivism is also implied throughout the book of Acts. Peter and Paul gave their lives to tell lost people about Jesus. Would they have made this sacrifice if they had been either pluralists or inclusivists? Paul's exclusivism appears even when he is not trying to make the point. In 1 Thess 2:16, he says God's wrath is falling on the Jewish leaders because they have been "keeping us from speaking to the Gentiles so that they may be saved." Paul's focus is on the Jewish opposition, but what is he assuming? If he does not tell the Gentiles about Jesus, they will not be saved.

Application

Daily life drains our attention. Our computer crashes and we fall behind at work. We come home and burn dinner or find mold growing in the shower. These are real problems, but we must not let them distract us from what is at stake. Everything is on the line. This life will determine where we will live forever, and with whom. Are you in Christ? Then you are okay, even on your worst day. Do you know someone who does not yet follow Jesus? Do not settle for small talk. Ask them if they know what they are playing for, and how to win.

CHAPTER 30

We Must "Preach the Gospel at All Times and If Necessary, Use Words"

The Legendary Belief

This popular phrase is commonly believed to have originated with Francis of Assisi. It sounds like something he might say, as his sermons emphasized a simple life of obedience. But we have no record that he ever said it. None of his disciples or early biographers report him using it. So, we do not know where the legend began. But if you have spent any time around Christians, there is a good chance you have heard someone say, "Preach the gospel at all times and if necessary, use words."

Unraveling the Legend

The legend is popular because it reminds us that our deeds must match our creeds. Few things are more infuriating than hypocrisy: people who talk a good game about loving Jesus and neighbor but exhibit no evidence that they think much about either. Our walk must match our talk. This is true. But we must elevate the former without diminishing the latter. There is only one way to preach the gospel. If we are going to tell people the good news about Jesus, we will have to use our words.

What Is the Gospel?

This is a relatively easy question because God answers it directly. The Spirit through and with Paul told the Corinthians, "I want to make clear for you, brothers and sisters, the gospel I preached to you, which you received, on which you have taken your stand and by which you are being saved" (1 Cor 15:1–2). Notice the gospel is something that Paul "preached" to the Corinthians. It was something they "received," not something they achieved. Paul did not think the Corinthians could share the gospel by how they lived, only using their words in a pinch. *Oh no! My lifestyle is not communicating the gospel effectively. I guess I have to add my words!* Paul thought words were the only way to share the gospel.

Why? Because the gospel is the good news that "Christ died for our sins according to the Scriptures, that he was buried, that he was raised on the third day according to the Scriptures, and that he appeared to Cephas, then to the Twelve" (1 Cor 15:3–5). The gospel is the message about what Jesus has done. How would anyone communicate that by their actions? We might impress others with our prompt service and cheerful demeanor, but no amount of goodwill would lead someone to guess the particular, historical facts about Jesus of Nazareth. There is no way to get from "Tom is a good neighbor" to "Jesus is the Son of God who came to earth and lived a perfect life and was crucified and rose again to forgive my sin." If Tom wants to communicate that part, he must use his words.

Of course, having told people the good news about Jesus, our sacrificial love adds credence to the message. Others can see what difference Jesus makes in our lives and note that we seem to sincerely believe and follow him. But our good works cannot replace our words about Jesus. Only Jesus is the good news. You and I are not the good news. We are not good; we are not even news.

The good news of Jesus not only requires our words; it inspires them too. What do you do when you have exceptionally good news? How did you notify your parents that your child was born? You did not send a text, "Congratulations, Mom and Dad. You are grandparents." Smiley emoji. No, you used the call function on your phone. You were excited to verbally tell them about the birth of your child. That is the right way to share this moment, to express your joy and hear their joy in return. Good news is meant to be spoken.

Martin Luther said this is why the gospel inspires preaching. Form follows function, so the Old Covenant Law was meant to be written. Nothing is lost when we read God's rules and judgment on our sins. But the new wine of the gospel breaks out of the old wineskin. The good news about Jesus cannot be contained in written form. It must be publicly proclaimed in worship services that invite participants to respond aloud in prayers and songs. Luther explained, "And the gospel should really not be something written, but a spoken word which brought forth the Scriptures, as Christ and the apostles have done. This is why Christ himself did not write anything but only spoke. He called his teaching not Scripture but gospel, meaning good news or a proclamation that is spread not by pen but by word of mouth."[1]

---

[1]   Martin Luther, "A Brief Instruction on What to Look for and Expect in the Gospels (1521)," in *Martin Luther's Basic Theological Writings,* 3rd ed., ed. Timothy F. Lull and William R. Russell (Minneapolis: Fortress, 2012), 75.

Preach the gospel without words? Not if we have the slightest idea what Jesus has done for us.

The Gospel of the Kingdom

Some Christians mistakenly include our good works in the gospel because they misunderstand our role in the kingdom of God. They read that "Jesus went to Galilee, proclaiming the good news of God: 'The time is fulfilled, and the kingdom of God has come near. Repent and believe the good news!'" (Mark 1:15). They wrongly infer that if the gospel includes the coming of the kingdom, then kingdom living must be part of the gospel.

Chapter 37 will say more about the kingdom, how it is something we receive from Jesus rather than something we do for him. Now it is enough to note that our life in the kingdom is not itself the good news. The good news, said Jesus, is that the kingdom has come. The good news is not what you and I have done. Our good works for the kingdom are our Spirit-fueled response to the kingdom's arrival. The arrival is the good news; not what we do after it has arrived. Our efforts are the necessary fruit of the gospel, yet they never replace the gospel. We must care for creation, serve the poor, and fight injustice, but these are not called gospel anywhere in Scripture. The gospel is not what you and I do for Jesus. The gospel is solely what Jesus has done, is doing, and will do for us.

When we smuggle our works into the gospel, we distract from Jesus and replace what is essential with what is merely good. Like Martha, who was angry with her sister for sitting at Jesus's feet rather than helping in the kitchen, we may hear from our Lord, "You are worried and upset about many things, but one thing is necessary. Mary has made the right choice, and it will not be taken away from her" (Luke 10:41–42). My good works cannot save. Your good works cannot save. Only Jesus saves.

Deeds, Not Creeds?

The message about Jesus and what he has done is told in stories, and the gist of these stories is communicated in the church's creeds. The Apostles' Creed tells the story of Jesus, who "was conceived by the Holy Spirit and born of the virgin Mary. He suffered under Pontius Pilate, was crucified, died, and was buried; he descended to hell. The third day he rose again from the dead. He ascended to heaven and is seated at the right hand of God the Father almighty. From there he will come to judge the living and the dead."

Faithful churches treasure this creed and the gospel it presents. But some churchgoers fear a preoccupation with the finer points of doctrine might cause division and distract us from serving our neighbor and doing good in the world. They use the slogan "Deeds, Not Creeds" to encourage professing Christians to set aside their doctrinal differences and unite with others for the common good. An extreme example is the Unitarian Universalist Association, which leverages "deeds, not creeds" to partner with people of all faiths to "work for a better world . . . as we harness love's power to stop oppression."[2]

This tactic overlooks the fact that no one loves from nowhere. Our deeds are driven by creeds; our actions are determined by what we believe. Everyone agrees we should love others, but what that means depends on what we think is true. If truth is person specific, so that each person is free to speak and live his or her own truth, then love requires us to cater to the whims of every individual. To use a severe but increasingly common example, if Sally's truth is that she is a man, a loving doctor will prescribe opposite sex hormones and perform radical surgeries in a futile attempt to make her into something she can never be. But if truth comes from God and is embedded in natural law, a loving doctor will prescribe counseling to help Sally accept herself and her sex as God's gift. This option may be mocked and possibly punished in Western culture, but we are beginning to hear stories of deep regret from transgender people whose broken bodies cannot be made whole.

We must not pit doctrine against ethics, as if too much of the former might squeeze out the latter. Doctrine drives ethics. Truth motivates and informs love. Have you noticed that you could draw a line down the middle of many of Paul's epistles? The first half is creed; the second half is deed. Paul begins by telling us the good news about Jesus; he ends by showing how this gospel compels us to love better and truer.

Application

If the gospel is what Jesus has done for us rather than what we do for him, then the key to the Christian life is resting in Jesus. We rest in Jesus in good times and bad, both when we succeed and when we fail. How comforting to rest in Jesus when we are driven to our knees in guilt and shame! How necessary to rest in Jesus when we are praised! Jesus alone is the good news, which is the relief we have been waiting for. If Jesus is the good news, we don't have to be. We can call it a day and go to bed, resting wholly in him.

---

[2] Unitarian Universalist Association, "Justice and Inclusion," https://www.uua.org/justice.

Suburban Legend

"Evangelism distracts from social justice."

Progressive churchgoers warn that conservative Christians' concern to tell others that Jesus died for their sin prevents them from joining the fight for racial, sexual, and economic justice. We are so focused on avoiding everlasting damnation in hell that we neglect to help victims escape their present suffering on earth.

I expect many Christians feel this tension to some extent. We are finite people with limited resources, and it is hard to care for a person's spiritual and physical needs at the same time. At any given moment we may be leading a Bible study or stocking a food pantry, but not both. I appreciate how one Christian ministry expresses the tension. It says evangelism and justice are two sides of the same coin, and we must continually flip the coin. We must care for the whole person, with all his assorted needs.

But evangelism and justice are not merely in tension. Evangelism aims to make disciples, and disciples fight for what is right and defend those who cannot protect themselves. The more people in a community follow Jesus, the less crime and abuse there should be. It was Christians who led the fight to end slavery. This is not a cure-all, as Christians remain sinners (and far too many owned slaves), but the best way to improve justice in your town is to bring people to Jesus and teach them his ways.

CHAPTER 31

———

God Helps Those Who Help Themselves

The Legendary Belief

This sentence may be the most quoted "Scripture" that is not in the Bible. It sounds so right, so American, we assume God must have said it. A Barna survey found 52 percent of practicing Christians strongly agree the Bible teaches "God helps those who help themselves."[1] But it doesn't. The line was attributed to Ben Franklin in the 1757 edition of *Poor Richard's Almanac.* It may have originated earlier, with Algernon Sydney's 1698 article, *Discourses Concerning Government.* Regardless of its origin, is it true? Does God help those who help themselves?

Unraveling the Legend

Not when it comes to salvation. There is an essential difference between the help God provides for salvation and the help he provides for general self-improvement. Social workers know the best way to lift someone out of poverty is to give them a hand up. Provide scholarships so they can go to school, seed loans to start a business, and affordable day care so they can manage work and parenting. Help them earn their way, and they will build confidence as they become financially independent.

But what works for social and economic improvement is lethal for salvation. We need infinitely more than a hand up to be accepted by God. We need a handout. God must do everything. The whole enchilada; the kit and the caboodle. God only helps those who cannot help themselves. Here's why.

---

1   "Competing Worldviews Influence Today's Christians," Barna, May 9, 2017, https://www.barna.com/research/competing-worldviews-influence-todays-christians/.

Pelagius

Pelagius was an early adopter of the urban legend "God helps those who help themselves." A fifth-century British monk, he was offended by the lackadaisical Christianity that accompanied its popularity as the empire's state-sponsored faith. He doubted socialite Christians were even saved, as they made no effort to be holy. They sat around waiting for God to change them. Pelagius said that when challenged by God's commands, they cry, "It's hard! It's difficult! We can't! We are but men, encompassed by the frailty of the flesh!"[2]

Pelagius gave them a kick in the pants. He said we need three things to do what is right: the power or capacity, the will, and the act. The power comes from God and is never lost. The will and the act of doing good are both up to us. Because our capacity to obey God remains in us, we never lose the ability to choose and follow his commands. We may seem hopelessly shackled by habitual sin, but if we wake up sick and tired of our miserable condition, we can choose to turn it around. Why not start today?[3]

While in Rome Pelagius attended a public reading of Augustine's *Confessions* and was outraged when he heard Augustine's prayer, "O charity, my God, set me on fire. You command continence; grant what you command, and command what you will."[4] Give me the ability to obey and I will do whatever you say. Pelagius thought, *That's the problem!* So many Christians think they cannot obey God unless he does it for them. He wrote, "What blind folly! What rash profanity! We make the God of knowledge guilty of twofold ignorance: of not knowing what he has made, and of not knowing what he has commanded."[5] God is our Creator, so he knows what we are capable of. If he commands us to be holy, he expects us to do it. No excuses. He has given us everything we need; now it is up to us.

Pelagius explained what God has given in his treatise *On Nature*. He said our Creator gave us healthy minds and free wills to choose what is right, the commands of Scripture to know what is right, and the example of Jesus to show us how it is done. Should we mess up and sin, we can ask God to forgive us, and he will. But though we need his grace for past blunders, we do not need any special grace in the present. Our Creator has equipped us with everything we need to obey him. If we are not holy, it is our fault. We only need to try harder.

---

[2] "Pelagius: Letter to Demetrias, 414," in *Creeds, Councils and Controversies,* 272 (see chap. 24, n. 1).

[3] "Pelagius' Doctrine of Human Freedom," in *Creeds, Councils and Controversies,* 270.

[4] Augustine, *Confessions,* Book 10.xxix (40), trans. Henry Chadwick (New York: Oxford, 1991), 202.

[5] "Pelagius: Letter to Demetrias," 272.

Augustine

Augustine responded to Pelagius with his essay *On Nature and Grace*. Nature is not enough. We also need grace, far more than Pelagius thought. Augustine said Pelagius properly praised our good natures that our Creator bestowed, but Pelagius forgot they are no longer good. Adam's sin has corrupted and spoiled our minds and wills, so we are born morally unable to keep God's commands. Using a pedestrian example, Augustine said it is easy for humans with "healthy feet" to walk. "But if their feet are broken, they do not have that ability, even if they will to walk. That nature has been injured . . . it begs the physician" to infuse the medicine of grace so they can be healed. Only repaired feet can walk; only repaired wills can choose and do what is right.[6]

Pelagius's teaching sounds uplifting. It inspires people to believe in themselves. *Up with people! You can do it!* But what if they can't? Pelagius compared our ability to do good to our ability to see. It is ludicrous for a person with healthy eyes to close them and complain they cannot see. They certainly should not blame God. *You can't see? Open your eyes already!* Augustine agreed our blindness is not God's fault. Adam's fall and our sin have blinded us to God's truth. The fault lies in us. But that does not change the fact that we are blind.

The debate between Pelagius and Augustine turns on humanity's condition after the fall. How healthy are we? If we have sound eyes and feet, Pelagius's encouragement to try harder is all we need to get going. But if we are blind and crippled, his cheering is cruel. We would not applaud for a blind person reading an eye chart, thinking if we clap louder he would be able to focus and tell us what he sees. We would not pat a paraplegic on the back. *Do you believe you can run? We believe you can run! Now get up and win this race!* That is not being inspirational. That is being a jerk.

God says we all "were dead in [our] trespasses and sins" (Eph 2:1). What can a dead man do? Not a lot. We can give him a standing ovation, read an inspiring poem, and put speakers in his casket that blast "Eye of the Tiger." We will not get a response. Similarly, we were spiritually dead until "God, who is rich in mercy, because of his great love that he had for us, made us alive with Christ even though we were dead in trespasses. You are saved by grace!" (vv. 4–5). If God helps those who help themselves, he will help nobody. Our rotting corpses are unable to lift a pinky finger in God's direction, and we look less promising by the day. If spiritually dead people are going to be saved, it is because the God who raises the dead has called their name and done for them what they are wholly unable to do for themselves.

---

6   Augustine, "Nature and Grace," chap. 50, 57, trans. Roland J. Teske, ed. John E. Rotelle, in *Answer to the Pelagians: The Works of Saint Augustine: A Translation for the 21st Century* (New York: New City, 1997), 250, 254.

Who Moves?

The defining question between Pelagius and Augustine is who is the mover in salvation? Who is ultimately responsible? Pelagius said it was us. God gives us a healthy nature and the commands of Scripture, then leaves it up to us. Augustine said this was heresy because it did not contain enough grace. We cannot save ourselves simply by choosing and doing what is right. We need the Holy Spirit to change our hearts and compel us to follow Christ. Augustine declared that God is the sole mover of salvation. From start to finish, our salvation rests in his hands. We must "work out [our] own salvation with fear and trembling," but we do so while relying on God, "who is working in [us] both to will and to work according to his good purpose" (Phil 2:12–13). We must strive, but all our efforts depend on God, who efficaciously calls us to himself and carries us across the finish line.

We are speaking solely of salvation. If our minds are strong enough, we can help ourselves break addictions, tamp down anxiety, and perform at our personal best. Willpower can accomplish much. But not when it comes to salvation. There we are spiritually dead, utterly unable to help ourselves.

Pelagianism is a known heresy, but a milder form of "God helps those who help themselves" has been accepted by multitudes of Christians. In the late Middle Ages, Franciscan theologians said, "To the one who does what is in him, God will not deny grace." Do what you can. Show up at church and receive the sacraments, and the grace that is in them will save you. This Semi-Pelagian view says there are two movers of salvation, God and us, and we come first. We cannot save ourselves. We need grace. But we can take the first move and reach for it.

An interesting and understandably controversial question is where to place Arminianism. This Protestant view says that before the world began, God chose for salvation those he knew would later choose him. God does not force anyone to follow Jesus; he gives everyone a general, prevenient grace that overcomes their depravity and enables them to choose him if they want. Arminians say God is the first mover of salvation because his election occurred in eternity past and his prevenient grace precedes our faith. However, some argue that since Arminians base God's election on his foreknowledge he is logically responding to our choice. God's eternal election is chronologically first, but our temporal choice is logically first. And though God's prevenient grace does precede our faith, it is easily resisted by most people and so may not count as a sufficiently robust first move. There are reasons for saying Arminianism is Semi-Pelagian (two movers, and we move first) and reasons for saying it is Semi-Augustinian (two movers, and God moves first). Arminians make fine Christians, but I believe it is biblical and more comforting to rest in the security of Augustine's view. There is one mover of salvation, and it is God. He will carry me home.

Application

It is dangerous to end this chapter with application. That is just the sort of thing Pelagius would do. He urged Christians to try harder and do more, so he loved when sermons closed with homework. Applications are particularly dangerous for Americans because Pelagianism is the quintessential American heresy. It is our default position. We are practical, get-it-done people. Do not bore us with abstract theory or highfalutin philosophy. Show us the cash value. Give us five steps to a better you; seven tips for intimacy with God; three things to do before next Sunday. Keep us busy, and we'll think we are getting ahead.

Applications are good. This book has nearly forty of them. But every now and again, and this is one of those times, it is helpful not to end with next steps. The application is there is no application. There is nothing more to do. Just stop. Put your book down and go to bed. As you transfer your weight to the mattress, imagine yourself putting all your weight on Jesus. The secret to salvation and the key to life are the same. Are you resting in him?

CHAPTER 32

Justification Means Just-as-If-I'd-Never-Sinned

The Legendary Belief

My Sunday school teachers used memory devices to plant God's truth into my little mind. They worked, because I still remember them decades later. They taught me that JOY comes from pursuing this order: Jesus, Others, You; GRACE means God's Riches at Christ's Expense; atonement makes us "at-one" with God; and justification is the clean slate I receive when I put my faith in Jesus. It is "just-as-if-I'd-never-sinned."

Unraveling the Legend

Now that I am older, I have learned to be suspicious of formulas that work only in English. The Spanish word for "joy" is *alegría*, which sounds like something that relieves allergies, and the Arabic term for "grace" is *niemat aw waqt samah*. The acrostics for joy and grace would look noticeably different in these languages! Still, the expression for justification says something important. When we put our faith in Jesus, God forgives our sin so we stand innocent before him. But our status is more complex than "just-as-if-I'd-never-sinned." The fact is we did sin, in high-handed and selfish ways that deserve hell. This must not be glibly waved away.

Sinful Me

"Just-as-if-I'd-never-sinned" risks minimizing my sinful past, my continuing sin in the present, and what must happen to me as a result. What would we make of a shooter who, forgiven by his victims' families, said, "Thank you for your grace! I feel so free! It's just as if I hadn't done any of this!" Wouldn't the grieving families have to forgive him all over again? Or consider a bomber who whistles as he walks through his city's smoldering rubble, smiling at the collapsed buildings because he knows in his heart that he has been forgiven. Isn't he a psychopath? A normal person takes the damage he has caused to heart. He knows it can never be just-as-if-he'd-never-sinned. Too many people have suffered at his hands.

Similarly, we have wounded others by our words and actions—sometimes recklessly and sometimes on purpose—and we continue to do so. Praise God that he stands ready "to forgive us our sins and to cleanse us from all unrighteousness" (1 John 1:9). But forgiving the past does not erase the past. And that is a good thing. If our past offenses could be whitewashed away, we might forget our desperate need for Jesus. Like Pelagius, we might thank Jesus for dying for our past sin and assume we can take it from here.

The severity of our sin requires an equally severe response. It is gloriously true that Jesus died in our place. But that does not mean we do not also have to die. Paul wrote, "I have been crucified with Christ, and I no longer live, but Christ lives in me" (Gal 2:20). Justification requires crucifixion: the shameful death of our old self so our new self can rise with Jesus. Paul explains:

> Or are you unaware that all of us who were baptized into Christ Jesus were baptized into his death? Therefore we were buried with him by baptism into death, in order that, just as Christ was raised from the dead by the glory of the Father, so we too may walk in newness of life. For if we have been united with him in the likeness of his death, we will certainly also be in the likeness of his resurrection. For we know that our old self was crucified with him so that the body ruled by sin might be rendered powerless so that we may no longer be enslaved to sin. (Rom 6:3–6)

Eleven times in the first fourteen verses of Romans 6 we read that we have died and/or are buried with Christ. Karl Barth picked up this thread and said, "That Jesus Christ died for us does not mean, therefore, that we do not have to die, but that we have died in and with him, that as the people we were we have been done away and destroyed, that we are no longer there and have no more future."[1]

There is no salvation without judgment. We are judged in Christ, and so graciously forgiven, but we are still judged. Our old self that identified with the pride and selfishness of the First Adam must be buried so our new self can rise with the Last Adam (Rom 5:12–21). I once preached a dreadful Christmas sermon entitled "The Baby Is a Killer." I noted how many people fear the second coming of Christ, when he returns to judge the world with fire. They much prefer the cuddly infant in the cozy manger, cooing at his mommy and kicking his

---

[1] Karl Barth, *Church Dogmatics* IV/1, ed. G. W. Bromiley and T. F. Torrance, trans. G. W. Bromiley (Edinburgh: T&T Clark, 1956), 295.

chubby little legs. They lean in for a closer look. Be careful! This tiny bundle of Christmas joy has come to take us out. Barth said the baby's arrival means "our hour has struck, our time has run its course, and it is all up with us."[2] Two thousand years ago Jesus came to earth to destroy us. When he returns he will finish the job. Our old self will be dead and gone, and our new, glorified self will rise to live forever. Then the ancient prophecy will come true, "Death has been swallowed up in victory" (1 Cor 15:54).

Just-as-if-I'd-never-sinned? No. More like "Just-as-if-I've-sinned, been judged and condemned for it, and risen with Jesus to new life!"

Righteous Jesus

We should not expect too much of slogans. It is hard to say everything that needs to be said in a pithy saying. In light of that, this next critique may be a bit unfair. Still, it is worth noting that "Just-as-if-I'd-never-sinned" covers only one side of what Martin Luther called "the joyous exchange." When we put our faith in Jesus, we become one with him, and we share what each other has. As a husband and wife combine finances—his car loan becomes hers and her student loan becomes his, his checking account becomes hers and her retirement account becomes his—so God assigns our deficits to Jesus and his earned righteousness to us.

Thank God that our sin, guilt, and shame are rolled onto Jesus. He dragged them down with him into the grave, and when he rose, he left them in the dust. "As far as the east is from the west, so far has he removed our transgressions from us" (Ps 103:12). But God has done even more. He not only forgives our sin, raising us from bankruptcy to zero; he also credits the righteousness that Jesus earned to our account. We are more than forgiven; we are flush with cash. We stand before God as righteous as Jesus. Who can fathom this?

The Bible does not explicitly say God imputes Jesus's righteousness to us, but it is implicit in our union with Christ and in Paul's desire to know Jesus. What else could Paul mean by wanting to "gain Christ and be found in him, not having a righteousness of my own from the law, but one that is through faith in Christ—the righteousness from God based on faith" (Phil 3:8–9). Paul fears standing before God clothed in his own righteousness; he knows he will not survive unless he is clothed with the righteousness of Jesus. And he is (cf. Zech 3:1–5).

Just as if I'd never sinned? No. Our salvation is infinitely better than that. It is "Just-as-if-I've-lived-perfectly-righteous."

---

2   Barth, 294.

Application

The topic of justification raises issues of justice and fairness. God is not fair. Jesus told parables that made this point. He said God is like a father who ran down the road when his prodigal son returned. He embraced his boy, forgave him for squandering his inheritance, and threw a party. This did not sit well with the elder son, who angrily denounced his dad in front of the village: "Look, I have been slaving many years for you, and I have never disobeyed your orders, yet you never gave me a goat so that I could celebrate with my friends. But when this son of yours came, who has devoured your assets with prostitutes, you slaughtered the fattened calf for him" (Luke 15:28–30). Jesus also said the kingdom of heaven is like a landowner who paid vineyard workers the same wage whether they worked all day or just one hour. When the best workers complained, the owner said he had the right to spend his money however he wanted and they agreed on their wage. Then he added this zinger: "Are you jealous because I'm generous?" (Matt 20:15).

God is not fair, but he is just. God never gives anyone less than they deserve—except Jesus—and he gives the rest of us a whole lot more. It is not fair that Jesus became "sin for us, so that in him we might become the righteousness of God" (2 Cor 5:21). It is not fair that Jesus suffered an excruciatingly painful and shameful death so we might live forever. It is not fair that Jesus bore the wrath of God so we might escape the hell we deserve. None of this is fair. But it is good, and it is love.

Life is unfair. Thank God. We pray for justice and grace, but the combination of these must be unfair, at least to Jesus. God must punish Jesus to maintain justice and create space for grace. Pray for justice and grace, but never ask God to be fair. It is not what you need—or want.

Mini Myth

"Jesus is my Savior but not my Lord."

The relation between faith and works is a recurring issue in Protestant churches. Some Christians so fear adding works to salvation that they insist Jesus can be their Savior without being their Lord. They are saved when they put their faith in Jesus as Savior. Whether or not they repent and submit to Jesus as Lord is a later, and optional, decision.

This begs the question, *What do we think Jesus saves us from?* The angel told Joseph to name his Son "Jesus, because he will save his people from their sins" (Matt 1:21). Not merely from the penalty of their sins, but from their sins, period. It is hard to say with a straight face that Jesus saves us from sin when we are wallowing in its filth, burying our head in its muck, and have no desire to change. We are like a drowning man who yells for an anchor, a man on fire who grabs for lighter fluid, or a man in the cardiac unit who orders a bacon double cheeseburger and a chocolate malt. How exactly are we "saved"?

Conversion means to change, and it naturally includes both faith and repentance. Faith describes our turning toward Jesus, and repentance describes our turning away from sin. It is the same turn, viewed from complementary perspectives. Both are necessary. Try turning toward something without turning away from something else. You will wrench your back! Similarly, those who attempt faith without repentance will need a spiritual chiropractor. We cannot claim Jesus as Savior without claiming him as Lord. No one is that limber.

Who is our Savior? The Lord Jesus Christ.

How are we saved? By believing "in the Lord Jesus" (Acts 16:31). "If you confess with your mouth, 'Jesus is Lord,' and believe in your heart that God raised him from the dead, you will be saved" (Rom 10:9).

___

CHAPTER 33

We Should Not Be Motivated by Fear

The Legendary Belief

Popular wisdom says we should not be motivated by fear. It is too negative. Fear might rouse short-term success, but it drains our energy over the long run. We become too conservative, playing not to lose rather than to win. And when we do win, we feel relief rather than the joy of accomplishment. Scared people are seldom happy.

And they are often alone. Fear shuts out the world. Frightened folks suffer the inevitable suffocation that smothers loners obsessed with their own safety. They would be much happier if they chose love. This positive emotion inspires us to focus on what we can give rather than what we might lose. So, even if our task ends poorly and we are not as successful as we had wished, our mental health will be okay.

Some Christians take this cultural wisdom to heart. They shake their heads at fellow believers who monitor their kids' Internet usage and do not give them cell phones. They say rather than live in fear of the world, we should teach our children to embrace the world for Jesus. Other Christians say we should not use fear when talking to people about Jesus. We may suspect they are headed for hell, but we do not want to "sell fire insurance," manipulating them with images of fiery torment. We prefer that people come to Jesus for noble, positive reasons.

Unraveling the Legend

There is one large rebuttal to this claim that we should never be motivated by fear: Jesus.

He told his disciples, "Don't let your heart be troubled," so he did not want them paralyzed by fear (John 14:1). But he did encourage a wary, discerning distance from the world. He said, "If the world hates you, understand that it hated me before it hated you. . . . However, because you are not of the world, but I have chosen you out of it, the world hates you. . . . If they persecuted me, they will also persecute you" (John 15:18–20). Jesus does not want us to be terrified of persecution, but he thinks we should be on guard and avoid it if possible. Right until the end, just minutes before his arrest, he asked his Father for any other way than the cross that might save us. If so, "take this cup away from me" (Luke 22:42). Jesus was willing to suffer, but he did not go looking for it. Neither do we. We are Christians, not masochists.

Even more, Jesus believes we should fear sin. Unlike Christians who indiscriminately watch R-rated movies because we are called to know and love the world, the Bible distinguishes the "world" as a valuable group of image-bearing people from the "world" as a gnarled jumble of predatory sins. God loves the people of the world (John 3:16) yet commands us not to love the sin of the world. He warns, "Do not love the world or the things in the world. . . . For everything in the world—the lust of the flesh, the lust of the eyes, and the pride in one's possessions—" are sins (1 John 2:15–16). We should fear lest they turn our hearts from our heavenly Father and destroy us with our own lusts.

Jesus also used fear to motivate people to follow him. We may not want to "sell fire insurance," but Jesus did. No one in the Bible spoke more about hell, and more forcefully, than Jesus. He frightened his listeners with the story of the rich man who was tormented in hell, begging Abraham, "Send Lazarus to dip the tip of his finger in water and cool my tongue, because I am in agony in this flame!" (Luke 16:24). Jesus described hell as "outer darkness" crawling with undying worms, searing with "unquenchable fire," and shrieking with "weeping and gnashing of teeth" (Matt 25:30; Mark 9:43, 48). He said hell is so awful it is worth mutilating yourself—cutting off your hand or foot or gouging out your eye if doing so would keep you from everlasting torment (Mark 9:43–47). Jesus came to save us from hell, and he was not above using fear to do it.

Fear Is Your Friend

In a fallen world, every gift of creation presents an accompanying danger. The flickering flame that heats our stove or supplies an aura of romance can burn our fingers or catch our drapes on fire. The electricity that brews coffee and irons shirts can electrocute if we stick a knife in the socket or curl our hair in the tub. The car that takes us to work can take away lives in a single, distracted instant. The sex that binds us to our spouse and produces the next generation will destroy those who pursue it outside the bonds of marriage. The higher the benefit—the more power a created or cultural gift offers—the more easily and fatally we can be injured. This high-reward–high-risk calculus is why we childproof our homes, talk to our teenagers about the dangers of driving and premarital sex, and vote to keep the nuclear power plant out of our backyard.

In each case, wisdom attempts to balance thankful enjoyment with appropriate fear. People with no fear of anything tend to not live long, while people with overwrought fear—who catastrophize about things that are unlikely to happen—do not live well. If you are a senior citizen who needs an electric recliner but are afraid to buy one lest the power goes out; a teenager who avoids parties because you might say something dumb; or a conspiracy theorist who does not have an Internet connection because that is how "they" get you, you are making life harder than it has to be. Get the chair, go to the party, and do your banking online. It is going to be okay, as long as your password is not "password."

This is the classic tension between fight and flight. If your instinct is to fight, like my little Bichon Maltese dog, you will get mauled unless you have attentive owners who pick you up and walk away. Those who always lean in get punched in the mouth. If your instinct is flight, you will likely live longer but you may lose your purpose. What is the point of preserving our lives if we never spend them on something we believe in? So, Christians, while not seeking persecution, may choose to stop running and become martyrs—a word that means "witnesses"—for their faith. How better to pledge our allegiance than to give our lives for Jesus?

Godly Motivation

Fear is not our only motivation. It is not even first. But it has a vital role in the Christian life. The Bible teaches three primary motivations: hope, fear, and gratitude. Perhaps you think love should top this list, or at least make it. I agree that love is the heart of the Christian life. The greatest command is to love God and our neighbor as ourselves (Matt 22:36–40). Love is what Christians do. But why? What motivates our love? Hope, fear, and gratitude. And the greatest of these is hope.

God leads with hope, which simply means faith in our promised future. God promised the children of Israel if they believed they would enter and thrive in the Promised Land (Deut 28:1–14). He promises us if we believe we will have everlasting life, union with Christ, and become the children of God who will live forever with him on the new earth. Our Father moves our hearts by promising a glorious future far beyond what our finite minds can imagine.

God leads with hope and closes the back door with fear. He warned Israel if they broke faith and disobeyed, they would suffer devastating curses and be ripped out of the land (vv. 15–68). He warns us that anyone "whose name was not found written in the book of life" will be "thrown into the lake of fire" (Rev 20:15). God offers us himself and the world, then warns of the catastrophe that awaits those who refuse to believe and obey. The options could not be starker and more substantial, so God employs the largest hope and the biggest fear. It is not possible to oversell either end. The high could not be higher and the low could not be lower.

Evangelical preachers should imitate God and include fear in our gospel presentations. Some speak only of hope: follow Jesus so you will live forever, fill the God-sized hole in your heart, and overflow with love for others. But what if our listeners do not repent and believe? What then? If we remain silent about hell, we communicate that at worst our listeners will remain unhappy and unfulfilled. Their God-sized hole will never be filled, they will never know true love, and they will never become all they could be. But the consequences of not following Jesus are infinitely worse! Our choice is not between everlasting life and nothing. It is between everlasting life and hell. If we love and respect people, we will tell them.

We who run to Jesus in hope and away from hell in fear are bursting with gratitude. Who can grasp the glory of our promised future? Who can fathom the horrors we escaped? Who can give enough thanks for our great salvation? We will never comprehend the depth of these motivations, but we will reach forward in hope, run away in fear, and rejoice in gratitude for the grace that delivered us from the worst possible outcome and brought us the very best.

Application

Christians who are too noble to be motivated by fear are too pious by half. Sometimes fear is the most fitting motivation. If you see a bear in the woods, it is not a good time to say, "I choose not to be motivated by base passions, such as fear. I choose to be motivated by love, the highest emotion." You may choose love—but the bear might choose lunch!

Similarly, when you feel the flames of hell licking at your legs and your sin pulling you in, your hair should stand on end. Do not worry that your motives may not be the best. Just get out of there. Jesus accepts impure motives—he died to forgive them too. He is not so pious that he will not accept you unless your motives are perfect. He spoke most about hell, so he does not mind if you love him now for what he saves you from. He is humble enough to start where you are, gently leading you until you love him for who he is and long for the day when you see him face-to-face. Your fear is not misplaced, though in time it will be displaced by the higher motivations of hope and gratitude.

Mini Myth

"Free grace encourages sin."

If this chapter's urban legend minimizes fear, this mini myth goes the other way and makes too much of it. It implies we must not let the followers of Jesus get too comfortable. If we tell them grace is free, they are liable to turn it into a license to sin. I understand this concern, but if we lose either part, the grace or the free, we lose the good news of Jesus.

How do we preach free grace without encouraging sin? Chapter 25 explained how grace produces gratitude, which is a sign we are saved. Have you given someone a card with cash and not received a thank you? It made you wonder whether they opened the card or perhaps lost it. Maybe they didn't see the money. Our gratitude to our heavenly Father is evidence that we have opened his gift. Thanksgiving is a sign of our salvation; we express it by avoiding sin and doing what pleases him.

What about the free part? Well, have you noticed things can be free for two vastly different reasons? Some things are free because they are worthless, like a box of VHS tapes at a garage sale. The whole box is free because no one wants them. Whatever is left is going in the trash. Other things are free because they are priceless. What value would you assign to your love for your spouse or child? What price would you sell your love for? You wouldn't. You couldn't. Your love for them is not for sale. You can only give it away for free.

Some things are free because they are worthless; some things are free because they are priceless. Which kind of free is God's love? God says he paid for us, "not with perishable things like silver or gold, but with the precious blood of Christ" (1 Pet 1:18–19). Our salvation cost God too much to be anything but free. When we remember why grace is free, we will be much less tempted to take advantage of it, to use its price as an excuse to sin. Salvation must be free because it cost Jesus everything.

CHAPTER 34

We Should Forgive Others for Our Own Good

The Legendary Belief

Anne Lamott expresses her vulnerabilities about faith and life in a way that readers can relate to. She understands the twisted pleasure of nursing a grudge, but she knows its weight falls heavier on the grudger than on the offender who needs forgiveness. We would be much happier if we let go and forgave the person who wronged us. She cites a wise saying, "Not forgiving is like drinking rat poison and then waiting for the rat to die."[1]

This is true. Oprah Winfrey says she has learned not to "hold grudges for anything, or any situation. And neither should you." Forgiveness is "letting go so that the past does not hold you prisoner, does not hold you hostage."[2]

Progressive Lutheran pastor Nadia Bolz-Weber makes the past explicitly personal. She says, "The bigger the @$$hole, the better to forgive and forget them." She explains: "I really believe that when someone else does us harm, we're connected to that mistreatment like a chain. . . . In the end, if we're not careful, we can actually absorb the worst of our enemy and on some level even start to become them. So, what if forgiveness . . . is actually a way of wielding bolt cutters and snapping the chain that links us. Like it is saying, 'What you did was so not okay that I refuse to be connected to it anymore.'"[3]

Why forgive? To wrest back control. The person who wounded us does not get a say. He does not get to hold power over us, victimizing us again as we flail through a helpless cycle of anger and revenge. We forgive so we can break

---

[1] Anne Lamott, *Traveling Mercies: Some Thoughts on Faith* (New York: Pantheon, 1999), 134.

[2] Oprah Winfrey, "Oprah's Favorite Definition of Forgiveness," Oprah Winfrey Network, https://www.oprah.com/own-digitaloriginals/oprahs-favorite-definition-of-forgiveness-video.

[3] Nadia Bolz-Weber, "Forgive Assholes," *Have a Little Faith* series, video by Makers, https://www.youtube.com/watch?v=VhmRkUtPra8.

the chains of bitterness, putting him and his transgression in the past so we can move on with our lives. We forgive him so we can forget him. We forgive for our sake, not his.

Unraveling the Legend

Thousands of therapists highlight the freedom of forgiveness. Foolishly refusing to forgive others hurts us more than it hurts them. This is true. But there is an insurmountable problem with making the benefits of forgiveness the reason for forgiveness.

Why is it hard to forgive? Because we understandably focus on ourselves and the hurt we carry. The other person must pay. We will get our due.

Why must we forgive? For our own sake, to reclaim our power and freedom.

Do you see the problem? The self is the reason we do not forgive, and the self is the reason we must forgive. How is this supposed to work? If focusing on me is the obstacle to forgiveness, how is focusing on me also the answer? Am I not digging my hole deeper? If the reason I forgive is to break your power over me or to put you in the rearview mirror, am I not still fighting you, and doesn't that indicate I have not forgiven? This "forgiveness" looks like another defensive move, dressed in its Sunday best but aimed at shoving you away. How can I forgive you when I am thinking mostly, or only, of me?

What Is Forgiveness?

Forgiveness is a tricky subject. The deeper we walk into the topic the more rabbits we kick up. This chapter can only start us down the path, but a good beginning will get us most of the way there.[4]

Forgiveness is a two-stage process. Step one occurs in our heart, as we resolve not to hold an offense against the person who wronged us. We prepare our hearts to absorb the moral cost, to eat what she owes, to release her from the moral debt of her offense. We cannot genuinely do this unless we are wishing what is best for the offender. If we try to forgive for our sake, we will be too self-focused to put anger and bitterness behind us. We must forgive for her sake, or we do not forgive at all.

Step one is seldom a one-off event, especially for deep wounds. We must forgive each time we think of her and what she has done. We slog down the path of forgiveness, taking frequent stops to gather ourselves for another push. Though we may not know how, one day we realize our bitterness has dissipated. We check the corners of our hearts and find to our delight that our rage

---

[4] See Chris Brauns, *Unpacking Forgiveness* (Wheaton, IL: Crossway, 2008) for a biblical and pastoral approach to forgiveness.

has transformed into love. We feel compassion for her and desire her best. We hear a snatch of good news about her and our heart nods its approval. We do not think about balancing the report with a tale about the time she hurt us, nor would we want to. We have finished the first, and most excruciating, task of forgiveness.

Step one may not be completed in this lifetime, but we who follow Jesus must commit to the journey. We will not quit until we reach the end or die. If forgiveness is entirely for our sake, step one would be the end of the process. We have put the pain behind us and are free to move on with our lives. But if forgiveness is about something larger than our own mental, emotional, and spiritual health, there must be a next step.

At some point in our journey of forgiveness we are ready for step two. We are far enough along in our heart work to extend a hand, informing the offender that we stand ready to pardon him for the wrong he has done if he owns his sin and repents. We have committed to forgiving him in our heart, and we have progressed far enough to offer our hand of forgiveness, so we will resist nursing a grudge if he does not repent. But we cannot shake hands unless he grabs ours, and this requires him to confess his guilt.

He must not offer a weasely confession in the passive voice. Not "Mistakes were made," or as Aaron told Moses, "When I threw it into the fire, out came this calf!" (Exod 32:24). Not "I'm sorry if you were offended," "We can't all be perfect," or "God has forgiven me so I hope you will too." We should not be surprised that the offender needs coaching, as the same character flaws that led to his offense are liable to mess up his repentance. We will tell him that we need to hear a sentence that begins with "I" and follows with a strong, active verb. "I" then fill-in-the-blank. I *stole*. I *slandered*. I *cheated* you. And I am sorry.

If he owns his sin and repents, we must grant forgiveness to him. This moment can be painful for men, who would rather not show their hand. Have you seen two guys try to patch things up? The penitent man nods toward the person he hurt, "Hey." The victim responds by looking away, "K." Done. "Let's shoot hoops!"

No! Halfway repentance leads only to halfway reconciliation. Half-hearted granting of forgiveness produces only half-hearted reconciliation. If the offender owns what he did, we speak graciously, directly, and redemptively. "Thank you for taking responsibility. I appreciate it very much. I forgive you. We will never speak of this again. Now, let's shoot hoops!"

Reconciliation may not eliminate all consequences. Forgiveness removes the moral debt, yet there may be appropriate legal and relational debts to pay. We must forgive the penitent drunk driver who killed our friend, but she is still going to jail. We must forgive the spouse who had an affair, but we may not trust him or her enough to stay married. We must forgive the uncle who molested our child, but he will not be joining the family for Thanksgiving dinner. We must forgive the gossip who shared our secret, but that is the last bit of news she will hear from us.

Consequences may also include financial restitution. Old Testament law required a man to repay five cattle for a stolen ox and four sheep for a stolen sheep (Exod 22:1). So David said the man who stole one lamb must repay four (2 Sam 12:6), and a penitent Zaccheus pledged to repay four times what he had taken (Luke 19:8). We must be vigilant lest enforcing consequences becomes a backdoor way to carry a grudge, yet we may fully forgive someone and still require financial, legal, or relational remedies. And if they are penitent, they will want to make it right.

Forgiveness may be the hardest thing we ever do. Even after we have formally pardoned the offender, we may catch ourselves brooding over the offense and needing to forgive all over again in our heart. It is much easier to carry a grudge and, at least initially, it feels better. The therapeutic benefits of forgiveness do not kick in until we reach the end of our journey and release the moral debt.

Breaking the chains of bitterness is a gift from God, but it is not the goal of forgiveness. The goal is reconciliation. We forgive for the other's sake, to call her back from the moral wilderness, to repair our relationship so our family, church, or friends can be whole. There are therapeutic benefits to forgiveness, but they are not why we forgive. We forgive because our Father commands us and to serve the person who needs our forgiveness.

Application

The last chapter warned about omitting hell when Scripture requires it, so I must add that another reason to forgive is to avoid going to hell. Jesus told a parable about a slave who was forgiven a ridiculous amount (10,000 talents, which equals 60 million denarii or 60 million days of work) but refused to forgive a fellow slave who owed him much less (100 denarii). His angry master handed the coldhearted servant "over to the jailers to be tortured." Jesus turned to his disciples and delivered the punch line, "So also my heavenly Father will do to you unless every one of you forgives his brother or sister from your heart" (Matt 18:34–35).

The master in the parable told the servant he should have forgiven his sizable loan because his comically high debt had been forgiven. The servant was not responsible to conjure the grace to forgive. He only needed to pass on the grace he had been given. So it is with us. We cannot manufacture the grace required to forgive egregious offenses. And we must not try. When we forgive, we are merely passing on to others the hard-won grace God has lavished on us. If we have not experienced the grace of God's forgiveness in Jesus, we can hardly forgive offenses that cut deeply and are done on purpose. But since we have, we can, and we must. Or there will be hell to pay.

Suburban Legend

"I must forgive myself."

An updated version of this chapter's urban legend doubles down on forgiving others for our own good. We elbow everyone else out of the picture and say, "I must forgive myself." We are both offender and victim, and that is the problem.

I understand what often inspires this suburban legend. Sometimes we are so ashamed of what we have done that we do not know how to get past it. We are angry at ourselves and do not think we deserve a second chance. We stew in our shame, beating ourselves up for our sin. Maybe our biggest need is to forgive ourselves?

That is not quite it. Our biggest need is grace. From whom? Not from ourselves. Giving ourselves grace is like paying ourselves a hundred dollars. No money changed hands. It merely changed pockets. What have we really done?

But forgiving ourselves is worse than futile. It obscures our fault and most pressing need. When we say, "I must forgive myself," we imply that part of us is innocent. If only the victimized side of us could forgive our offending side, we could move on with life, unshackled. But no part of us is innocent. Our whole self is the offender. What we need is not our own forgiveness. What we need is to humbly accept the forgiveness of God and the others we have wronged.

But that may be the problem. Saying "I must forgive myself" allows us to retain a bit of pride. Some part of us is pure and has the right to be angry at our other, evil side. This is a surefire way to mess up our repentance. Halfway repentance produces halfway reconciliation, so we will not experience the full joy of being reconciled to God unless we humbly confess that in this instance we are nothing but the penitent. Our sin does not entitle us to play the role of innocent forgiver; rather our sin drives us to repent and rest in the forgiveness of God. When we trust—really believe—that God has forgiven us, we will no longer worry about forgiving ourselves.

PART IV

———

Church and Last Things

CHAPTER 35

Christianity Is Not a Religion—It's a Relationship

The Legendary Belief

This urban legend is repeated so often it has become a cliché. What is the difference between Jesus and all other gods? Jesus loves you so much. He is crazy about you. If you are tired of rules and rituals, if your heart thirsts for communion with Almighty God, then come to Jesus. Christianity is not a religion. It's a relationship.

Unraveling the Legend

Those who use this urban legend usually intend to make three important and related points. First, Christianity is superior to all other religions because it surpasses the entire category. It does not even call itself a religion. Second, the Christian faith is personal. It is not primarily about religious ritual. Other religions demand their adherents perform prescribed prayers, sacrifices, and ceremonies. They follow the rules, checking religious boxes to appease their fickle god and gain his favor.

Third, the Christian faith is not about such futile human works. Karl Barth said religion is a human effort to locate and satisfy God. It is "the realm of man's attempts to justify and sanctify himself before a capricious and arbitrary picture of God." He explained, "From the standpoint of revelation religion is clearly seen to be a human attempt to anticipate what God in His revelation wills to do and does do. It is the attempted replacement of the divine work by a human manufacture. The divine reality offered and manifested to us in revelation is replaced by a concept of God arbitrarily and wilfully evolved by man."[1] By contrast, Christianity says God has found us, and we respond to the

---

[1]   Barth, *Church Dogmatics* I/2 (Edinburgh: T&T Clark, 1956), 280, 302.

revelation he has graciously given. Our faith moves from God to us, not from us to God.

These are weighty reasons to distinguish Christianity from religion. Nevertheless, there are two problems with claiming Christianity is not a religion.

James and Jesus.

James believed his relationship with Jesus counted as a religion. He wrote, "Pure and undefiled religion before God the Father is this: to look after orphans and widows in their distress and to keep oneself unstained from the world" (Jas 1:27). James sought pure religion, not no religion.

Jesus himself was religious. Judaism is a religion, and Jesus was and remains a faithful Jew. He kept the law perfectly, attended synagogue every Sabbath (Luke 4:16), celebrated Passover with its prayers and hymns (22:7–20), and joined other pilgrims in Jerusalem for religious festivals (2:41–42; John 2:13; 5:1; 7:2–10; 10:22–23). No one would be more surprised than Jesus to learn he was not religious.

Christianity does not distinguish between religion and relationship but between false and true religion and between broken and reconciled relationship. Jesus offers the true religion that restores our relationship with God. Or to say it from the other way, Jesus restores a relationship that we pursue religiously.

Is Christianity a Religion?

Religion is the worship of God or gods. An expanded definition would include specific beliefs and practices, usually grounded in a revelation that governs our lives and discloses the human problem and way of salvation.

Christianity meets all these criteria. Christians believe particular doctrines about God, the world, humanity, sin, salvation, and the future. We glean these truths from the Bible, God's revelation that authoritatively rules every aspect of life. Christianity is more than a religion, but it is not less. The church has always assumed this. When John Calvin wrote his systematic theology in the sixteenth century, he named it the *Institutes of the Christian Religion*. Preachers who say we are not a religion sing a different tune to the tax man. Every church in the United States claims a religious exemption to avoid paying income tax. We qualify as nonprofit organizations because the government recognizes we are religious institutions.

So, the urban legend is wrong about what it denies: Christianity is obviously a religion. Perhaps surprisingly, the legend may also be confused about what it affirms: Is Christianity a relationship?

Is Christianity a Relationship?

Generations of Christians love the schmaltzy hymn *In the Garden*. We sing, "I come to the garden alo-o-ne, while the dew is still on the ro-o-ses; and the voice I hear, falling on my ear, the Son of God disclo-o-ses. A-a-a-nd he walks with me and he talks with me, and he tells me I am his own. And the joy we share as we tarry there, none other has ever known."[2] We yearn for an intimate experience with Jesus, and if you believe you have it, I do not want to talk you out of it. But I worry about the impression we leave with those who pray to their heavenly Father but do not get "the feels." They hear us talk about having morning coffee with Jesus and wonder why they are missing out. *What is wrong with them?*

Nothing. Absolutely nothing.

Peter was Jesus's lead disciple. Imagine the stories he could tell about his three years traipsing around Galilee with Jesus. Peter knew the timbre of Jesus's voice and how his eyes gleamed when he smiled. He knew how to make Jesus laugh and he had made him cry. He had experienced the depths of denial and crucifixion and the height of resurrection. He knew Jesus personally. He also knew we do not know him in the same way.

Peter wrote to Christians who had never seen Jesus but were faithfully suffering for him. Peter told them to hang on until Jesus returned, then encouraged them with this realistic assessment: "Though you have not seen him, you love him; though not seeing him now, you believe in him, and you rejoice with inexpressible and glorious joy, because you are receiving the goal of your faith, the salvation of your souls" (1 Pet 1:8–9). You have not yet seen Jesus. You would not recognize his face in a lineup or his voice on a recording, yet you love him and you believe in him. You are willing to die for a man you have not physically met, and so you are gloriously saved.

Jesus's personal absence is one of the takeaways from his ascension. Peter and his fellow disciples were shocked to see their resurrected Lord rise into the sky. Angels appeared and asked why were they "looking up into heaven? This same Jesus, who has been taken from you into heaven, will come in the same way that you have seen him going into heaven" (Acts 1:11). Jesus has been taken from us. Praise God that our ascended Lord sent the Holy Spirit to dwell in and among us (John 16:7). Praise God that we may sense the Spirit's presence as we read Scripture, pray, and gather with God's people. But it is okay if we do not. The important thing is not that we feel Jesus's presence, but that we continue to believe and love him as we await his return.

Christianity is a relationship, but it is unlike any other relationship with any other person. We love a Savior we have not physically met, so it is going

---

2   C. Austin Miles, "In the Garden" (1940).

to look and feel a bit different. Let's not oversell the relationship we currently have. What we have is real, but it is the appetizer before the marriage supper of the Lamb. The kingdom of God is both already here and not yet in its fullness. When we play up the "already" as if the "not yet" has arrived, we overstate the personal relationship we presently have with God and may make others feel like second-class Christians. We are thrilled that we can talk to Jesus now and hear his voice in Scripture. But just wait until we see him face-to-face (1 John 3:2).

Application

If Christianity is a relationship and not a religion, it is easy to see why Christians view church as optional. What are we missing if we do not gather with the body of Christ? We would be further ahead if we stayed home and worked on our personal relationship with Jesus. We go to the garden *alone*. Who needs church?

But if Christianity is a religion, with the start of a promising relationship with a God we have not seen, then of course we need church. How better to make progress in this religion? How better to grow in this relationship? What could possibly help us more than joining the bride of Christ as we worship Jesus with other members of his body?

Jesus went to Jewish church (synagogue) every Sabbath (Luke 4:16). If we follow him, so will we.

Suburban Legend

"The Bible doesn't teach church membership."

The New Testament does not command Christians to join a local church, probably because it did not need to. What New Testament follower of Jesus would refuse to join his body? On the day the church began, 3,000 people believed and were baptized and added to the church. In ensuing days, "all the believers were together," and "every day the Lord added to their number those who were being saved" (Acts 2:41–47). This pattern of believing and joining the church continued throughout the book of Acts. Is it possible to believe in Jesus and not belong to his local assembly? Maybe, but it never occurred to an apostle that anyone would try. If someone refused baptism and membership in a local assembly, they would not be counted as a genuine believer. The church assumed everyone who was baptized by the Spirit had by that baptism become a member of the body of Christ. They belonged (1 Cor 12:12–13).[3]

We do not know how the New Testament church kept track of its members (did they keep membership rolls?), but there are several Scriptures that assume they had them. Paul tells Christians directly, "Now you are the body of Christ, and individual members of it" (v. 27). The New Testament church held elections for deacons and to send men to Antioch with Paul and Barnabas (Acts 6:1–4; 15:22). Surely, they knew who had a vote and who did not. Membership is also required for church discipline. Jesus said if our offending brother will not listen to our rebuke, we should "tell the church" (Matt 18:15–17). How do we tell the church if we do not know who belongs to the church? If our erring brother does not repent, Paul said we must "remove the evil person from among [us]" (1 Cor 5:13). How do we remove a person from among us if we do not know who counts as us? Paul said God judges those outside the church and we judge those inside, so when we evict people from membership, we are leaving them to the judgment of God (vv. 12–13). How do we do this without a clear boundary between those inside and outside the church?

Finally, God says the elders of the church are responsible for the people under their care. They must "be on guard for yourselves and for all the flock of which the Holy Spirit has appointed you as overseers, to shepherd the church of God" (Acts 20:28). They "will give an account" to God for how well they kept "watch over your souls" (Heb 13:17). If they "shepherd God's flock among you, not overseeing out of compulsion but willingly," they "will receive the unfading crown of glory" when Jesus returns (1 Pet 5:1–4). The elders are not responsible for everyone, or even every Christian. They are responsible for the people in their flock, which assumes they know who is a member of their church and who is not.

New Testament Christians could not imagine uniting with Jesus but not his church. Neither should we.

---

[3] Although it is important to ask whether and how Spirit baptism is linked to water baptism, this would have been a moot point to the New Testament church. Everyone who was Spirit baptized was water baptized as well.

CHAPTER 36

———

I Don't Need Church to Have a Relationship with God

The Legendary Belief

The man had not been to church since the start of the pandemic, and he did not see a need to return. He and his wife watched their favorite television preacher every week, which he said brought them closer to God than all the years they had spent in church. They realized now they did not need church to have a relationship with God. After all, going to church does not make you a Christian, any more than parking in a garage makes you a car.

Unraveling the Legend

It is true that walking through the doors of a church does not make you a Christian, just as entering a garage does not make you a car. But if you are a car, you will park in the garage. And if you are a Christian, you will go to church. The New Testament does not have a category for born-again Christians who refuse to join a local body of Christ. It never came up. Do-it-yourself Christianity did not become a significant problem until the rise of the modern world. As we will see, there are historical and cultural reasons for this shift, but fundamentally it arises from a misunderstanding of the Protestant principle of the priesthood of all believers.

Priesthood of All Believers

Medieval Christians believed the church was necessary for salvation because its priests dispensed saving grace through the sacraments. Priests baptized infants with the waters of regeneration, distributed the body of Christ in the form of communion wafers, and applied the merits of saints to the bankrupted accounts of penitent sinners. Martin Luther's discovery of justification by grace alone through faith alone disrupted this sacerdotal system and emphasized the priesthood of every believer. Ordinary folks no longer needed to go through a priest to access God and his grace. They could now come to God directly, through Jesus, their "great high priest" (Heb 10:19–23).

Evangelical Christians sometimes think this priesthood of all believers means we no longer need the church. God disagrees. After saying each Christian may boldly enter the heavenly "sanctuary through the blood of Jesus" (without the aid of an earthly priest), the author of Hebrews commands us to "consider one another to provoke love and good works, not neglecting to gather together, as some are in the habit of doing, but encouraging each other, and all the more as you see the day approaching" (vv. 19–25). The priesthood of every believer points us to the church because we serve as priests together in the community of faith. Peter testifies, "But you are **a chosen race, a royal priesthood, a holy nation, a people for his possession, so that you may proclaim the praises** of the one who called you out of darkness into his marvelous light" (1 Pet 2:9).

Priests represent God to the world and the world to God. They stand between God and the world to intercede on the world's behalf. Luther said each believer shares in their brother Christ's priesthood as they are baptized, born again, and anointed with the Holy Spirit.[1] We function as priests when we pray for each other and for the world, and as we proclaim the Word and assure one another of God's forgiveness in Christ. Ordinary Christians gather as a community of priests, to give and receive intercession. None of us are meant to walk with Jesus alone.[2]

Luther's priesthood of all believers was inherently communal and focused on the church, but each succeeding wave of Protestantism washed away more of this ecclesiastical beach. Luther leveled the church hierarchy but insisted that regeneration and forgiveness of sin came through the sacraments of baptism and the Lord's Supper. The Reformed church went further, saying baptism is merely the sign of the covenant and Jesus is only spiritually present in the Lord's Supper. The church's sacraments no longer regenerate; only personal faith in Jesus saves. Anabaptists took an additional step. They reduced the sacraments to ordinances and said they were merely symbols of our faith in Jesus (baptism) and of his sacrificial death (Lord's Supper). I was born Mennonite and am an ordained Baptist pastor, so I appreciate the necessity of personal faith in Jesus. Baptism and the Lord's Supper do not save. But they, and the church that practices them, are more important than many Christians suppose. Our personal faith in Jesus too often becomes individualized, leaving

---

[1]   Baptists reverse Luther's order. We are born again, then baptized.
[2]   Paul Althaus, *The Theology of Martin Luther,* trans. Robert C. Schultz (Philadelphia: Fortress, 1966), 313–18.

us with an impoverished view of our local church. Here is briefly how this happened in America.

Made in America

Many of the colonists who came to America were Puritans who had fought unsuccessfully to cleanse the Church of England from its Roman Catholic sympathies. Crossing the Atlantic Ocean turned these Puritans into functional Separatists, because they were now 3,000 miles from the Anglican bishops back home and their new colonies were too vast and too sparsely populated to be governed by a central church. Puritans who had been Presbyterian in England made the practical decision to become Congregationalists. Each church would have to govern itself.

This brought its own set of problems. The Puritans aspired to establish a "city on a hill," a shining light that would show the world how to run a pure church and Christian society. They did not have enough man power. When a church disciplined a heretic or dissenter, the person might simply move twenty miles out of town and hunker down. The church did not have the time or energy to search for him and bring him to heel. The Puritans slowly realized the logistical necessity of religious freedom. On that score, they were all Anabaptists now.

The existence of different colonies also promoted individual choice. Roman Catholics congregated in Maryland; Congregationalists in New England; Anglicans in Virginia; Dutch Reformed in New York; and Baptists, Quakers, and every sort of dissenter in Rhode Island, which the Puritans sniffed was the "latrine of New England." America was too diverse to impose a state church. Each person could choose their best fit from a smorgasbord of options.

Many second- and third-generation Puritans selected none of the above. They had been raised in church but were more invested in the wealth and wanderlust of the new world. Pastors realized their churches had many unconverted attenders, so they began preaching revival sermons, such as Jonathan Edwards's "Sinners in the Hands of an Angry God." The eighteenth century's First Great Awakening featured sinners getting saved by gospel preaching. How exciting! This preaching need not occur only in church, so it didn't. George Whitefield toured the colonies, preaching in fields; his entertaining sermons drew immense and captivated crowds. Lives were being transformed outside normal church services (even Edwards's "Sinners" sermon did not become famous until he delivered it as a guest preacher in Enfield), which encouraged the rise of dynamic parachurch, transdenominational ministries.

The nineteenth century's Second Great Awakening amplified this parachurch trend. Camp meetings featured spectacular conversions. Charles Finney held revival meetings for weeks at a time (often competing with local churches). D. L. Moody preached evangelistic conferences and founded a Bible Institute, while others started parachurch organizations such as the American Board for Foreign Missions (1810) and the American Bible Society (1816).

The twentieth century's divisive fundamentalist-modernist controversies turned many conservative Protestants against the institutional church. They had been evicted from the Roman Catholic Church in the sixteenth century, the Church of England in the seventeenth century, and now from their mainline Lutheran, Presbyterian, and Baptist churches. They concluded they did not need the blessing of their church, but only faith in Jesus and the support of like-minded, born-again people. So they started more parachurch ministries: conservative Bible colleges, publishing houses, mission agencies, radio programs, campus ministries, and conferences and retreat centers that crossed denominational lines. Some created the first ever nondenominational churches—independent, Bible-believing churches that retained their autonomy by not identifying with any denominational structure. As these churches separated from other churches, so their members might leave them for another that suited better. This was easy to do, given the following cultural factor.

Expressive Individualism

Our modern world encourages expressive individualism: the freedom to live as we desire. Earlier agrarian societies required people to conform to the external world. They had to master crop rotation and seasonal weather patterns. Plant too early, too late, or too often, and they might not survive. Technology changed that. We now have control over the external world. The coldest winter is no longer a problem. We have insulated homes with gas furnaces. Summer too hot? Turn on the air conditioning. Need to travel hundreds of miles? Get in your car and go. Need to go farther? Hop on a plane. Does that seem too long? Then text or call. You can talk to anyone in the world, as if they are sitting next to you.[3]

Technology also produced the Industrial Revolution, which enticed people to leave their communal farms for the individualism of the big city. On the farm, people belonged to extended families that gave them an identity and held them accountable. Everyone knew everybody. The city made them anonymous. Everyone knew *of* more people, but they knew them less well. They knew them only in certain contexts, such as work or a favorite restaurant. Their neighbors were largely invisible to them, and they to them. Most could live

---

[3]   Carl Trueman, *The Rise and Triumph of the Modern Self* (Wheaton, IL: Crossway, 2020), 40–42. Expressive individualism was popularized by Robert N. Bellah, Richard Madsen, William M. Sullivan, et al., *Habits of the Heart* (New York: Harper & Row, 1985) and Charles Taylor, *A Secular Age* (Cambridge, MA: Belknap, 2007), 473–95.

as they pleased, without fear of being found out or disappointing their family back home.

With this background of rising individualism, consider how two technologies, cars and computers, have changed our commitment to our local church. Before the onset of the automobile, Christians could only attend a church in their neighborhood or at most a carriage ride away. They put up with a lot they did not like, because what were their options? Now think of all the churches you pass on the drive to yours, churches that would be good enough in a pinch but are not quite up to snuff. You have a car; there is no need to settle. But why get in your car at all? You can stay home and watch your church's worship service on your computer, or any other church you might prefer, in the comfort of your pajamas.

The COVID pandemic piqued what had been percolating in American Christianity for several centuries. As moderns, we focus on ourselves. As modern evangelicals, we focus on our own faith. When considering a church, our first questions are *How is the preaching? How is the worship? How will this church help me grow?* The answer may not matter much anyway. Since our most memorable spiritual moments happened at concerts, around campfires, and in college chapels, we may assume we don't even need the church to have a vibrant relationship with God.

Application

The Christian faith is personal, but it is not individual. Jesus would have died for you alone, but he did not die for you to remain alone. He died to save you and unite you to his body, the church. This church is universal, and it is also local. You cannot have one without the other. The universal church is present when your local church meets, and your local church is what connects you to the universal church. Saying you belong to the universal church but not a local church is like being married to no one in particular. If you love Jesus, you must love his bride. And how can you love his bride if you won't even join her? Changing New Testament metaphors, we cannot say we are joined to the head (Jesus) if we do not belong to his body. We are an amputated body part, unconnected, of no use, and bleeding out.

Do you want Jesus to love you? Then join the object of his affections. Become one with his bride, and Jesus will become one with you.

Suburban Legend

"Nature is my church."

Some people say they feel closer to God fishing on a lake or hiking in the mountains than sitting in church. When pressed, they might claim that nature is their church.

They are right that nature often provides a religious experience. Paul says, "[God's] invisible attributes, that is, his eternal power and divine nature, have been clearly seen since the creation of the world" (Rom 1:20). Creation does lead us to a general knowledge of God. However, though the sun reveals some basic facts about God, only God's Son can reconcile us to the Father. And how do we know the Son? Through his church. The Spirit of God uses the Word of God proclaimed in the church of God to unite us to Jesus and his body. This is not something that can happen as we stare at a mountain, but only as we gather as the church. The church alone is the heart of God's kingdom, where Jesus empowers his priests to intercede for each other with God. Nature is good for many things, but it is not the church. It will not bring you all the way home.

Are you content to merely know something about God, or do you recognize your need to be reconciled with the Father? Get to church.

CHAPTER 37

——

We Are the Hands and Feet of Jesus

The Legendary Belief

When a church group presents their service project, there is a better than average chance someone will say they are going into the community "to be the hands and feet of Jesus." This popular phrase does not come from the Bible. It seems to have originated with a poem that many believe was written by Teresa of Ávila, a sixteenth-century Spanish mystic (1515–82), but may instead be the combined effort of a Methodist minister and a Quaker missionary.

> Christ has no body now but yours,
> No hands, no feet on earth but yours,
> Yours are the eyes through which he looks
> Compassion on this world,
> Yours are the feet with which he walks to do good,
> Yours are the hands with which he blesses all the world.
> Yours are the hands, yours are the feet,
> Yours are the eyes, you are his body.
> Christ has no body now on earth but yours.[1]

Perhaps we do not know who came up with this urban legend because it is so common that any number of Christians could have done it. For example, counselor Diane Langberg urges fellow therapists to "incarnate God" when they counsel trauma survivors. They should aim to imitate "Jesus, in the flesh, explaining God to us. Jesus, bringing the unseen down into flesh and blood actualities." If counselors want their clients to know God is a faithful and

---

[1] The poets are Mark Guy Pearse and Sarah Elizabeth Rowntree, respectively. See Mockingbird's Imitations, "Whose Hands? Another possible case of cumulative authorship," November 7, 2011, http://mimuspolyglottos.blogspot.com/2011/11/whose-hands-another-possible-case-of.html?m=0.

225

patient refuge, the counselors must become a faithful and patient refuge. They must ask God for grace to represent him well.[2]

Unraveling the Legend

This urban legend aptly says the followers of Jesus represent their heavenly Lord on earth. For better or worse, this is true. But the legend's strong words risk sliding beyond *representation* into *replacement.* Are we truly the hands and feet of Jesus? Are we expected to perform another incarnation of God for trauma survivors? Is this boilerplate Christian ethics or borderline blasphemy?

Body of Christ

The church is the body of Christ, but this does not mean its members are the hands and feet of Jesus. The body of Christ is a metaphor that Paul uses to express that each born-again church member is united to Jesus, the head, and to the other members in the body. Paul does not use the body metaphor to depict the church's witness to the world (as the hands and feet of Jesus) but to describe our mutual belonging and interdependence. We all belong: "If the foot should say, 'Because I'm not a hand, I don't belong to the body,' it is not for that reason any less a part of the body" (1 Cor 12:15). And we need each other: "The eye cannot say to the hand, 'I don't need you!' Or again, the head can't say to the feet, 'I don't need you!'" (v. 21). The higher members depend on the lower parts, so that together we "are the body of Christ, and individual members of it" (v. 27).

Okay, so Christians are not the hands and feet of Jesus to the world. But aren't we the hands and feet of Jesus to each other? Paul does not say this either. He sandwiches his metaphor of Christ's body between two paragraphs on spiritual gifts. He argues that as hands, feet, and other parts of the body of Christ, we use our spiritual gifts to empower the church to flourish and grow. What are we to each other? Not the hands and feet of Jesus, but variously apostles, prophets, teachers, and those gifted with faith, miracles, healing, helping, administration, a message of wisdom or knowledge, and tongues and their interpretation. We serve each other through these gifts that the Spirit distributes to us (vv. 1–11, 27–31).

Bottom line: The hands and feet of Jesus do not exist on earth. They exist in heaven, attached to the risen, glorified, and ascended body of our Lord. We have only one Savior, and we are not him. When we say we are the hands and feet of Jesus, we imply he is limited to our feeble efforts, and we distract from

---

[2]   Diane Langberg, *Suffering and the Heart of God: How Trauma Destroys and Christ Restores* (Greensboro, NC: New Growth, 2015), 97.

the hands and feet that were pierced for our salvation. If we are the hands and feet of Jesus, what is uniquely special about him? We minimize his unrepeatable redemptive work when we attempt to "incarnate God."

Incarnational Ministry

Other Christians are more theologically responsible. They know we cannot incarnate God, yet they urge us to use the incarnation as a pattern for ministry. Missiologists often advocate following Jesus's example of leaving home and becoming incarnate in his target culture. Alan Hirsch explains: "The Incarnation not only qualifies God's acts in the world but must also qualify ours. If God's central way of reaching his world was to incarnate himself in Jesus, then our way of reaching the world should likewise be *incarnational.*[3]

Incarnational ministry correctly instructs us to join the people we are seeking to reach and immerse ourselves in their culture, yet it suffers from similar problems as the urban legend to become the hands and feet of Jesus. First, incarnational ministry is impossible, both because we are not God and because we cannot become one with the target culture. The Son of God became fully human, but we can never identify wholly with any culture that is not ours. I will never be Chinese, French, or a Michigan Wolverine.

Second, incarnational ministry contains an ethnocentrism that distorts the gospel. The divine Son did not leave one culture for another, because deity does not have a culture. But we do. Culture is a category of creation; it is what humans make of the world. If Jesus leaving heaven is our pattern, and my "heaven" is Northeast Ohio, then I begin with my Midwestern, evangelical view of the gospel and attempt to translate that into the target culture. But this elevates my culture to the same level as the Word, and because it is intertwined with the Word, I "incarnate" both together. I may not know what cultural baggage I am smuggling alongside the gospel, but my target audience may be able to tell. And I hope they do, so we can keep the gospel clean.

Third, incarnational ministry distracts from the unique person and work of Jesus. There is only one incarnation, only one Word that became flesh, only one divine Son who left his Father's side to give himself for the life of the world (John 1:14–18; 3:14–18). Our presence, no matter how loving and sacrificial, is not enough. We cannot save. Contrary to Hirsch, "our very lives" are not "our messages." Our incarnational presence is not redemptive, and neither

---

[3] Alan Hirsch, *The Forgotten Ways: Reactivating the Missional Church* (Grand Rapids: Brazos, 2006), 133; emphasis his. See also Sherwood G. Lingenfelter and Marvin K. Mayers, *Ministering Cross-Culturally: An Incarnational Model for Personal Relationships,* 3rd ed. (Grand Rapids: Baker, 2016); and Paul Hiebert and Eloise Hiebert Meneses, *Incarnational Ministry: Planting Churches in Band, Tribal, Peasant, and Urban Societies* (Grand Rapids: Baker, 1995).

is it "revelatory."[4] God has not given us the impossible task of imitating his Son's incarnation. He simply asks us, by the power of his Spirit, to point others to Jesus.

Be Like Jesus?

Advocates for incarnational ministry attempt to ground their method in Phil 2:5–11, which urges us to "adopt the same attitude as that of Christ Jesus," who humbled himself by becoming incarnate and dying on the cross in our place. But Paul does not tell us to imitate the Son's incarnation. We are not divine, and we are already human, so an incarnation is not going to happen. Neither will we be "highly exalted" and given "the name that is above every name." There is only one "name of Jesus" before which "every knee will bow" (vv. 9–10). Paul commands us to imitate the Son's humility. We cannot duplicate the incarnation, but we can copy our Savior's attitude by setting aside our own interests and looking out "for the interests of others" (v. 4).

This imitation is not something we do on our own. Paul does not command us to grit our teeth and try harder to be like Jesus. He grounds his command in our union with Christ—our "fellowship with the Spirit" that supplies divine power "both to will and to work according to his good purpose" (vv. 1, 13). The Spirit unites us to Jesus in a saving, reorienting event that infuses us with spiritual life and transfers Jesus's earned righteousness to our account. All that we do flows from our resting in Jesus, as a branch rests in the vine (John 15:1–10). We do not strive to become incarnate; we rest in the one who became incarnate. Our exalted Lord sent the Spirit to baptize, fill, and unite us to his body. We gather with the other members, not to pretend we are the hands and feet of Jesus, but to use the Spirit's gifts and power to bear witness to Jesus and lead others to put their faith in him.

Application

The Christian life is simpler, and more feasible, than our urban legend suggests. Our hands and feet do not become the hands and feet of Jesus. We do not make Jesus visible to the world, and it is exhausting to try. The Spirit manifests Jesus to us and to the world, through his Word in his gathered church, and he uses our hands and feet to serve others and point them to him.

This chapter began with a wearisome, guilt-inducing poem, "Christ has no body now but yours. No hands, no feet on earth but yours. . . ." Here is a more

---

[4] Hirsch, *Forgotten Ways,* 133. For a constructive critique of incarnational ministry, see J. Todd Billings, *Union with Christ* (Grand Rapids: Baker, 2011), 123–65.

encouraging, doable verse about the Spirit's use of our limbs, from the hymn "Take My Life and Let It Be."

> Take my hands, and let them move
> At the impulse of Thy love,
> Take my feet and let them be
> Swift and beautiful for Thee.[5]

Suburban Legend

"We are building the kingdom."

My seminary once used this marketing slogan: "Building the kingdom, one leader at a time." It may have worked, as we attracted enough students to keep the lights on, but it was not biblical. Scripture never implies the advance of the kingdom comes from us. It rests solely on the shoulders of King Jesus, who established the kingdom at his first coming and will consummate it when he returns. In the meantime, we may enter (Matt 5:20), receive (Mark 10:15), inherit (Matt 25:34), and possess the kingdom (5:3). We may seek (6:33), pray (6:10), and look for it (Luke 23:51). We may sacrifice for the sake of the kingdom (18:29), but we cannot build, bring, or extend its reach. Only Jesus does that.[6]

This does not mean we sit on our hands. While we wait for Jesus to return and consummate his reign, we bear witness to the kingdom by doing the sorts of things that anticipate his return. When people look at our homes, churches, and seminaries, they should snap their fingers and say, "Like that. When Jesus returns, the whole world is going to look a lot like that."

---

[5] Frances Ridley Havergal, "Take My Life and Let It Be" (1876).
[6] George Eldon Ladd, *The Presence of the Future* (1974; repr., Grand Rapids: Eerdmans, 1996), 193.

CHAPTER 38

Death Is Not a Tragedy for Christians

The Legendary Belief

Steve Saint, grown-up son of martyred missionary Nate Saint, spoke at the funeral of Veronica Bowers and her daughter Charity, whose missionary plane had been mistakenly shot down by the Peruvian Air Force. Steve told six-year-old Cory, who survived the attack, that many will tell him, as they told Steve, that his parent's death was a tragedy. Steve said they are wrong. Cory's mother and sister and Steve's father went to live with Jesus, which is where we all want to go. They just got to go sooner than the rest. "Now when people say, 'That was a tragedy,' I know they were wrong."[1]

David Platt agrees. In his best-selling book, *Radical,* Platt tells about Genesa Wells, a young woman who gave up a middle-class American life to become a missionary in the Middle East, only to die in a bus accident in the Sinai desert. What a tragedy! Not so fast, says Platt. Her death "is not a story of tragedy but a story of reward," because the moment she died "she was ushered into the presence of Christ. There she glimpsed his glory in an amazing beauty that you and I cannot even fathom." Platt says viewing "death as reward . . . is *the key* to taking back [our] faith from the American dream." Only when we "focus our lives on another world," and realize that death is the doorway to get there, will we free ourselves from worldly desires, values, and ambition. Do we love Jesus more than the things of earth? Then "to die is gain" (Phil 1:21).[2]

---

[1] John Piper, *Providence* (Wheaton, IL: Crossway, 2021), 379–80.
[2] David Platt, *Radical* (Colorado Springs: Multnomah, 2011), 179–81; emphasis in original.

Unraveling the Legend

I appreciate Saint's and Platt's emphasis on the glory of seeing Jesus. Paul said "to depart and be with Christ . . . is far better" than "to remain in the flesh" (Phil 1:23–24). But though God gloriously brings good things out of death, he does not call death a good thing. In the next chapter, Paul said Epaphroditus "was so sick that he nearly died. However, God had mercy on him" and spared his life (2:27). Saving Epaphroditus's life was not merely a mercy for Paul. It was good for Epaphroditus too. Death may be the doorway to Jesus, but it is still something bad that we hope to avoid. Paul longed to be with Jesus, and if necessary he was willing to die to make that happen. But he preferred to be with Jesus not by his death but by Jesus's return, so he exclaimed, "Our Lord, come!" (1 Cor 16:22).

Psalm 116:15 declares, "The death of his faithful ones is valuable in the Lord's sight." This does not mean death itself is precious but that God's people are. He cares so much for his saints that he is with us in our worst, weakest moment. There is only one book of the Bible that says death is good. Can you guess? Job sobbed in his misery, "Why is light given to one burdened with grief, and life to those whose existence is bitter, who wait for death, but it does not come, and search for it more than for hidden treasure, who are filled with much joy and are glad when they reach the grave?" (Job 3:20–22). Job understandably pined for sweet death to come and end his suffering. Yet he did not consider death to be unequivocally good; he longed for the day when his death would be swallowed up in resurrection. He testified, "But I know that my Redeemer lives, and at the end he will stand on the dust. Even after my skin has been destroyed, yet I will see God in my flesh" (19:25–26).[3]

The Enemy

The Bible does not say death is our reward. From start to finish, Scripture says death is our enemy. Death is the first clearly negative reference in the Bible. One chapter before the serpent slithers into the story, God warns Adam not to eat from the tree of the knowledge of good and evil, "for on the day you eat from it, you will certainly die" (Gen 2:17). When Adam and Eve disobeyed, God said now they would die, "for you are dust, and you will return to dust" (3:19). Death is our first enemy, and it is our last enemy too. Paul declared, "The last enemy to be abolished is death" (1 Cor 15:26). He meant that literally. Death shows up before the devil, and it lingers a little after he is gone.

---

[3] The Hebrew of Job 19:26 could be translated "apart from my flesh I will see God," in which case Job is not expressing hope in his future resurrection. No matter. The rest of Scripture emphatically states that our bodily resurrection defeats the cold grip of death (Isa 26:19; Dan 12:2; 1 Cor 15:1–58).

Satan is thrown into hell in Rev 20:10; four verses later, death is thrown in (v. 14). Death is destroyed after the devil. It is our last enemy to go.

We must remember death is our enemy or we will lose the plot of the biblical story and miss the meaning of Jesus. Every religion tries to solve some problem. Islam claims it has the answer to pride, Buddhism the solution to suffering, and Hinduism the answer to bad karma. What is the problem the Christian faith solves? Sin and death. If we minimize death, if we say it is no big deal or even our reward, we minimize Jesus's victory that conquered it. Have you heard a winning coach trash the losing team in his postgame press conference? Me neither. Even if his team beat the Detroit Lions, because everyone does, he goes out of his way to praise the perennial losers. "They're professionals too. They fought us for four quarters, as we knew they would." The coach knows the better his opponent, the greater his accomplishment.

Death does not need puffing. It is as tragic and demonic as it feels. We must be honest about this so we can celebrate our hope in Jesus. If you have never been troubled by death, if you have never worried about what happens when you die, there is little chance you have put your faith in Jesus. Why would you? He is the answer for a problem you do not care about. Let's make much of death so we can make much of Jesus. There is only one Savior who has conquered death. Follow Jesus, and you will too![4]

Living in the Moment

Those who say death is a reward rather than a tragedy properly point to our redemption in Christ. What can match looking into Jesus's face and collapsing into his long embrace? Who can imagine our tears of gratitude? To be fully known, and fully loved, and fully saved from the hell we deserve. The end of our story puts death and the difficulties of this life in perspective.

Still, we must resist the temptation to cut to the chase. We live with our glorious goal in mind, but we live in this frequently agonizing moment. We cannot jump ahead to the story's end; we must walk through the chapter we are in. So we long for our redemption while knowing that we live in this present, fallen age. God's creation has been ravaged by sin, unleashing disease and disaster on our world. Until Jesus returns, we and everyone we love will die. This hurts. As it should.

If you grew up in church, what is the first verse you memorized? Nope, not John 3:16. Wasn't it John 11:35? "Jesus wept." You stuck out your hand. "Lollipop, please!" Scripture's shortest verse packs a theological punch. Jesus wept at Lazarus's tomb because he was sad. He did not rejoice that death was

---

[4] For an honest and hopeful study of death, see Michael E. Wittmer, *The Last Enemy* (Grand Rapids: Discovery House, 2012).

Lazarus's reward; he did not say Lazarus was safe in Abraham's bosom and we would not wish him back now. Jesus not only wished Lazarus back, he was about to bring him back into this fallen world where Jesus's enemies would seek to do him harm. Poor Lazarus! He already had died once, and soon the chief priests would try to kill him again (John 12:9–11). Jesus knew all this, as he knew he was about to save the day by raising his friend from the dead. Yet he remained in the moment and had a good cry.

Good Christians cry. An entire book of our Bible is called Lamentations! Paul said we do not grieve like most people, who have no hope (1 Thess 4:13). This is gloriously true. But this does not mean we do not grieve. We grieve, but not as those who have no hope. And we hope, but not as those who do not grieve. Our grief is a sign of our hope. We grieve because we know that something is deeply wrong, and we know the One who can do something about it. No one should feel the sting of death like Christians. We feel its weight deep in our bones, for we know this is not the way God made the world and it's not the way the world will be when his Son comes again. So we pray the closing prayer of Scripture, "Come, Lord Jesus!" (Rev 22:20). Raise the dead and restore all things! Let's do this already!

Application

If Jesus alone has conquered sin and death, then our only hope is to turn from sin and throw all our weight on Jesus. We may practice this each night as we go to bed. When I was a child, my parents taught me this bedtime prayer: "Now I lay me down to sleep, I pray the Lord my soul to keep. And if I die before I wake, I pray the Lord my soul to take." What a great prayer! As we transfer our physical weight to our mattress, so we place our spiritual weight on Jesus. Practice this each night, and we will be prepared for the sleep of death when it finally comes.

My friends called one night and asked if I would come over to see Jan, who was dying of cancer and might not make it through the night. Jan was a straight shooter. When I walked to the couch where she was lying, she looked at me and said, "How do I do this? I've never died before." I stumbled for a moment, then the Spirit gave me the words to say. I said, "Jan. You don't do this. You've walked with Jesus for seventy years, and tonight is when you cash in. Climb on Jesus's back and let him carry you home. You don't do anything tonight but rest in him." How long must we follow Jesus? Until our last night. Why do we follow him? For that same night.

Mini Myth

"Death is natural."

Most books on death say it is natural. One popular book declares, "Death is as natural as life. The fact that we make such a big hullabaloo over it is all because we don't see ourselves as part of nature. We think because we're human we're something above nature. We're not. Everything that gets born, dies."[5]

Even if this were true, how would it help? What if you came home to find someone had ransacked your house and set it on fire? You called 911 and the operator said, "Yeah, we have been getting a lot of calls like this lately; we think arson and burglary are the new normal." Wouldn't you scream, "Normal! I don't care how normal this is! Get somebody out here! My house is on fire!" Or say you are on a flight when the engines sputter and go silent on one wing, then the other. The intercom crackles, "Attention, passengers. We have just lost our engines. They ran well for years, and now have come to the end of their natural life. What did you expect? Assume crash positions."

Saying death is natural should fill us with despair. If death is natural, nothing can be done about it. If death is natural, nothing *ought* to be done about it. Death is just the way life is. The Bible offers hope because it says though death is common—everyone does it—it is not natural. Death is an unnatural intruder into God's good creation. It is not the way this world is supposed to be.[6]

God is not content to watch death slowly decimate his people and the love they share. He sent his Son to be crucified with the sin that causes death. Death died in the death of Christ. Jesus pulled death with him into his tomb and buried it forever, so we who believe in Jesus will not stay dead. Jesus told Lazarus's sister, "I am the resurrection and the life. The one who believes in me, even if he dies, will live. Everyone who lives and believes in me will never die. Do you believe this?" (John 11:25–26).

Do you believe this? Your life hangs on your answer.

---

[5] Mitch Albom, *Tuesdays with Morrie* (New York: Doubleday, 1997), 173.

[6] More specifically, it is human death that is unnatural, a consequence of Adam's sin (Gen 2:17; Rom 5:12–21). Vegetative death seems natural (the flowers that Adam cut for Eve would eventually wilt), while animal death is disputed (stepping on an ant is no big deal, but would puppies die in an unfallen world?). Scripture does indicate that animal predation is a consequence of the fall (Gen 1:30; Isa 65:25).

CHAPTER 39

Grandpa Went to Heaven and Plays Outfield for the Angels

The Legendary Belief

Eulogies often say the deceased is now doing in heaven whatever he did on earth, only better. If the man loved golf, he is driving celestial fairways. If he played guitar, he is jamming in heaven's band. If he was mildly annoying, he is really a pain in the neck now! It may have been years since Grandpa played semipro baseball, but he is now batting cleanup on God's lineup card. And not just for any team. He is slugging home runs for the angels, rounding the bases with other celestial spirits! So the eulogy ends, "We may have lost our father and friend, but heaven got another angel."

Unraveling the Legend

Such eulogies are vaguely comforting, but only if we do not think too hard. Because we are clearly making stuff up. We have no reason to think any of this is true. Worse, we have solid, biblical reasons to believe all of it is false. We do not become angels when we die, and we do not carry on in heaven as we lived on earth. Let's take each of these urban legends, in order.

Forever Human

First, humans never become angels. We are an entirely different class of being. We do not turn into angels any more than a robin becomes a giraffe. Of course, God can do whatever he wants, but we know he will not change us into angels because he has a much higher goal. He aspires to conform us "to the image of his Son, so that he would be the firstborn among many brothers and sisters" (Rom 8:29). God saved us to be like Jesus. We cannot be like Jesus in his deity (talk about a wholly different class of being!), but we will become like the holy human that Jesus is (Eph 4:20–24; 1 John 3:2–6). Jesus is 100 percent God and 100 percent human. He is 0 percent angel. When God makes us like Jesus, no part of us will be angel.

The book of Hebrews explains the relationship between Jesus, us, and angels. The Son of God is higher than the angels because of his divine nature—"The Son is the radiance of God's glory and the exact expression of his nature"—and because of his redemptive work—"After making purification for sins, he sat down at the right hand of the Majesty on high. So he became superior to the angels" (1:3–4). After citing several Old Testament texts that elevate the Son beyond the angels, the author of Hebrews quotes the Septuagint version of Psalm 8, "What is man that you remember him, or the son of man that you care for him? You made him lower than the angels for a short time" (Heb 2:6–7). The original Hebrew of Ps 8:5 does not explicitly say "angels." It uses the term *'elōhîm,* which means "gods" and can be translated either as "God" or as "heavenly beings/angels." Psalm 8:5 refers to humans and says, according to the Christian Standard Bible, "You made him little less than God." The book of Hebrews switches out humans for Jesus and God for angels and says that Jesus fulfills our mission. We do not yet see humans fully exercising authority over creation, as God intended for his image bearers, "but we do see Jesus—made lower than the angels for a short time so that by God's grace he might taste death for everyone—crowned with glory and honor because he suffered death" (Heb 2:9).

As God, Jesus transcends the angels. As man, Jesus lowered himself beneath the angels so he could die for humans. Hebrews emphasizes that we are the target of Jesus's redemption: "For it is clear that he does not reach out to help angels, but to help Abraham's offspring" (2:16). Now ascended to the right hand of his Father, Jesus has authority over all creation, including angels. And somehow, remarkably, we who are being made like Jesus will become a junior partner with him, sharing in his authority. Paul declared, "Or don't you know that the saints will judge the world? . . . Don't you know that we will judge angels"? (1 Cor 6:2–3). God will not turn us into angels; he has much bigger plans.

Temporary Heaven

Second, we will not do in heaven whatever we did on earth. We know this because we can see our dead friend's body. How do we suppose our loved one is planting peonies and baking pies in heaven? Wouldn't she need her body for that, as well as ovens, flour, and apples? But her body is in the casket, awaiting her resurrection.

Christians repeat this urban legend because they run together the events of our promised future. They seldom stop to think that God delivers his glorious, promised future in two parts. The first part happens when we die and go to heaven. The second part happens after that, when Jesus returns to resurrect our body and restore all things. We know almost nothing about the first part except that we are with the Lord. Jesus told the thief on the cross, "Today you will be with me in paradise" (Luke 23:43). Paul said he prefers to leave his body and be "at home with the Lord" (2 Cor 5:6–8). He longs "to depart and be with Christ" (Phil 1:21–23). When Jesus returns, he "will bring with him those who have fallen asleep" (1 Thess 4:14). What do these passages say happens after we die? We are with the Lord, nothing more. God does not share more details because what theologians call "the intermediate state"—the interlude between this life and our future resurrection—is not his focus. He is much more excited about what happens at the end.

The Christian hope focuses on the three *R*'s: the return of Jesus, the resurrection of the body, and the restoration of all things. This is our final and promised future, none of it happens the moment we die. Praise God that when we die our soul goes to heaven. It beats going the other direction! Praise God even more that our soul goes to be with Jesus. His presence is the high point of heaven. Seeing Jesus will be the best gift we have ever received, but it is not all that God has planned for us. As wonderful as it will be to be a disembodied soul in heaven with Jesus, there is one thing better: to be a whole person, body and soul, with Jesus on earth. This is precisely what Scripture promises: Jesus will bring our souls with him when he returns; he will resurrect our bodies and put us back together; and we will live with him forever here, on this renewed planet (Isa 65:17–25; 2 Pet 3:10–13; Rev 21:1–5).

The next chapter will say more about our final home on the new earth. For now, consider what John's vision of heaven implies about what we might do in our intermediate state, before we get to the new earth. Humans do not indisputably appear in Revelation's description of heaven until chapters 6 and 7, and since the humans there are martyrs of the "great tribulation," they may yet be future (7:14). Nevertheless, the activities of these tribulation saints suggest what our heavenly souls will be capable of, and perhaps do.

The heavenly saints praise God. John saw "a vast multitude from every nation, tribe, people, and language, which no one could number, standing before the throne and before the Lamb. They were clothed in white robes with palm branches in their hands" (v. 9). It is not clear how souls can wear robes and wave palm branches in their hands. This is par for the course for Revelation, whose apocalyptic genre drops puzzlers into every paragraph. Perhaps John is describing spiritual realities in physical ways. Or perhaps God supplies the saints in heaven with loaner bodies, like a mechanic might give a customer a loaner car. If so, these bodies must be inferior to the saints' resurrection bodies, which they will not receive until Jesus returns to earth. Regardless, they shout their praises with the angels to their beautiful Savior: "Salvation belongs to our God, who is seated on the throne, and to the Lamb!" (Rev 7:10). Can you imagine a more satisfying experience, praising God in heaven with uncountable numbers of new best friends?

The heavenly saints not only praise, they also pray. John heard the martyred souls crying "out with a loud voice, 'Lord, the one who is holy and true, how long until you judge those who live on the earth and avenge our blood?' So they were each given a white robe, and they were told to rest a little while longer" (6:10–11). The saints in heaven are not suffering, but they are impatient. They left the earth as losers, beheaded or burned alive by leaders who thought they deserved to die. *How long, Lord, until you return and vindicate us? Show our enemies that we were right all along! That we are on the right side of history!* They are given white robes and told to wait a little longer.

Likewise, we may be impatient in heaven. Not for our vindication, unless we suffered for our faith, but because we long for Jesus to return, resurrect our bodies, and consummate his righteous reign over the earth. Our impatience may inspire our prayers. I used to think heaven was a celestial hammock, where my soul rested in Jesus until his return. But several church fathers believed the departed saints have a job in heaven: to pray for those left behind. Origen wrote that "all those fathers who have fallen asleep before us fight on our side and aid us by their prayers." Gregory of Nazianzus said his dead father "accomplishes there now by his prayers more than he ever did by his teaching." And Martin Luther told his friend, "I shall pray for you, I ask that you pray for me. . . . If I depart this life ahead of you—something I desire—then I must pull you after me. If you depart before me, then you shall pull me after you. For we confess *one* God and with all saints we abide in our Savior."[1]

Luther was alluding to the communion of saints. This encouraging line in the Apostles' Creed means the saints on earth remain connected to the saints in heaven through Jesus. If we are in Christ and they are in Christ, then nothing can separate us from each other. Not even death. We may talk to Jesus about them, asking him to pass along a word or a hug. And they may talk to Jesus about us. We do not know what they know about our current lives, but if the saints in heaven pray, we may assume they pray for us.

Application

God's promised future does not come true all at once, which complicates Christian funerals. We must walk people through where our friend is now

---

[1] Quotes from Origen, Gregory, and Luther appear in Donald Bloesch, *The Last Things* (Downers Grove, IL: InterVarsity, 2004), 156, 170–71; emphasis Luther's.

(heaven), and where she will ultimately be (the new earth). We must tell them what happens when we die and what happens after that.

A Christian funeral must do three things. First, we mourn our loved one. She is gone and it is not okay. We miss her terribly. Second, we take comfort that her soul is with Jesus. What a relief! How do people cope without him? Third, we recognize she has not yet received all that God has promised. So, without lessening our present comfort, we long for what is yet to come. We raise a fist of defiance and declare that death does not have the last word. We will see our loved one again—not merely up there but down here, on this redeemed earth. Her body will rise from the dead! This will happen when Jesus returns, so with grieving hearts we shout the closing prayer of Scripture, "Amen! Come, Lord Jesus!" (Rev 22:20).

CHAPTER 40

———

We Will Live Forever in Heaven

The Legendary Belief

Give four guys microphones and a banjo, and you are sure to hear the gospel hymn "I'll Fly Away." Christians love to clap along to its eerily joyful lyrics, even at funerals.

> Some glad morning when this life is o'er, I'll fly away.
> To a home on God's celestial shore, I'll fly away.
> I'll fly away, O glory, I'll fly away.
> When I die, hallelujah, by and by, I'll fly away.[1]

Just reading those words, you are probably humming it now. It is a fun song that sticks in your head. But is it right?

Unraveling the Legend

The Bible agrees that we fly away at death, but it is not happy about it. Moses wrings his hands over his inevitable demise: "Our lives last seventy years or, if we are strong, eighty years. Even the best of them are struggle and sorrow; indeed, they pass quickly and we fly away" (Ps 90:10). Moses would not understand why middle-class Christians, blessed with far more joys than sorrows, are so excited to die.

Is it because, as verse 2 of "I'll Fly Away" says, this life is but a shadow and this world is a prison?

> When the shadows of this life have gone, I'll fly away.
> Like a bird from prison bars has flown, I'll fly away.

---

[1]   Albert E. Brumley, "I'll Fly Away" (1932).

But this is a heretically low view of creation. The idea comes from Plato, who said our material world is a shadow of a higher, spiritual realm, and that enlightened souls should yearn to return to heaven. Scripture teaches the opposite. Far from being a prison that we should pray to escape, this world is the home that God prepared especially for us. The earth is God's gift. Enjoy it!

Or is it because, as verse 3 implies, our final home is somewhere above the skies?

> Just a few more weary days and then, I'll fly away.
> To a land where joy shall never end, I'll fly away.

But as we learned last chapter, heaven is the believer's intermediate state. Praise God that our souls go to heaven when we die. What a comfort to be with Jesus! But as wonderful as it will be to exist as a soul in heaven with Jesus, it is better to live as a whole person, body and soul, with Jesus on this restored earth. This is precisely what Scripture promises.

The New Earth

The Bible repeatedly says our final home will be a new heaven and earth. Isaiah quotes the Lord God, "For I will create a new heaven and a new earth" (Isa 65:17). Peter says that "based on his promise, we wait for new heavens and a new earth" (2 Pet 3:13). And John concludes Scripture with his vision of "a new heaven and a new earth" (Rev 21:1). Our promised future brings the story of our world full circle. The Bible opens with "In the beginning God created the heavens and the earth" (Gen 1:1). The Bible ends by returning to these heavens and earth, now made new by the redeeming work of Jesus. Our promised future is not some Platonic flight into heaven but unending life with our Savior in the new creation!

But wait. What about the "heaven" part of the "new heaven and new earth"? Might that imply that Plato's fantasy is partly right? No. The term "heaven" can mean (1) an indeterminate space above the earth, from our sky through outer and intergalactic space; (2) the abode of God: that place in creation where God most fully reveals his glory (2 Cor 12:2–4; Rev 4–7); and (3) the intermediate state where dead saints go until the return of Jesus and their resurrection. God does not redeem his abode or the intermediate state, so the meaning of heaven in "new heaven and new earth" must be the first definition: the sky where airplanes fly, the area above the earth that belongs to God's creation. The Bible opens with creation and closes with the new creation.

To help Christians keep this straight, I often omit the mention of heaven from the phrase "new heaven and new earth." When many Christians hear "new heaven and new earth," their minds stop at the word "heaven" and, mistaking it for the abode of God or the intermediate state, assume they will live forever "up there" in the celestial clouds. The "earth" part does not register. The phrase "new heaven and new earth" is biblical, so it is fine to use, but it is easily misunderstood by Platonically influenced Christians. "New earth" or "new creation" communicates the biblical message more clearly to this audience, and it is what I will use for the remainder of this chapter.

The phrase "new earth" contains an important question. Something about the new earth is "new" or different, and something stays the same, or recognizably earth. What is new about the new earth, and what remains the same? We find a clue in 2 Pet 3:13, "We wait for new heavens and a new earth, where righteousness dwells." When Peter anticipates our final home, one thing stands out as new, and it is not a thing. Remember chapter 12's distinction between ontology and ethics? What does the term "righteousness" describe: ontology or ethics, things or actions? Doesn't righteousness describe ethics, actions, what we do?

Peter does not see new things on the new earth. He sees new actions. Unlike our present fallen age, which is broken by the ravages of sin, our final home is "where righteousness dwells." The new earth may have some new things. Who knows? There might be new kinds of animals or new laws of physics. But I doubt it. If the new earth is too different from this one, this earth has not been redeemed. It has been replaced.[2] That is not what God promises. The new earth is this earth that has been fixed.

God says as much when he speaks from his throne, "Look, I am making everything new" (Rev 21:5). He does not say, "Look, I am making new things," but "I am taking everything that is here and I'm making it new. I am restoring all things." This fits with God's goals all along. His biblical story is creation, fall, and redemption. He made all things good; all things have been savaged by sin; and he wants it all back. Satan wins nothing in the end. Everything that sin destroyed, God's grace will restore. The Christmas carol expresses it well: "No more let sins and sorrows grow, nor thorns infest the ground. He comes to make his blessings flow far as the curse is found." *Far as the curse is found?* Far as the curse is found. Joy to the world![3]

Rule of Thumb

We often wonder about life on the new earth. Will we travel? Hold jobs? Live as families? See our pets? We have more questions than answers about the new earth, but here is a rule of thumb. Since redemption restores creation, we may assume that whatever belongs to creation will be here while whatever belongs

---

[2]   The same is true for you. If your resurrection body is too different from your present body, you have not been redeemed. You have been replaced. Expect your resurrection body to be gloriously indestructible, and it will still be you.

[3]   Isaac Watts, "Joy to the World!" (1719), arranged by Lowell Mason, 1848.

to the fall will be removed. For instance, Isaiah sees houses, vineyards, money, and lions and lambs on the new earth (Isa 60:3–11; 65:21–25). Yes, animals will be here, perhaps one that looks suspiciously like your beloved Labrador.

There seem to be only three exceptions to this rule. First, marriage is the one good of creation that does not appear on the new earth. Because of the fall, people die and divorce and their spouses remarry. Some people, through no fault of their own, have had multiple husbands and wives. Who will they be married to on the new earth? The Sadducees tried to trick Jesus with this question. A woman had seven husbands one after the other, as each stepped up to marry his brother's widow. By the way, how dumb was brother number six? How did he think this would end? Jesus said the Sadducees' question was moot because there will not be marriage on the new earth (Matt 22:23–33). Divorce and death have so scrambled marriage that God cannot restore one union without violating another. If you love your spouse and cannot imagine living without that person, remember that you will know him or her on the new earth. You will not enjoy less intimacy, but it will not be sexual and it will not be exclusive. As the bride of Christ, you both will be married to Jesus—the deeper mystery of which your present marriage is a picture (Eph 5:32).

Second, there are two consequences of the fall that will never be fixed. The serpent was cursed in Eden, and he remains cursed on the new earth. Wolves and lambs will dine together, and lions will chew "straw like cattle," yet "the serpent's food will be dust!" (Isa 65:25). The other consequence that remains are the scars of Christ. When our resurrected Lord appeared to Thomas, he invited him to touch the wounds in his hands and side (John 20:27). God keeps these two reminders of sin to point us to his grace. When we've been here ten thousand years, bright shining as the sun,[4] we won't become proud and think somehow we deserve this. Every time we see a snake we will remember our sin, and every time we see Jesus's scars we will remember the price he paid to win us back. And we will praise his amazing grace!

Consummation

God does not merely redeem his creation. He also consummates it, taking our world to the higher place it was always intended to go. The end of our story is better than the beginning in at least five ways.

First, God will live here with us. God created the earth as his cosmic temple, with humans as his image and Eden as his Most Holy Place. He intended Adam and Eve's children to extend the courts of the temple outward until the whole earth was filled with the knowledge of him. We failed, so Jesus will do it himself. God walked with Adam in Eden, but he came and left. Came and

---

[4] From the anonymously written verse 6 of John Newton's "Amazing Grace" (1779), added at least a century after Newton penned the original hymn.

left. In the end, God will live here permanently. John "heard a loud voice from the throne: Look, God's dwelling is with humanity, and he will live with them. They will be his peoples, and God himself will be with them and will be their God" (Rev 21:3). What did you hear three times? God will be "with humanity." He will be "with them." He will be Immanuel, God with us.

Second, we will have spiritual bodies. Our bodies will still be physical, for the resurrection is physical, but they will be more than physical. They will be patterned after Jesus's glorified body and animated by his life-giving spirit (1 Cor 15:42–49). They will be indestructible. I am afraid of heights, so I'm saving hang gliding, zip-lining, and bungee jumping for the new earth. If something goes wrong, my spiritual body will probably bounce and I'll try again.

Third, we will enjoy ever-escalating culture. God told us to develop culture in Eden and he never rescinds that command (Gen 1:28; 2:15). When Jesus returns, we will enter the new earth with whatever cultural level we have achieved and then keep going from there. Can you imagine the music of the new earth when Bach has forever to write without the handicap of the fall? Our return to the new earth means you do not need a bucket list. Don't worry that you didn't get to see and do all that you wanted to in this life. If you are in Jesus, you will live more than once. You will return to the earth, and you will have forever to see and do what you did not get to this time around.

Fourth, we will have the peace of mind that comes from the absolute certainty that we will never sin. Adam and Eve were created good, but they could and did fall. How much better to know that God has glorified us, and he promises to preserve us so we will never mess this up (Rom 8:30)!

Fifth, there is one feature of the consummation that exists, not despite our fall, but in part because of it. Angels stand on tiptoe, trying "to catch a glimpse" of God's gracious salvation (1 Pet 1:12). Adam and the angels knew God was good, but they had no idea how good. Only forgiven sinners can appreciate the depth of God's love. No angel has experienced grace: the good angels did not need it and the fallen angels did not receive it. But we have, so we understand God better than any other creature can.

Application

Our final destiny is not a choice between heaven and hell but between hell and here. Would you like to escape hell and live forever here, with Jesus and all those who love him? Then repent of your sin and throw all your weight on Jesus, and you will inherit the earth (Matt 5:5). Who can imagine life on this restored earth, with all the ravages of sin removed? I love peaches, oranges, and strawberries, but I've only eaten these fruits from cursed soil. How luscious will fruit taste on the new earth! How bright and deep will be the color blue! How heightened will all of our earthly pleasures be when the curse is reversed! If you enjoy being human and enjoy living here, you're going to love the new earth.

Jesus is the center of the new earth. Nothing will be more satisfying than praising him with uncountable numbers of our brothers and sisters. We were made for this. Jesus is the center, yet there is a circumference. We will thrill to worship Jesus, and we will also enjoy doing what humans do—traveling, chatting, snorkeling, playing cards, dining on rooftops overlooking the ocean, and riding bears bareback. We will not choose between praising Jesus and enjoying culture. We will do both, with a priority on Jesus, our God who created and died for us.

I changed the lyrics to "I'll Fly Away" to correct this chapter's urban legend and emphasize our promised future.

What happens when we die? We go to be with Jesus.

What happens after that? We rise again.

Some sad morning when this life is o'er, I'll fly away.
To my Lord and Savior, Jesus Christ, I'll fly away.
And I'll rise again, O glory, I'll rise again.
When I die I will not have risen yet,
But I'll rise again!

Subject and Name Index